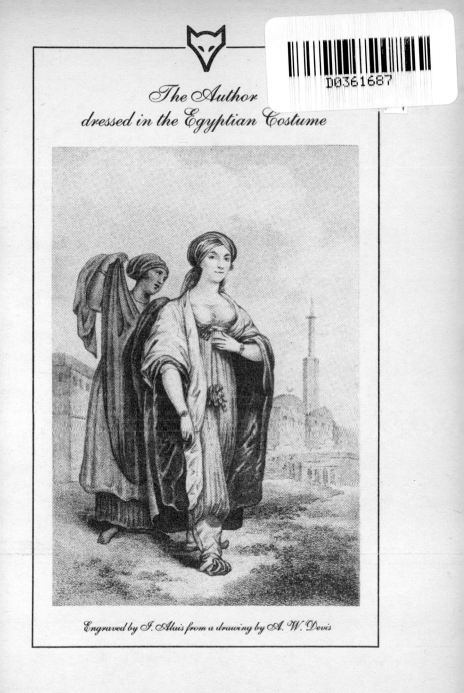

The Author
dressed in the Egyptian Costume

Engraved by I. Aluis from a drawing by A. W. Devis

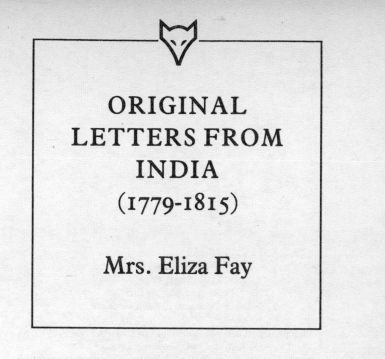

ORIGINAL LETTERS FROM INDIA
(1779-1815)

Mrs. Eliza Fay

With Introductory and Terminal Notes
by
E.M. Forster

New Introduction by
M.M. Kaye

THE HOGARTH PRESS
LONDON

Published in 1986 by
The Hogarth Press
Chatto and Windus Ltd
40 William IV Street, London WC2N 4DF

First published in Great Britain by The Hogarth Press 1925
This edition offset from the original British edition
Introductory and terminal notes by E.M. Forster © The Provost and Scholars
of King's College, Cambridge
New introduction © M.M. Kaye 1986

British Library Cataloguing in Publication Data

Fay, Eliza
Original letters from India (1779-1815)
1. India – Social life and customs
I. Title   II. Forster, E.M.
954.03'1'0924   DS421

ISBN 0 7012 1000 1

Printed in Great Britain by
Cox & Wyman Ltd,
Reading, Berkshire

CONTENTS

INTRODUCTION

There are any number of things I would like to know about Eliza Fay, but sadly never will. So many questions that I would have liked to ask her. The most important of these being how on earth did she come to have this fixation about going to Calcutta in the first place? It can never have been a salubrious city, and although its imposing public buildings and the Georgian mansions that the merchant-princes of the East India Company built for themselves on the banks of the Hoogli at Garden Reach may have looked impressive enough in the latter half of the eighteenth century, when they were spanking new, the climate must have been just as bad then as it is now. While the smell was probably worse – if that is possible.

Today it is, frankly, a horrific place. And in my day it was a pretty nasty one. Yet the thought of travelling to India in order to live there seems to have been an obsession with Eliza, and a long standing one at that; for I do not believe that when she eventually got there it was merely because the man she married happened to have been offered the chance of practising as an advocate at the Supreme Court of Calcutta. She was, after all, only twenty-three and newly married when she set out with him to find her chosen Shangri-la. And from what we know of her, she probably gave him the idea in the first place and personally engineered the whole thing from start to finish. I wouldn't put it past her.

My guess is that the talk of some elderly East India Company nabob living in gilded retirement in or near her native town of Blackheath, overheard at some local function or repeated to her by gossiping neighbours, fired her youthful imagination and made her picture Calcutta as a modern El Dorado: a Tom-Tiddler's Ground where anyone of spirit could make their fortune simply by 'picking up gold and silver'. Or was it social status that she hankered after? Possibly. For everyone knew that Anglo-Indian society was not nearly as hidebound or exclusive as the home-grown variety, and it was common knowledge that the then wife of His Excellency Governor Warren Hastings, although a divorced woman and a foreigner, ranked as Calcutta's First Lady.

Whatever Eliza's reasons, the fact remains that she had made up her mind to go to Calcutta. And in 1779 to Calcutta she went. Nothing and no one was allowed to stop her. Not even the knowledge that the first leg of the journey involved crossing France, with whom her own country happened at the time to be at war. But then Eliza took no interest in wars. A large number of them were waged with spectacular and ferocious enthusiasm during her lifetime, but she ignores the lot. Neither Wellington nor Bonaparte get so much as a mention, and one would never have guessed that America was engaged in fighting the War of Independence if that particular conflict had not, in an oblique way, caused her some trifling inconvenience – though only briefly.

Eliza and her husband, Anthony Fay, sailed from Dover on the tenth day of April 1779, disembarking at Calais without the official 'enemy' asking them to produce any proof of their identity or, it seems, showing the smallest interest in them. Only when they reached Paris did they strike the first of many snags when the French police suddenly (and Eliza clearly thinks unreasonably) demanded passports.

Considering that the two countries were at war, the French treated the Fays extremely well; although the disgruntled Eliza, annoyed by all this red tape and the endless delays, describes their capital city as 'a sink of impurity'. The reference is presumably to smells rather than morals, and she does have the grace to add later: 'When I wrote the above I was in a great rage, and not without reason.' But war or no war, she indulged in an orgy of sightseeing – no one saying her nay. And when, at last, they are able to leave Paris and are on their way again, she is pleased to discover that 'tolerable Burgundy' is obtainable for 'about fourpence a bottle'. She seems to have been a good trencherwoman with a proper respect for the quality of food and drink.

Their intention had been to make for Marseilles and take a ship from that port, but having been strongly advised against it, they changed direction and boldly set off instead to cross the Alps into Italy. Even reading her account of that perilous crossing gave me vertigo, but Eliza merely writes gaily, 'being happily as you know very courageous, I made light of all difficulties'. She could say that again. What an endearingly comic, as well as impressive traveller she is, with her combination of impetuosity, fortitude and innocence.

Sadly, her husband Anthony, to whom she always refers as either 'Mr Fay' or 'Mr F—', is soon exposed as a total loss. In the first of many anecdotes that illustrate his inadequacy, she tells us how 'Mr Fay had most unwisely and contrary to my earnest entreaty, pinned our passports to the book of roads, which he usually carried with him on horseback'. He lost them of course. Without those passports they could not have got anywhere, but 'happily' (it is a favourite word of Eliza's) Mr F— rode back and found them near their last stopping place. And despite the fact that he behaves in a foolhardy and deplorably stupid manner in the mountains, his wife is still able to write buoyantly that 'A good night's rest put us all in good humour'. Not for long I imagine, judging by his subsequent exploits.

Their next stop is Genoa, followed by a short trip in a felucca that brings them to Leghorn, from where, on July 2nd, they board a ship for Alexandria. The weather is vile, and one suspects from her tone that the redoubtable Eliza was sea-sick. Yet no sooner are they on dry land again than they are off sightseeing. There was no Suez Canal in those days, so on leaving Alex they sailed up the Nile to the city that Eliza refers to as 'Grand Cairo' – the voyage being enlivened by Mr Fay having to fire two pistols at a boat that was overtaking them and whose occupants were suspected of 'preparing to plunder, and perhaps, to murder us'. (Eliza's punctuation is apt to be as individual as her style.)

After an entertaining stay and the usual round of sightseeing, the Fays left 'Grand Cairo' in a caravan across the desert to Suez. And in no time at all found themselves involved in a series of hair-raising adventures and enduring such appalling discomfort that the intrepid Mrs Fay remarks tartly: '– if ever they catch me on their Desert again, I think I shall deserve all they can inflict.' That's my Eliza!

Her husband, writing a brief account of this nightmare journey to his father-in-law, says: 'Your daughter behaved most courageously and is extremely well, considering the extraordinary fatigue she has undergone.' While the daughter herself, never one to indulge in mock modesty, adds in a hasty postscript to her husband's letter: 'I bore the fatigues of the desert like a Lion.' Their use of the word 'fatigue' must rank as the understatement of the year – which is still 1779.

At Suez they boarded the sailing ship *Nathalia*, which after a brief stop at Mocha headed out across the Indian Ocean toward Bombay. It was obviously not a happy ship and we find Eliza writing: 'Dissensions have run very high on board.' No one seems to have been sorry when at long last the Malabar coast was sighted, for they were happily unaware that they were about to leave the frying pan for a very nasty fire indeed. On December 5th their ship dropped anchor at Calicut, and almost everyone on board was imprisoned by order of the local Governor, one Sudder Khan, a brother-in-law of the Nawab of Mysore who had been enraged by the British capture of Mahe, which he regarded as his property, from his allies, the French.

Anthony Fay gave his celebrated imitation of a boneless wonder throughout the terrifying series of alarums and excursions that followed, and which, after weeks of fear, near-starvation and confinement in conditions of squalor and extreme discomfort (Eliza is far too prudish even to hint at how they coped with the everyday sanitary problems, but imagination boggles!), ended only just in time, for a week later war broke out in earnest between Hyder Ali and the British. They escaped with little more than their lives and reached the safety of Cochin on February 19th, 1780. The remainder of their journey included a hideous sea voyage round the southern tip of India, Cape Cormorin, and two weeks in Madras, before they landed at last in Calcutta: that 'place for which I have so long sighed,' writes Eliza, ' . . . and where I have long rested my most rational expectations of future prosperity and comfort.' It was as though she had come home.

If we include those two-and-a-half months of captivity in Calicut, it had taken Eliza exactly twelve months and eighteen days to reach Calcutta. The same journey that in my day took about three weeks.

Since I, and many thousands like me, made that passage from England to India, it is interesting to contrast our journey with Eliza's. Most of us went all the way by sea, a voyage that was the greatest fun even when – or perhaps especially when? – one had to do it on the cheap. And was it cheap! Right up to the end of the Thirties, the return fare, Tourist Class, from London to Bombay, was only £40. True, the accommodation was a bit cramped. But as most of the young and impecunious travelled Tourist, there was a great deal of laughter and never a dull moment; and, best of all, we were allowed to disembark at whatever port where the ship happened to stop, to go shopping or, like Eliza, sightseeing: for in the halcyon days of the Pax Britannica there was no nonsense – as Eliza doubtless would have appreciated – about passports or visas to stop us landing in droves wherever we chose.

We explored Gibraltar, Tangier and Naples, danced and dined in Malta which, at that time, was almost a second home since everyone seemed to know someone there and the liners would stop for at least one night, often two, while their passengers held high revel ashore. And who can ever forget Port Said or Simon Artz's shop where we used to buy endless duty-free goods and acquire new topis – those khaki-coloured, regulation pith helmets that were required wearing East of Suez? From Port Said our ships edged slowly down the Suez Canal and through the Bitter Lakes by the light of a bone-white Egyptian moon, to Port Tewfik on the Red Sea; and from there to 'Old Aden', like a barrick-stove that no one's lit for years and years' (Kipling's description cannot be bettered) and out into the midnight-blue waters of the Indian Ocean with its flying fish, dolphins and whales.

No one who was not actively anti-social and determined to be bored or cross, or both, could complain of those voyages being dull. By night, there were dances on the deck – one or two of them fancy-dress affairs – or amateur concerts and cabaret shows. By day, there were shuffle-board, quoits, and deck tennis for the energetic, a library and two card-rooms for the sedentary, a sweepstake on the ship's run for those who liked to bet, while almost everyone, young and old, either walked briskly round the decks for a set number of times, or dutifully swam a given number of lengths in the canvas swimming pool in order to offset the effects of eating the four very lavish meals that were placed before them daily.

It intrigues me to discover that some of the things Eliza writes about were not all that different in my day – or in my mother's either. To take only one example: shipboard romances. These were an accepted feature of all the long, eastward voyages, and the average unattached damsel invariably lost a portion of her heart to some young man who danced and played deck tennis with her, stood her lemon squashes or sherry (as a non-drinker, I must have saved my beaux a lot of money) and escorted her to the bows on moonless nights to 'look at the phosphorus'. Nor was it only the unattached who indulged in these delightful shipboard flirtations. Many an eager young or not-so-young sahib, whose work lay in India, has, in his day, hurried down to the dock at Karachi or Bombay, Colombo, Madras or Calcutta, to meet a liner bringing his betrothed out to marry him, only to see her descend the gangway on the arm of Another, and discover that she has changed her mind in transit. The silt must still hold innumerable returned engagement rings that have been angrily flung by embittered ex-fiancés into the turgid waters of one or other of India's famous docks. Romance was a recognised hazard – or bonus, depending on the point of view – of any long voyage. (But no chaperone, however strict, would have taken such extreme measures to protect her charges from its baleful influence as Eliza did on one of her later voyages, when she kept the three young ladies whom she had undertaken to convey safely to India locked in their cabin for the entire trip.)

But even in the hey-day of the big ocean liners, shipboard life was not always restful or romantic, and dissensions tended to run high in my time as well as in Eliza's. There were, too, the occasional patches of wild and stormy weather when the more prudent (myself included) took to their berths. And should anyone trip over the leg of a deck-chair, fall down a companion-way or come out in spots, there was a well appointed hospital section with a doctor and qualified nurse to deal with them (or, if necessary, to operate).

In general, though, I remember those voyages to India as three weeks of non-stop fun, sightseeing, or just plain lazing. Nowadays, a jumbo jet will take you there in less than twenty-four hours, and any delay, whether caused by climatic conditions, NATO exercises, a strike, a hijack, or engine repairs, will be greeted with angry protests from the passengers. How Mrs Fay would have despised us!

One of the many puzzling things about Eliza is why, after all the unpleasant and frequently terrifying things that befell her during the interminable journey, she should ever have considered, even for a moment, repeating it again once her foot was safely back on her native Blackheath. Yet she did just that; and not only once! In all, she made four journeys to Calcutta, and we can only conclude that she was either a glutton for punishment or else, like those intrepid characters who go in for driving racing cars at Le Mans or climbing the north face of the Eiger, she thrived on danger. Probably the latter, for although Eliza, like her great namesake Elizabeth Tudor, may have had 'the body of a weak and feeble woman' (though I very much doubt it – despite those frequent and always well timed 'bursts of tears', occasional swoons and repeated references to ill health), she certainly had the heart and stomach of a merchant-adventurer. And of a British merchant-adventurer too!

The greatest puzzle, however, is how a woman blessed with such a liberal supply of that admirable quality our forebears called 'gumption', could ever have married such a spineless poop as Anthony Fay. The attraction of opposites perhaps? Or was he the only man to offer for her? Yet to judge by Davis's drawing – and even making allowances for an artist's desire to flatter his sitters – she was by no means unattractive, and there should have been others. Several others. But the marriage appears to have been doomed from the start. Those bright expectations of 'future prosperity and comfort' in Calcutta received a sharp setback when it finally disintegrated and she parted from him (acrimoniously, I have no doubt, but not a moment too soon) and returned to England in the spring of 1782.

Calcutta, however, like some dancing, shimmering, treacherous Will-o'-the-Wisp, lured her back again and again. She returned there in 1784 to set up as a milliner and quarrel briskly with the church authorities, and when that venture failed, sailed home again – only to return briefly in 1796. Six months later she is off once more to England; encountering en route the usual quota of disasters, even a small proportion of which would have broken the spirit of any less resolute member of the human race. Yet, after that, undaunted, she turns her gaze westward to America and tries her hand at making her fortune in the New World instead.

That scheme, too, appears to have foundered, for in 1816 she sailed yet again for Calcutta. It seems as though she could not keep away. And this time Calcutta caught her and has held her fast ever since, for she died and was buried there in the early autumn of that same year. She was sixty. *Ave atque vale*, Eliza.

M. M. Kaye, Sussex 1985

INTRODUCTORY NOTES

Eliza Fay is a work of art. But she was also a historical character, who wielded and resumed a pen, and from that point of view some brief notes may be acceptable; the reader can be trusted to forget them as soon as he enters her tremendous presence and gazes upon her prepotent form. (See Frontispiece.)

Manuscript of the Letters

She died in Calcutta, in 1816, and her MSS. were probably destroyed there after her death. As arranged for publication, they consisted of (i.) twenty-three letters to her family, covering the period from April 1779 to February 1783. (ii.) Letters composed at Blackheath, at the instance of a certain Mrs. L. Mrs. L. may be only a literary device, for these letters are really an autobiography. They continue her story from 1783, and doubtless carried it down to 1815, the date at which she was writing. Unfortunately the administrator of her estate did not consider the letters to Mrs. L. sufficiently interesting to print in their entirety, and the reminiscences end in September 1797 in consequence; the last twenty years of her life are almost unknown to us.

Editions of the Letters

(i.) In the *Calcutta Gazette* (May 9, 1816) Mrs. Fay " respectfully gives notice that the Narrative . . . is now

in the Press, and will be completed with all possible des-
patch "; subscriptions are invited.   She died the following
September, intestate and insolvent, and the book was published in an unfinished state, with a tepid ' advertisement '
by the administrator, who hopes it will benefit the creditors
(p. 272).   This is the original edition (1817).   The Library
of the India Office possesses a copy; I know of none other
in England.

(ii.) The book brought in a profit of Rs.220 in four
years,[1] and was reprinted in 1821, also at Calcutta.   This
reprint is identical with the 1817 edition, except that the
title page is reset and the ' advertisement ' omitted.   The
British Museum possesses two copies of it.

(iii.) In 1908 a new edition was published by Messrs.
Thacker, Spink & Co. of Calcutta, under the auspices of the
Calcutta Historical Society; edited by the Rev. W. K.
Firminger (now an Archdeacon), who further contributed an
introduction and notes.   I am grateful to this volume, for it
was here I met Eliza first, and the notes contain much valuable local matter.   Nevertheless it is an indifferent piece of
work.   There are numerous slips and—what is worse—
the text has been tinkered and repunctuated unpardonably.
Believing Mrs. Fay's English style to be inferior to his own,
the Archdeacon has made on an average one alteration in
every line she wrote—alterations which always lead us away
from her spirit, and occasionally from her meaning.

The present edition—the first to be published outside
India—makes no claim to scholarship but it does restore
the original text.   A few obvious printer's errors have been
corrected, full names have often been substituted for initials
when my knowledge permits, and in one place (p. 221) I have

---

[1] India Office Records: Bengal Inventories, 1821, vol. 3.

ventured an emendation.   Elsewhere Mrs. Fay speaks for
herself, as was indeed her constant custom while alive:
" this story must be told in my own way, or not at all."

In preparing the notes, I have been under much obliga-
tion to Sir William Foster, C.I.E., who has not only allowed
me access to the India Office records, but has given me the
benefit of his great experience and knowledge.   It is entirely
through him that I am able to present a few additional facts
about Mrs. Fay.   There are still some problems awaiting
solution: *e.g.* What was her maiden name?   What was the
date and the fate of the portrait of her by A. W. Devis?

Mrs. Fay's Career

There is little to relate, beyond what she herself tells us.
She was born in 1756, perhaps at Blackheath.   Perhaps
her father was a sailor, for she refers to his familiarity with
the wind's eye, and to her own resemblance to him when
disguised in a pair of striped trousers.   He died in 1794.
There was a mother—dead by 1783.   There were two
sisters, one of whom apparently married a Mr. Thomas W.
Preston.   The initial letter of Mrs. Fay's maiden name
was apparently C.   And that is all we know of her origins.
So obscure were the C. family that a very few years have
sufficed to conceal them from the historian.

Nor will her education detain us more than it did her.
Something vaguely commercial is indicated—perhaps connected with dressmaking and France.   She could splash
about in French, also pick up and drop Italian, Portuguese,
shorthand and Hindustani.   In music she loved a Nicolai
Sonata, and she was capable of backgammon and cards,
though rapidly fatigued by either, and invariably worsted at
chess.   On one of her voyages a pair of globes accompanied

her, but geography could never have been her strong point, for she thought that the Alps were only one mountain thick, and the Malabar Hills the third highest range in the world. Writing she adored—never happier than when the pen is in the hand—but her grammar was most personally her own, and Archdeacon Firminger observes with concern that " she frequently arranges her words in such an order that she is bound to get into trouble with her relative pronouns." She does. Indeed her mental equipment was that of an intelligent lady's maid or courier, who has read Mrs. Radcliffe, Pope, and *Nubilia in Search of a Husband*, and can allude at a pinch to Queen Christina of Sweden. Her religious instruction was that of the Established Church of England: pious without enthusiasm, she censures the bigotry of Rome and deplores without attempting to correct them the errors of the heathen. She thought that the Mohammedans worship Mohammed. She believed in Nature. She detested indelicacy.

When we meet her (spring of 1779) she is twenty-three years old, confused and vigorous, and recently married to Anthony Fay. Nothing is known about Fay either. He was Irish by extraction, and the only son of a " Francis Fay, gentleman, late of Rotherhithe, Surrey." [1] He had recently been called to the Bar at Lincoln's Inn, and was now going out to practise as an Advocate at the Supreme Court of Calcutta. At this point Mrs. Fay's letters to her family start. The first fourteen of them—the most brilliant she ever penned—describe the journey out. The ride across France, the adventures in Egypt, the voyage down the Red Sea, all lead up with unintentional art to the stupendous tragi-comedy of Calicut, where the East hit her, bang, and

---

[1] Lincoln's Inn Admission Registers, July 3, 1778.

incidentally revealed to her both her husband's character and her own.   The enormous letter recounting their imprisonment by Hyder Ali ranks among the more remarkable documents of Anglo-India; intensity, passion, venom, humour conscious and unconscious, are sustained page after page, and the pæan of deliverance that follows adds a grotesque yet genuine touch of beauty.   Nothing as exciting as Calicut happened to her again.   It is her high-water mark of sensation.   In time the Fays reached Calcutta, he was admitted an advocate (June 16, 1780) and began to practise, but their married life did not last.   They were both of them underbred and quarrelsome and he was a fool to boot. In less than two years he had run into debt, alienated their professional friends, and produced an illegitimate child, and his wife had to leave him.   He went back to England, in connection with a big political intrigue, and we hear no more of him (dead by 1815).   She went back to England herself in 1782, *via* St. Helena; chastened but indomitable.

Her second voyage.   Off to Calcutta again in 1784. Humbler social outlook; thought of starting a seminary for young ladies: but resumed mantua-making instead: bankrupt in 1788: returned to England in 1794 and acquired a financial interest in a boat called the *Minerva*, which promptly burst into flames owing to the explosion of a bottle of aqua fortis, and had to be scuttled.

Third voyage.   Off to Calcutta in the repaired *Minerva*. Arrived in 1796 but only stopped six months.   Another boat is acquired, the *Rosalia*, and is laded with costly muslins with which she hopes to make her fortune in the United States.   Before she can reach the mouth of the Hoogli, the *Rosalia* fills with water and the muslins are ruined.   New York is attained by other agencies on September 3, 1797.

At this point the administrator lost enthusiasm and stopped publishing the MS., so that our next glimpse of the wanderer is in 1815 at Blackheath, where she probably sponges on her sister, Mrs. Preston. She writes her reminiscences for Mrs. L.——older and more formal now, but still cattish. Her last movements can be pieced together from various sources.[1] Next spring she sails for Calcutta for the last time, on the *Sir Stephen Lushington*, to die there on September 9, 1816, aged sixty.[2] Since she left no will, her estate was administered by the Registrar of the Supreme Court. Her Indian creditors got eight annas in the rupee. Mrs. Preston, of Point Cottage, Blackheath Hill, was owed £300 and got £61 : 1 : 0. The *Sir Stephen Lushington* was owed Rs.800 for passage money and got Rs.400. Her effects were put up for sale by her old enemy, the auctioneer Tulloh.[3] Prices did not run high. A book entitled *Thoughts and Remarks on Establishing an Institution for the Support and Education of Unfortunate respectable females* only fetched one rupee fourteen annas, while *Thoughts and Remarks on a Protestant Nunnery* went for even less. Scott, Mrs. Barbauld, Hannah More, Lady Morgan and introductions to chess also occur on the list, also oddments of household furniture and millinery, also a Welch wig, two pianos and a gold watch—perhaps the very one into which she had stuck pins at Calicut, so many years before: anyhow it went cheaply. She was buried the day after her death, in one of the Calcutta cemeteries, no one knows in which, and there her second-rate career comes to an end. She had been neither rich

[1] Among them are Archdeacon Firminger's notes to his edition, and MS. notes in the possession of Sir W. Foster.

[2] *Asiatic Journal* for 1817, pp. 407 and 517.

[3] India Office Records: Bengal Inventories, 1816, vol. 3.

nor well-educated nor well-connected nor good-tempered nor beautiful nor improper; what hope had such a female of attracting the attention of her contemporaries? And why does she attract us now?

Her Style. Her Character

" I reserve to myself the option of resuming the narrative style whenever I shall deem it necessary." She was in prison when she wrote this, and a tea-kettle had just been stolen from her by another lady, so that one would not expect her to reserve options, but the remark is typical of her. It expresses her character, like all her remarks. Every word she wrote is personal. Not a single sentence is dead, and even when she seems to function mechanically —to praise Providence, for instance—there is always some little turn at the end, such as " But to resume," or " You must however be all impatience to know how we fell into this pickle, take then the particulars," which pulls the paragraph into shape and makes it her own.

How very differently do human beings pass the time alloted them in this probationary existence! Surely, to consume it in supine indolence or " vain repetitions " can never render us more acceptable to Him who is the fountain of light and knowledge. We ate some preserved peaches with them, which the Consul paid for; and then took our leave; but were forced to submit to a salute from the sisters, which we would gladly have dispensed with, for they all took an enormous quantity of snuff.

Thus does she get her own back upon some unattractive Ursuline Nuns. Or consider the following trifle: it begins with all the dreariness and unreality of an ocean log, then curdles into daily life suddenly.

Numbers of man-of-war birds and eggs, were taken, which proved to be good eating; they likewise caught the finest turtle I

ever saw, weighing near 400 lbs., but by an act of unpardonable
negligence in people so situated, it was suffered to walk overboard in
the night.

Suffered to escape, and she so partial to nourishing food!
Her opinions and desires are always sticking out like this,
and ripping the chaste mantle of literature.

Were she only frank and naïve, it would be something,
but she is much more: a soul courageous and gallant, an
eye and ear always on the watch. She does not conceal
her sufferings, but not once does she whine over them, and
we get after a few pages a wonderful impression of hardness. Hard as steel? Scarcely, because that suggests
nobility: but harder than her blockhead of a husband.
When the verandah in which they had hidden their savings
was twitched off the house by a monsoon, he abandoned
himself to lamentations while she calculated the direction of
the wind and finally discovered the money in a far away
tuft of grass. In her sense, as in her sentiment, she is the
child of her century, which despite its palpitations never
lost grasp of the main chance. Her floods of tears and
fainting fits are always postponed until a convenient
moment: they never intrude while she is looking after her
luggage or outwitting her foes.

To this strength of will she joins high powers of
observation. Her little character sketches are delightfully
malicious; Mr. Hare, the Tullohs, the grand Mrs. Hastings,
Captain Ayres, Captain Lewis.—" I want to make you see
them," she says, and we see them. She is also shrewd
about national characteristics; quick to detect the callous-
ness of the lower class Frenchwoman; nor, if one is to
generalise about the myriads of India, could it be better
done than this:

I wish these people would not vex one by their tricks; for there is something in the mild countenances and gentle manners of the Hindoos that interests me exceedingly.

And the liveliness of her eye! People and articles passed before her not as they do for most of us, in a blur, but with definite outlines. Read her description of the costume of the Consul's wife at Alexandria, or of the costume she herself donned before entering Cairo, or of the scenery of East Africa, with which she so nearly collided. All she says of it is " before we tacked *flies* were seen on the shore—had this happened during the night nothing could have saved us ": yet no words could bring East Africa nearer and she does not weaken the effect by remembering that night might have concealed the flies. And her ear: like her eye it is always alive; how the cries of the sepoys at Calicut sink into her! And her mouth: how she does relish her food! She is constantly registering through her senses, and recording the results with a powerful though untrained mind. The outcome is most successful, and it is strange that her letters are not better known in this country. Though they have value historically, their main interest is human; they show us a highly remarkable character, triumphant over the difficulties of life and narrative style.

Style is always being monopolised by the orderly minded; they will not admit that slap-dash people have equal literary rights, provided they write slap-dash. If Mrs. Fay got her relative pronouns correct she would be a worse writer, for they can never have been correct in her mind, she can never have spoken quite proper even when calling at Government House or learning sweet little Miss Rogers the use of the globes. She wrote as well as she could, she wrote nothing that she herself was not. Even the tatters of the Grand Manner are hers, for she was full of aspirations, and loved to embark upon the billows of the grandiose. Her humour, irritability, power of description, sense of little things, all gain their full force because she was at the same time wishing she could write as feelingly as Mrs. Radcliffe or as wittily as Fielding. Her age produced many greater letters, but few that so faithfully reflect the character of their author. Every word tells its story. Cherchez le style; c'est la femme.

THE HISTORICAL BACKGROUND

Two facts must be kept in mind while we read the earlier letters: England and France are at war, and the English in India are preparing to fight Hyder Ali, the ruler of Mysore.

(i.) England went to war with France (also with Spain, America and Holland) in 1778, so when the Fays travel across France in the following year they are in enemy country. They are treated, and expect to be treated " with great politeness "; she is quite affronted when their papers are looked at, and though she sometimes sighs for Old England, she never thinks it her duty to suffer. With a clear conscience she admires Marie Antoinette, sight-sees, hob-nobs with the enemy, gives her letters to St. Lubin. The French, under Admiral Suffren, treated Hickey and his Charlotte with similar courtesy at Trincomalay three years later (Wm. Hickey, iii., 34 *seq.*). Eliza has not Charlotte's charm, yet even she finds little to resent, and her letters are an interesting example of eighteenth-century war mentality.

Peace was made in 1783 to the advantage of France.

The war had been mainly naval—West Indies, coasts of Southern India; in the latter theatre it connects with the more intimate operations of Hyder Ali.

(ii.) The " fell tyger Hyder Ally " was a Mohammedan soldier, who started in Hindu employ, established himself in the uplands of Mysore, and was trying from that central position to dominate southern India, and to reach the Malabar coast on the west and the Carnatic and Coromandel on the east. He succeeded in the Malabar and occupied Calicut, its capital: but to the east he had already collided with the English in Madras (1767–69), and a second and greater war was impending when the Fays blundered on the scene. Hyder Ali had two main grievances against the English: they had taken the port of Mahe during their operations against the French, and he regarded it as under his protection; and they were intriguing with his mutinous subjects, the Nairs. In the confusion and tension his brother-in-law, the governor of Calicut, thought it wiser to detain all English people there. For further details see note on the Fays' imprisonment at Calicut (p. 276). Soon after their release the actual war broke out.

This is the war that so roused the eloquence of Burke. Hyder Ali swept down into the Carnatic and nearly took Madras. When the French fleet arrived under Suffren he operated in conjunction with it. He died in 1782, but his son, Tipu Sahib, continued to give trouble.

Subsequent upheavals, such as the French Revolution and the Battle of Waterloo, do not appear to have incommoded Mrs. Fay. But it is as well to remember that she lived through them. She saw a little of the Portuguese possessions, and a little of the Cape, both before and after

the expulsion of the Dutch: and probably she saw a good
deal of America towards the close of her life, but " having
arrived in the land of Columbia, I will bid you adieu."

CALCUTTA IN 1780

When the Fays landed in Calcutta, certain very celebrated and rather dull historical events were in progress,
events well known to Macaulay and every schoolboy, and
the object of careful research on the part of Sir James
Fitzjames Stephen. Eliza herself was more interested in
the price of mutton and the shapes of hats, nevertheless the
celebrated events influenced her life, so some reference must
be accorded to them; it will be followed by short references
to Calcutta society and to Calcutta topography.

(i.) *History.* — In 1773 the British Parliament had
passed a " Regulating Act " to provide for the government
of Bengal, a province which was technically part of the
Mogul Empire but actually under the control of a politico-
commercial enterprise, the Honourable East India Company.
The Act created (*a*) A Supreme Council at Calcutta, with
Warren Hastings as Governor-General and four councillors,
of whom the most famous is Philip Francis; (*b*) A Supreme
Court of Judicature, with Sir Elijah Impey as Chief Justice
and three other judges, of whom Sir Robert Chambers will
concern us most (p. 174). Council and Court were independent of each other and their spheres not clearly defined,
so there was friction between them (p. 176), but far more
serious was the friction that arose inside the Council itself.
A prominent Hindu, who had accused Hastings of corrup-
tion, was himself subsequently accused of forgery; he was
tried before the Supreme Court, and probably fairly tried,
he was found guilty and was executed (1775). This is the

famous and interminable Nuncomar case; Mrs. Fay does not refer to it in her letters, but it must have been often on her lips, for it convulsed Calcutta, and finally crippled the careers both of Hastings and of Impey.

Warren Hastings is far above our heads; an Imperial Pioneer and a fine fellow, feared for his ability, liked for his charm. He had just made a somewhat imprudent second marriage with a divorcée, but was living down the slight scandal it had raised. Impey was a man of inferior calibre; however, he was neither dishonourable nor weak, and, though he and Hastings had been at the same public school, there is no reason to suspect conspiracy between them on the occasion of the Nuncomar trial. The evil genius of the tangle was certainly Philip Francis. Brilliant, bitter, ambitious, immoral, and probably the author of the *Letters from Junius*, Francis came out East in the hope of advancing his career on the newly created Council, but he met with a personal mishap: he climbed up a bamboo ladder into the room of a Mrs. Grand, was discovered, sued by the husband, and condemned by Sir Elijah Impey to pay Rs.50,000 (1779). Hence his hatred of Impey; which, combined with his jealousy of Hastings on the Council, induced him to rake up the Nuncomar trial (although he had not tried to save Nuncomar at the time), and to search for anything else that was likely to injure his enemies. He drew a Colonel Watson into his schemes, and Watson drew in poor blustering Anthony Fay (p. 198) and Fay deserted his wife; celebrated events wrecked little lives.

Francis and Hastings fought a duel (p. 185), but this was only an incident in their feud. Francis returned home after it to stir up trouble in England. He aimed at the impeachment of Hastings and of Impey for High Treason; both men had subsequently to return for the purpose of defending themselves. Hastings was tried and acquitted, amid much social publicity. The motion to impeach Impey was dropped.

Books: Fitzjames Stephen, *Nuncomar and Impey*, gives a thorough analysis of the episode; for gossip, turn to Busteed, *Echoes from Old Calcutta* (4th edition), an entertaining and accurate miscellany.

(ii) *Society*.—To the student of British deportment overseas, the end of the eighteenth century in Calcutta is an interesting period. A change is at hand. The English are no longer merely traders, soldiers, adventurers, who may take up what attitude suits them towards the aborigines; they are acquiring racial consciousness and the sense of Imperial responsibility.

> O never let conscience molest or offend you,
> For conscience should keep all the time we're in India,

sings a local poet in the *Bengal Gazette*, but his advice was ignored and his paper suppressed. A Supreme Council and a High Court brought solemn social consequences in their train. Viceregal airs begin, the king's birthday is already a religious event although he was George the Third, Lady Governess and Chief Justice hold their state, and apart from them, with a pride exceeding their own, Charles Grant lays the foundation of Protestant Missions in Bengal. What would be the relation of this new society to the old oriental societies through which it was sprouting? No one asked the question yet, nor knew that a very peculiar brand—Anglo-India—was being added to the existing distractions of the peninsula.

A social routine soon evolved, which has partially

continued down to the present sterner epoch. Ride or walk before breakfast. Breakfast about nine. Then the gentlemen went to their work, and the ladies passed their morning as best they might, in a state of deshabille.

The fashionable undress, except in the article of being without stays (and stays are wholly unworn in the East) is much in the English style, with large caps or otherwise, as fancy dictates. No care or skill is left unexerted to render the appearance easy and graceful, a necessary circumstance, as gentlemen in the course of their morning excursions continually drop in, who say the prettiest things imaginable with an air of truth that wins on the credulity and harmonises the heart

Thus writes Miss Sophia Goldborne, a contemporary of Mrs. Fay's and sometimes her rival in the narrative style. Dinner burst on the world at two — enormous (p. 181); the gentlemen each drank three bottles of claret, after which both sexes fell asleep, only regaining consciousness towards sunset. Perhaps a little more work was done in the evening, but the great event was a ride or drive on the Course, or an airing on the Hoogli; then tea or coffee, formal calls, and supper at ten. Mr. Mackrabie (another contemporary) writes in his diary: " *Entre nous*, the evening was stupid enough, and the supper detestable; great joints of roasted goat with endless dishes of cold fish." Bed at midnight.

Mrs. Fay's early connections were with legal circles— the Impeys, Chambers, Hydes. But after her husband deserted her she sank into what would now be termed " second society." Perhaps she did not mind much. She had soon seen through the world and its little tricks and discovered that " grand parties so much resemble each other that a particular detail would be unnecessary and even tiresome," and that even Mrs. Warren Hastings was mildly absurd.

The delightful *Memoirs of William Hickey* (3 vols.: 1749–1790) form a perfect social pendant to our authoress. If she is a lady, Hickey is a gentleman. He was an Irish attorney, etc., who ran in and out of Calcutta during her period, and in and out of the same section of society. They never allude to one another, and it is improbable they ever met—dates just preclude it. But they had numerous friends and aspirations in common, and both clung to what either would have called the wheels of fashion's car. Their value to us to-day is that they were not first-rate, never at the top. They give an account of Calcutta that would never occur to the well-bred, the highly educated, the sincerely pious, or the satisfactorily introduced. If any one wishes to know what ordinary social life there was like a hundred and fifty years ago, let him read them; their modest careless stuff is true as a mirror and also pleasant as a design.

(iii.) *Topography.*—The city, like its inmates, was just assuming modern airs. Its territory already stretched over three miles along the Hoogli and about a mile and a half inland. As Mrs. Fay sailed up the animated stream she passed on her right the recently built residences on Garden Reach, and, after them, the imposing mass of the new Fort William, the river Esplanade, and the old Fort William. The Old Fort was under demolition, for bitter memories were not as carefully cherished in India then as they are to-day, and Eliza and her friends were not exercised by an episode which had happened in the debris twenty years previously, and which was to thrill the nineteenth century with increasing indignation:—the Black Hole of

Calcutta. The site of the tragedy was—as it still is—
the geographic centre of the city, and the bungalows of
the English and the buildings they constructed for business,
amusement, and religion lay mostly within a half-mile radius
of this Old Fort; hereabouts stood the Government Offices,
the Court House, the residences of the judges, the " Harmonicon," the Playhouse, and other buildings mentioned
by Mrs. Fay, and here, shortly after her arrival, rose the
classical colonnade of St. John's Church. It is not known
where she and her husband set up house, but in later years,
after his desertion of her, she had a shop abutting on to
the St. John's churchyard, i.e. in Old Post Office Street,
now called Hastings Street (see note, p. 282).

North, east, and south of the English area dwelt " the
blacks " in some congestion, the richer blacks repairing
to the north. Also apart, though for other reasons, dwelt
the Governor-General, Warren Hastings, together with his
wife, the Lady Governess. Until recently the magnificent
couple had lived out at Belvedere, Alipore, but Hastings
had sold this house just before Mrs. Fay arrived, and the
house in which she pays her respects and which she calls
" Belvidere " must be some other mansion, at present
unidentified.

There was no bridge over the Hoogli, and consequently
little expansion on the western bank.

Those who care to evoke Mrs. Fay's Calcutta should
look at the charming set of coloured engravings of the
city by T. Daniell (1786–88), which breathe the very
spirit of Anglo-Indian origins; here are porticoes and
street scenes, esplanades, equipages, and mendicants, just
as they met her appraising eye. Among contemporary
maps Upjohn's (1791) is good. Literary assistance may

be found in Firminger's notes, Busteed's *Echoes from Old Calcutta*, and the pages of *Bengal, Past and Present*, an excellent periodical which specialises on topography.

THE DEVIS PORTRAIT

(*See Frontispiece*)

This amusing picture raises a small problem. It is reproduced from the engraving " by T. Alais " in the 1817 edition. I have failed to trace the original drawing. As the inscription states, Mrs. Fay is in Egyptian (not in Indian) costume—the clothes precisely correspond with her description of what she wore in Cairo—so one would assume that the portrait was made shortly after her arrival in Calcutta, *i.e.* about 1780, while she still had money, friends, youth, and interest in her escapade. But A. W. Devis, the artist, would then have been very young indeed— scarcely eighteen—nor can I find proof that he came East at so early a date. He was on an E.I.C. boat, the *Antelope*, in 1783, and was wrecked on the Pelew Islands, where he took part in the tribal wars of savages, and sketched them and their womenfolk between whiles (see *An Account of the Pelew Islands*, by George Keate, 1788—a fascinating work, replete with adventures that put the Fays' to shame). He was in Calcutta by 1784, and perhaps he drew Mrs. Fay then, but she had parted with her husband, lost her mother, and visited England in the interval, and it seems unlikely that she should retain either her Egyptian clothes or her enthusiasm about them through so many vicissitudes.

ORIGINAL LETTERS

FROM INDIA;

CONTAINING A NARRATIVE OF A

JOURNEY THROUGH EGYPT,

AND

THE AUTHOR'S IMPRISONMENT AT CALICUT

BY HYDER ALLY.

TO WHICH IS ADDED,

An Abstract of three subsequent Voyages to India.

―――――

BY Mrs. FAY.

―――――

PRINTED AT CALCUTTA.

――

1817

PREFACE

THE volume now submitted to the public, exhibits a faithful account of certain remarkable occurrences in the history of an individual, whose lot has been to make frequent visits to several distant regions of the globe, to mingle in the society of people of different kindreds and tongues, and to experience many vicissitudes of fortune. At a time when fictitious representations of human life are sought for with so much avidity, and constitute one of the principal sources of amusement in the hours of solitude, such a work as the present will, it is presumed, not be unacceptable. Those whose curiosity is attracted by the recital of incidents that never took place, or whose sensibility can be awakened by the description of emotions that were never felt, may perhaps derive a similar gratification from the following unembellished narrative of simple facts and real sufferings.

Five and thirty years ago, it was the fate of the author to undertake a journey over land to India, in company with her husband the late Anthony Fay Esq. who, having been called to the bar by the onorable society of Lincolns Inns, had formed the resolution of practising in the courts of Calcutta. They travelled through France, and over the Alps to Italy, whence embarking at Leghorn they sailed to Alexandria in Egypt. Having visited some of the curiosities in this interesting country, and made a short stay at Grand Cairo, they pursued their journey across the Desert to Suez. After passing down the Red Sea the ship in which they sailed touched at Calicut, where they were seized by the officers of Hyder Ally, and for fifteen weeks endured all the hardships and privations of a rigorous emprisonment.

When, after residing two years in India, the author, on account of circumstances explained in the course of the work, returned to her native country, she was repeatedly urged by several of her friends to publish some account of the events that had befallen her, which, it was supposed would engage the attention of the public, being connected with important circumstances in the lives of well known and respectable individuals, and illustrative of the character of a Potentate whose movements were the subject of serious alarm in India. But, at this period a woman who was not conscious of possessing decided genius or superior know-ledge could not easily be induced to leave " the harmless tenor of her way," and render herself amenable to the " pains and penalties " then, generally, inflicted on female authorships; unless inspired by that enthusiasm that tramples on difficulties, or goaded by misfortune which admits not of alternative. Being utterly uninfluenced by either of these motives, and having all the fear of criticism and aversion to publicity which characterizes the young women of her day, the author at that time declined com-plying with the wishes of those she yet highly honored, and never enquired farther after the fate of her letters, than to learn that they were duly received by those dear friends, to whom all her peregrinations and the knowledge of her eventual safety could not fail to be highly interesting.

Since then, a considerable change has gradually taken place in public sentiments, and its developement, we have now not only as in former days a number of women who do honour to their sex as literary characters, but many unpretending females, who fearless of the critical perils that once attended the voyage, venture to launch their little barks on the vast ocean through which amusement or instruction is conveyed to a reading public: The wit of Fielding is no longer held over them in terrorem, and the delineations of Smollet would apply to them in vain. The race of learned ladies ridiculed by these gentlemen is extinct. A female author is no longer regarded as an object of derision, nor is she wounded by unkind reproof from the *literary Lords of Creation*. In this indulgent era the author presumes to deliver her letters to the world as they have been preserved by the dear sister to whom they were partly addressed, trusting that as this is, in its nature, the most unassuming of all kinds of writing, and one that claims the most extensive allowances, they will be received with peculiar mercy and forbearance.

Since the period to which these letters refer, the Author has made voyages to India, touching in the course of them at various places in all the quarters of the globe, and has been engaged in commercial and other speculations. Her trials and anxieties, however, have produced only a long train of blasted hopes, and heart rending disappointments.— An account of these subsequent occurrences is therefore subjoined in a series of letters lately drawn from the original Journals and Memorandums, and addressed to a lady, whom the Author has the happiness to rank in the number of her friends.

Shadows, clouds, and darkness still rest on the remainder of her pilgrimage, which calls for the pilotage of kindness and the Day-star of friendship. She has, however, by the blessing of Providence been constantly enabled to rise superior to misfortune, and will not now in the evening of her days, derogate from the unostentatious energy of her character, or seek to solicit the pity of her readers by wearisome retrospect or painful complaints. With feelings acutely alive to kindness and truly grateful for every expression of it, she most thankfully esteems the generous patronage with which she has been honoured, and is rendered the more sensible of its value, because she is conscious, that it was not meanly solicited or unworthily obtained.

To the inhabitants of Calcutta, she begs more particularly to render her thanks. Long acquaintance, high esteem, and unfeigned affection call for this peculiar tribute. Five times has she visited this city, under various circumstances, and with different feelings, yet never had cause to regret the length or the dangers of the voyage, secure of ever meeting here all that could encrease the joys of social life, in its happiest moments, or soothe the hours of languishment in the days of adversity.

CALCUTTA, *Anno.* 1816.

ORIGINAL LETTERS

LETTER I.

FROM MRS. FAY.

Paris, 18*th April,* 1779.

I BELIEVE before I left England it was agreed that, my Letters should not in general be addressed to any one particularly, as they will be something in the style of journals; therefore a contrary method would be rather embarrassing—I suppose you begin to think that I have forgotten you all; but it really has not been in my power to write till now, of which assertion an account of our route will furnish abundant proof.—We reached Dover at about seven in the evening of the (*in my* eyes,) ever memorable 10th of April. The thoughts of what we all suffered on that day, can never be banished one instant from my recollection, till it shall please God to grant us a happy meeting. My constant prayers are that, we may be enabled to support this dreadful separation with fortitude—but I dare not trust myself with the subject; my very heart seems to melt as I write, and tears flow so fast as to compel me to shut one eye while I proceed. It is all in vain, I must leave off. And must weeks, nay months elapse before I can have the satisfaction of even hearing from you? How shall I support the idea! oh my dear Father! my beloved Mother! for your poor girl's sake, take care of your precious health; do not be unhappy. The Almighty will, I doubt not, preserve us to each other; something tells me that we shall meet again; and you have still two excellent children left to be your comfort; they I know will use every effort to keep

up your spirits; happy to be so employed! but let me not
repine; this trial is not permitted, but for all wise purposes.
I will now lay down my pen and endeavour to acquire a
calmer set of ideas, for I must either write with more
fortitude or not at all. Adieu for a little while; I will try
to take some refreshment, and then resume my pen.—Half-
past four P. M.—In vain I strive, the thoughts of home still
prevail, and totally preclude every other consideration. I
know no better method of chasing these intruders, than by
proceeding with the narrative of our journey; *allons donc*.
We embarked at Dover for Calais on the 11th at 5 P. M.
and had a most delightful passage of just three hours, from
port to port. I wished for a little sea sickness but either
the wind was not high enough, or I am become too good a
sailor, to expect benefit this way, for I remained perfectly
well. I assure you there is a deal of ceremony used here
now. On coming within gunshot of the Fort, we hoisted a
French flag, and were permitted to sail quite up to the
Quay. We met the other packet coming out, which
accounts for my not writing by that mail.—I have neglected
to mention that Mr. B— the young gentleman whom
Captain Mills recommended as a travelling companion,
joined us before we left England. His appearance is by
no means prepossessing; he seems a dissipated character
and more calculated to shine in convivial parties than to
render himself agreeable in the common routine of society;
whether this opinion be just or not, time will discover. On
landing we were all drawn up together, and ordered to the
Custom House, where we gave in our names, occupations,
&c. they next marched us about half a mile farther to wait
on the Governor, in order that he might put any questions
he chose to us; his Lordship not being visible, we were
forced to arm ourselves with patience and proceed to his
Commissary, where we found it a mere matter of form,
they asking but what was known before. However I assure

you, we thought more than we dared to express on the occasion. Only imagine how disagreeable to be dragged about in such a manner immediately after a Sea voyage instead of reposing ourselves. After all was settled, we first took places in the Diligence for the next day: then called on Monsr. Pigault de l'Epinoye, to whom you will remember I had been formerly introduced. He received us with his usual kindness and hospitality. This gentleman is descended in a direct line from one of the six brave Citizens of Calais, who so nobly offered themselves as victims to save their beloved country from the barbarous sentence pronounced against it by our third Edward. He is much esteemed by his countrymen on this account.

This being my fourth visit to Calais, I must of course have formerly described every thing worth notice there, so shall merely say we sat off from thence on the 12th Inst. at 8th A. M. and reached Boulogne about noon. The sight of this place brought to my mind many pleasant recollections of the social hours passed there. I called on several friends, and was much urged to prolong my stay among them, but that you know was impossible. Indeed far rather would I, had time permitted, have taken *one* turn round the ramparts, to enjoy the melancholy satisfaction of once again beholding the white cliffs of my dear native land, so frequently viewed from thence.

You must expect me to make frequent omissions and mistakes, for two men have just placed themselves under my windows with humstrums; and indeed there is constantly some noise or other through the day and evening; sometimes two or three dancing bears; and a few hours ago they exhibited a poor little Porcupine. I pitied the miserable animal from my heart. What can these unhappy creatures have done to merit being so tormented? (now by way of parenthesis, I could almost wish that a London mob had possession of the two musicians, as possibly the discipline

of a horse-pond might be of use in teaching them for the
future, better employment on Sunday evenings); but to
proceed: We left Boulogne (a place I shall ever admire, and
perhaps regret), and about ten at night reached Montreiul,
from whence we departed at three on Tuesday morning,
dined at Abbeville, and by eight in the evening were set
down at the same Inn, where you may remember we stopped
when travelling this road before, but were hurried away
when we had scarcely tasted a morsel, under pretence of the
Diligence being ready, and afterwards detained in the yard
an hour; nor did our hostess in any respect deviate from her
former character, as you shall hear. As a lady in company
and myself were greatly fatigued we chose tea, but none
being procurable there, were forced to use our own; the rest
sat down to supper, which I had predetermined to avoid
doing. Before they had a quarter finished, in came the
woman; never did I behold such a horribly looking great
creature. " Well " said she " the coach is ready " and on
being asked if she wanted to get rid of us, replied that it
was equal to her whether we went or staid provided she
were paid for our suppers: at last when compelled to
relinquish her claim on that score from the lady and me,
she insisted on being allowed twenty-four sous for the hot
water, this we complied with; to oblige our hospitable
countrywoman, (tell it not in Gath I blush to acknowledge
the claim) but persisted in remaining till on being summoned
by the driver, nearly an hour afterwards, we set off and
travelled sixty miles without alighting, to Chantilly, where
is a famous palace belonging to the Prince of Condé, but
to my great mortification, I was through weariness obliged
to remain in the house while the rest of the party went to
see it. Well never mind, you can read better descriptions
of it, than mine would have been. From thence we proceeded to St Denis, where I was fortunate enough to obtain
a cursory view of the ancient abbey; a most magnificent

structure, the burying place of the Kings of France. Such scenes naturally induce reflections on the vanity of all human grandeur, and lead to a melancholy, rather soothing than otherwise, to minds wearied by exertion, or irritated by disappointment. Having however little leisure to indulge these reveries, we passed on to the Library, where among other trophies is deposited the sword of our illustrious Talbot; a pang shot across my heart at the exulting manner in which it was exhibited; in short I felt as an English-woman, a more severe degree of national mortification than this Memento of an event so long gone by seemed calculated to produce. The sacred relics were next displayed, amongst which are, an eye of St Thomas the apostle, the shoulder blade of I forget what saint, and a small phial of the Virgin Mary's milk; at the sight of these absurdities I silently blessed God, that my religious instruction had not been blended with such cunningly devised Fables. If all the gems they shewed us were genuine, the Treasury must be immensely rich, for many of the shrines were almost covered with them. We arrived at Paris about eight on Wednesday; and most dreadfully fatigued was I; nor will that appear strange when one considers that, for the last sixty miles the carriage went as fast as eight horses could draw it, over a strong rough pavement; never stopping but to change horses, and at St. Denis to repair a wheel. As the post went off next morning, I could not recover myself sufficiently to write by it; but now feel quite strong again, and having brought you to Paris, may venture to take a little repose as it is past eleven. 9th 7 A. M. I have arisen thus early on purpose to finish my letter (which must be in the Office before ten). I find little alteration in this Place; the people behave as politely as if there were no War, or even dispute between us. This you know is not the region of Politics, therefore little can be mentioned under that head. I could communicate some few observations, but as perhaps this may be inspected, judge it more prudent to suppress them. A variety of circumstances has contributed to detain us here much longer than we intended; and I am fearful we shall not leave Paris before Thursday; however this will be the only letter I shall write until I can give you intelligence of our safe arrival at Marseilles, which will be I suppose in about a fortnight. From thence to Leghorn we must coast it in a Feluca. So if you write by the mail of the 29th addressed to me at the Post Office Leghorn, your letter will be sure to meet me there. I have a thousand things more to say, but must reserve them for my next, for if I miss the post it will I am sure, make you very uneasy—God bless you.

Your's affectionately.

LETTER II.

My dear Friends,

Being detained for want of our passports, I find
it necessary for my comfort to hold the only communication
now in my power with you. Last night we were at the
Colissée, a place resembling our Ranelagh; there were some
brilliant fire works to be exhibited, and as it is the custom
for Ladies to stand upon chairs to see them, a gentleman of
our party having placed us with our backs against a box,
went to procure some. During his absence the Queen [1]
entered the box attended by the Duchess D'Alençon, and
several other ladies. I had seen her Majesty before at
Verooilloo, and thought her at that time very handsome, but
had no idea how much better she would look, by candle
light. She is delicately fair and has certainly the sweetest
blue eyes that ever were seen; but there is a little redness,
a kind of tendency to inflammation around them, and she
is likewise slightly marked with the small pox; both which
trifling blemishes were then imperceptible, and she appeared
perfectly beautiful. On entering the box she sat down,
and pressed the Dutchess to sit also, which the latter in
terms of great respect declining, the Queen in a tone of
kindness that it is impossible to forget, said, "Then you
will oblige me to stand," rising as she spoke. The Duchess
then complied, and they conversed together very agreeably
during their stay. Her majesty seemed highly gratified
by the entertainments, and expressed her approbation, in

[1 N.B.—These small figures refer to terminal notes, p. 273.]

what I could not help thinking, rather too familiar a way for a person of her exalted rank: frequently clapping her hands and exclaiming aloud, " Ah! mon Dieu que c'est charmant, ah! que c'est joli." The Royal party soon retired, and we afterwards walked in the Rotunda! than which a more brilliant spectacle can scarcely be imagined. The ladies were all splendidly dressed, and their heads adorned with feathers in greater profusion, and far more lofty, than is customary with us. But enough of this, I must now turn to a very different subject, having hitherto neglected to inform you of a singular conversation (and its result) which passed in the Diligence, as we came to this place. We had among the passengers a Mr. H— an English Jew, and two brothers, named Ar—f diamond merchants, who were just returned to their native country after a long residence in London. The former had left Paris some years and resided in a provincial town. Speaking of this circumstance he observed that, his principal reason for quitting the Capital was his dread of assassination, to which he thought it probable that his religion might render him more liable, than other inhabitants; although he admitted he had no proof that persons of his persuasion were among the more frequent Victims. This statement, of course, excited both surprize and curiosity in us, who were foreigners; and the elder Mr. A—f evidently mortified at such discourse, and doubting a representation of facts from so prejudiced a quarter, and about which it had not fallen in his way to inquire, stoutly denied the charge; but the Jew would not give up the point. He said that in a certain part of the City, where there were many houses of ill fame, it was but too common to rob and murder those, who were inveigled into them, and afterwards throw the bodies into the Seine; when taken out they were conveyed to the Petit Chatelet to be owned, and that who ever would take the trouble to visit that place would find that, out of the numbers deposited there were very few (as reported) merely drowned persons; but evidently such as had died by violence. This conversation ended (as that of men frequently does) by a wager between the parties, both of whom agreed to refer the matter to Mr. Fay. The Jew was to lose, if, in one week seven bodies under such suspicious circumstances should not be found exposed at the Petit Chatelet. I thought this a monstrous supposition; for though I had often heard of people being drowned in the Seine, and the explicit detail of Mr. H— led me to fear that, the manner in which they met their fate, was but too truly described, yet I could not believe the number of victims to be so great. The result of Mr. F—'s researches has unhappily placed the fact beyond a doubt. Within the last seven days, ten miserable wretches have been exposed, who had marks of violence on their bodies, and of these, there were two dreadfully mangled. But I will say no more on this shocking subject than merely to observe, that there must be either some radical defect in the police, or a degree of ferocity in the people, not to be repressed by the severe penal Laws, which in other countries are found nearly adequate to the purpose. The slight degree of feeling expressed by the lower order in speaking of such things, even when pressed on their senses, evinces a hardness of heart approaching to absolute insensibility, that to me seems quite revolting: I myself asked a young woman, who had been peeping through the gate at the Petit Chatelet, what was to be seen there? "Oh" replied she, with great apparent indifference, " seulement quelques bras et jambes " (only some arms and legs). I have written myself into a train of most uncomfortable thoughts, so lest I infect you with the gloomy ideas that fill my mind, the wisest way will be to say adieu! We shall now soon be out of Paris.

Ever your's,

&c. &c.

LETTER III.

MY DEAR SISTER.

As I do not propose sending this before Monday,
I shall have full time to write every particular.   I date once
more from this sink of impurity, contrary to my expectation.
We have been detained thus long that the Lieutenant de
Police might have time to make the necessary enquiries
about us, but have at last obtained our passports, and thank
Heaven shall soon breathe a purer air.   From the first
place we stop at, I purpose giving you a further account of
our accommodations in the superb and elegant city of Paris,
famous throughout the world for its superiority over all
others, especially in the points of cleanliness and delicacy.
I assure you that, so long as I before resided in France, I
never till now formed an adequate idea of it: but adieu
for the present: I am going to drink tea.   How do you
think I make it?   Why in an earthen pot an inch thick
at least, which serves the double purpose of tea kettle and
teapot, so it is all boiled up together and makes a most
curious mess.

AUXERRE EN BURGOYNE,
130 *Milles De Paris.*

When I wrote the above I was in a great rage and not
without reason, pent up as we were in a street scarce wide
enough to admit the light; our chamber paved with tiles,
which most likely have never been wetted, nor even rubbed,

since the building of the house; add to this two *Commodités*
in the same state, on the stairs, and you will not wonder
that my constitution was not proof against the shock; the
very air I breathed seemed almost pestilential.   However
thank God I escaped with one of my feveretts of four days
continuance.   When I began this letter I was but just
recovering: no creature to do the least thing for me in the
way I had been accustomed to; obliged to prepare for my
departure the next morning, though scarcely able to crawl;
and to crown the whole a most extravagant bill for being
poisoned with Dirt.   Well we sat off, and the fresh country
air soon restored me to myself—but I have not told you
how we travel.

   We found the route totally different from what we
expected, and that we must be positively under the necessity
of going by land to Chalons sur Soane, which is three
hundred miles from Paris: now as we could get no remittances till our arrival at Leghorn, it did not suit us to
take the Diligence, so after mature deliberation we determined on purchasing two horses, and an old single horse-
chaise; but how to avoid being cheated, was the question;
for Mr. Fay did not care to depend on his own judgement
in horseflesh.—He made enquiry and found that there were
many englishmen employed in the stables of Noblemen
here; so putting a good face on the matter he went boldly
to the Duc de Chartres' Castle,[2] and scraped acquaintance
with his head groom, who was very proud to see a countryman, and immediately on being told the affair, offered his
assistance.   Accordingly they went next day to the cattle
Fair, where he pitched on an excellent draught horse, only
a little touched in the wind, on which account he procured
him for six guineas, so there cannot be much lost by him,
even if he turn out amiss.   But I dare say he will prove a
most useful beast, for he has drawn Mr. B—r, and myself
in our chaise (which by the bye we bought for seven guineas)

at the rate of thirty five miles a day: and does not seem in
the least fatigued, though we had our heavy trunk at our
back: so much for Azor—now for his help-mate Zemire.
In the course of conversation with his new friend, Mr. Fay
found that, there was a very pretty mare in the Duc de
Lausanne's stables, which had been intended for the course,
but would not bear training; so he agreed to give eight
guineas for her. Mr. B.— was to ride her next day to a
horse-race in the Bois de Boulogne, and we were to accompany him in a post chaise. But alas! poor man! it was
an unfortunate attempt. It seems he had never been used
to riding, and was ashamed to own it, (one of the weaknesses
to which I really believe men are almost invariably subject),
so wishing to pass for an excellent horseman, he mounted
with pretended courage: but through actual fear, reined her
in so tight that miss, knowing the weaknes of her rider,
reared up on her hind legs, threw him first, and then fell
backward over him. We thought by the violence of the
fall that he must have been killed, but he came off with a
few bruises; we had him bled immediately, put him to bed
and left him in good hands till our return. Mr. Fay
mounted Zemire, and we proceeded to the course, where we
were very agreeably entertained, only it grieved me to see
so many beautiful English horses galloping about; I could
hardly believe myself in France, for all the gentlemen were
dressed after our manner. The Count D'Artois might
very well have been taken for a Jockey in his buck-skin
breeches, and round hat. The bets were chiefly between
him and the Duc de Chartres; the horses were all rode by
englishmen: as to our little mare she would fain have been
amongst them, but she had now a rider who knew how to
manage her, and is punished for her audacity; for Mr. B—
has not the courage to mount her again, and she is forced
to carry Mr. Fay with a portmanteau of twenty pounds
weight—You will wonder at my temerity when I acknow-

ledge having myself ventured to mount Zemire, after Mr.
B——'s accident. I first however saw her tried by several
persons, and wishing to be able to vary the exercise by
riding now and then, during our journey, was induced to
make the attempt. She performed twice very well; but
on the third day, an umbrella being snapped close to
her nose, just as I was going to set off, she began to
rear, on which I instinctively abandoned both whip and
reins, and throwing my whole weight forward, clasped
her round the neck with all my might, this sudden
manœuvre fortunately kept her down: I seized the critical
moment and alighted in safety with no other injury, than
a little fright, and the consciousness of looking rather
foolish. Nor has she ever been guilty of the like towards
any one; so that my character for horsemanship is completely established. We have been certainly very lucky
in our purchases: the horses perform well, and the chaise,
without being particularly uneasy, seems very strong. I
am told they will bring a good price in the South, but you
shall hear.

I have nothing particular to say of the country; perhaps
it may be national prejudice from which no person is entirely
free, but notwithstanding all their boasting, I do not think
it equals my own dear England. It must be allowed that
the present season is not the most favourable for making
observations, for they cut the Vines close to the stumps in
the winter, and as they are not yet much sprouted, one sees
nothing but a parcel of sticks in the manner of our hop
poles, but not above thirty inches high, which gives an air
of barrenness to the prospect. I do not know what my
mother would do here, as she is not fond of wine; for there
is nothing else to drink. For my own part, and I believe
I may answer for my companions, I cannot say that I find
any great hardship in being obliged to put up with tolerable
Burgundy at about four pence a bottle; it is not at all

heady, so no creature thinks of drinking it with water. A
pint every meal is the allowance of each. We have all
necessaries with us, such as tea, sugar, bread, butter, corn
for the horses &c: so we have little to do with the Inns,
except at night, when we provide ourselves with meat for
the next day. As to breakfast and dinner we fix on a place
where there is water at hand, and there sit down under the
shade of a tree, and make a fire, while the horses graze
comfortably, and eat their corn. Ask my dear father if he
does not think this a good plan? at least we find it pleasant,
and much more to our taste, than spending more time as
well as money, in the wretched public houses we have
hitherto met with — I wish we were hardy enough to
make the grass our pillow; but that is impossible, so
we must submit to be disgusted and pillaged once a
day. You may remember my remarking that, I was
afraid we should suffer during our journey, for the fine-
ness of the spring which has proved to be the case. The
weather has been excessively boisterous for the last fortnight with much rain, than which nothing can be more
disagreeable on a journey, especially when conducted on
a plan like ours.—We were obliged to stop at Fontainbleau on account of the weather by which means we
saw the Palace, and gardens, and were almost wet through,
for our pains. It is an immense place; the Chapel
has been beautiful, but the paintings are much injured
by time. There is an elegant theatre which I was
much pleased with. The apartments of the royal family
are truly superb. We were shewn the council chamber
where the last peace was signed, and I, as an Englishwoman,
beheld it with *great pleasure* you may be sure. We saw
likewise the gallery of *Stags*, famous for containing above a
hundred stags' heads all ranged in order with an account,
when they were killed and by whom, and infamous (at least
in my opinion) as being the place where Christina, Queen

of Sweden, caused Monaldeschi her chief chamberlain to be beheaded, if not absolutely in her presence, at least while she remained in an adjoining room. I cannot bear that woman. She abdicated her crown from sheer vanity but retained that passion for despotism which shewed what kind of feelings she had cherished, while seated on the throne. I think that in her, the faults of either sex were blended, to form a character, which without possessing the firmness of a man or the gentleness of a woman, was destitute of the virtues expected in both. Christina may have been an accomplished female; but she can never be called great, even by her admirers.

The gardens of Fontainbleau are all in the old fashioned-gingerbread - style, ornamented with box in a thousand fantastical shapes. The Swiss who shewed us the Palace, was very thankful for a shilling, which is more than any person in the same situation would be in England for twice as much. The forest of Fontainbleau is thirty miles across, and nobody can hunt there without the Kings permission; he comes here every season.—We found the roads very heavy, but Azor was strong enough to go through them; however we have given him a day's rest, and after dinner shall set off Jehu like.

Now don't you envy us all this pleasure? I assure you I should be very glad to go all the way in the same manner, for we travel without fatigue, and the way of living just suits me; for you know I always preferred wine to beer, but I would not have you imagine that I can shake off all thoughts of home; they return but too frequently, and I really believe now, that my illness at Paris, was brought on principally by uneasiness of mind: but I find myself un-equal to this subject. I must make a resolution never to enter upon it; for what service can it do to either of us, to be continually recalling unpleasant ideas; especially when I have need of every possible consolation to support me in the arduous task, which Providence has called upon me to undertake.

I have now literally exhausted my paper, and must therefore leave you to imagine every thing my heart says to all, and how truly

I am,

your affectionate

&c. &c.

LETTER IV.

Leghorn, 17*th June,* 1779.

MY DEAR SISTER.

I suppose you have been long uneasy at my silence, but indeed it has not been in my power to write sooner—In my last I gave you reason to imagine we should arrive here in less than three weeks, by way of Marseilles; but after we reached Lyons we were informed, that this would prove a very uncertain and dangerous method; as between the English and French scarcely any vessel can pass free: therefore after mature deliberation, we determined as we had still our carriage and horses, to push our way boldly through Savoye, and cross the Alps to Italy. We stopped several days at Lyons, which as you and all the world know has long been famous for its incomparable silks, and velvets; I think it ought to be so for its asparagus which is the finest I ever tasted; and remarkably cheap. Being a vegetable I am very fond of, and having found it at all times beneficial to my constitution, I wished to eat it freely; but was almost disgusted by the manner in which it was constantly brought to table at the Inn, covered with a thick sauce composed of eggs, butter, oil and vinegar.

Having in vain remonstrated against this cookery, I at length insisted on seeing the Cook himself; and when he made his appearance, arrayed as is customary, in a white waistcoat, cap, and apron, with a meagre face almost as sharp as the large knife he held in his hand, I calmly represented to him that the sauce he had sent up, totally disagreed with my stomach, and requested to have the asparagus simply boiled with melted butter, the poor man looked much distressed " What without oil! " yes! " Without eggs "? certainly! this answer completed his misery, " Ah madame " exclaimed he, with clasped hands and uplifted eyes " de grace un peu de vinaigre ". Madame was inexorable, and the shrug of contemptuous pity with which he retreated was ludicrous beyond expression.

On arriving near the Alps, it appeared that I had formed a very erroneous idea of the route, having always supposed that we had only one mountain to pass, and that the rest of the way was level ground; instead of which when we came to Pont de Beauvoisin (50 miles from Lyons, and the barrier between France and Savoye) we heard the agreeable news, that we had a hundred and twelve miles to travel thro' a chain of mountains, to the great Mont Cenis.

You may imagine how uncomfortable this information made us all; with what long faces we gazed upon each other, debating how the journey was to be performed; but being happily you know very courageous, I made light of all difficulties, and whenever there was a hill, mounted Zemire, while the two gentlemen took it by turns to lead me as I had not a proper side saddle, so poor Azor made shift to drag the chaise up pretty well, and in the descents we made him pay for the indulgence. I forgot to mention that they were very particular about our passports at this Barrier, and detained us while the Governor examined them minutely, though justice compels me to acknowledge that in general we were treated with great politeness in our passage through France; no one ever attempted to insult us, which I fear would not be the case were three French people to travel in England; I wish I could say as much for their honesty; but I must confess that here they are

miserably deficient, however my being acquainted with the
language saved us from flagrant imposition.

Our method was this: we always if possible, contrived
to stop at night in a large Town, (as to dinner we easily
managed that you know how), but never did we suffer the
horses to be put into the stable till I had fixed the price
of every thing; for they generally ask four times as much
for any article as it is worth. If I found there was no
bringing them to reason, we left the house. In particular,
at Chalons sur Soane, the first Inn we stopped at, the woman
had the conscience to ask half a crown for each bed; you
may suppose we did not take up our abode there, but drove
on to another very good house, where they shewed us two
rooms with six excellent beds in them, at the rate of four
sous a bed, for as many as we wanted; so for once I committed an act of extravagance by paying for the whole; or
we might perhaps have been disturbed in the night by
strangers coming to take possession of those left vacant.
For they are not very nice about such matters in France.
I have seen rooms with six beds in them more than once
during our route. I only mention the difference of price
by way of shewing what people may gain by choosing their
houses, for we were really better accommodated at less than
one fourth of what we must have paid at the other house.
Speaking of Chalons reminds me of a very unpleasant
circumstance that occurred to us at the following stage.
Mr. Fay had most unwisely and contrary to my earnest
intreaty, pinned our passports to the book of roads, which
he usually carried with him on horse back, and as might
be expected, they, in a short time worked themselves loose,
and we were on our arrival at the end of the next day's
journey alarmed with the idea of their being intirely lost,
and that we should be compelled to return all the way to
Paris to procure others: happily Mr. Fay went back &
found them at a place where we had stopped, I need not

tell you what fright and vexation, this folly and obstinacy cost us: but I hope it will have a salutary effect for the rest of our journey.

In further proof of my assertion on the subject of honesty, I must relate a little incident which occurred on our way to Lyons. Mr. Fay had changed as many guineas at Paris, as he thought would be sufficient to bring us to Chalons, and received by weight twenty four livres ten sous, for each, that is seven pence halfpenny profit: well, the last day but one we finished our current money, but as we were in a city, doubted not of being able to obtain nearly the value of our guineas. On inquiry we were recommended—to a very religious goldsmith who by the landlord's account spent almost his whole life in acts of piety: after waiting an hour and a half till he returned from mass, Mr. F. delivered him a guinea, confident of receiving its full value: when behold this conscientious gentleman after the most minute inspection and weighing it in a pair of sugar scales generously offered eighteen livres as a fair price: which so enraged Mr. Fay that he immediately left him and went to another shop, where the utmost they would give was *twelve* livres: only think what wretches! since it was impossible for them to be ignorant of its real value. Mr. Fay declared that he would rather fast all day than submit to become such a dupe. This subjected us to great inconvenience; after discharging the reckoning we had only thirty sous remaining; and sat out with a sum not sufficient to procure a single refreshment for our poor horses; so that at every Inn we were obliged to represent our situation: but found none who had honesty enough to offer us a fair price for our guineas, or the charity to give us even a glass of wine or a morsel of bread. I leave you to guess if our appetites were not pretty keen by the time we arrived at Lyons. I shall never forget how foolishly we looked at each other all day; however a good supper obliterated all grievances, and the next morning we found a way to change our guineas for Louis-d'ors on equitable terms. So much for our starving adventure. To proceed on our journey.

On the 20th we reached Lanneburg, a village at the foot of Mont Cenis situated in what is called a valley, which though really so with respect to the mountains that surround it, is even with the clouds. I had a tolerable proof of its elevation, for the weather was so sharp, that I could not keep a minute from the fire. By the way I must observe, that having travelled through North Wales, I supposed myself to have acquired a tolerable idea of mountains and their appendages, such as cascades, torrents, and apparently air-hung-bridges &c. but the passage of the Alps set at defiance all competition, and even surpasses whatever the utmost sketch of my imagination could have pourtrayed.

The valley of Lanneburg is itself, the most strange wild place you can conceive, in some parts grotesque, in others awfully terrible. The rocks rise around you so fantastically, that you might almost think yourself transported to a place which nature had made a repository of these stupendous productions, rather with a view of fixing them hereafter in appropriate situations, than of exhibiting them here.

But above all, the cascades throughout the road are charming beyond description; immense sheets of water are seen sometimes, falling from rock to rock; foaming fretting and dashing their spray on every side; and sometimes descending in one grand flow of majestic beauty: in short they went so far beyond any idea I had formed of such appearances in nature, that they seemed to communicate new powers of perception to my mind, and if I may so express it, to expand my soul, and raise it nearer to its Creator. The passage has been so ably described by various writers that any formal account I could give you of it, would rather waste your time than add to your

information.   I shall only tell you how I felt and acted for I
know your affection prompts the wish to travel in imagination with the sister you love; come then let us ascend
Mont Cenis together.—After various deliberations it was
concluded that I should go up across a mule, as the safest
way; both the gentlemen determined on walking, which
Mr. Fay knew not to be very difficult, having made the
experiment the evening before.   I was strictly forbidden
to touch the reins, being assured that the animal would
guide himself, and that any attempt to direct him could
hardly fail to prove *fatal*.   Under this charge, judge what
I must have felt when my mule, in the very steepest part
of the ascent and when I had become fully sensible of the
" high and giddy height," all at once, thought proper to
quit the pathway, and with great sang froid stalk out upon
one of those precipitous projections, where only the foot of
a wild Goat or Chamois ought to tread.   What did I not
suffer!   I durst not touch the rein, durst not even call to
the guide for help.   Every instant appeared fraught with
destruction, it seemed madness to die without an effort to
save one's self, yet to *make* an effort was to invite the fate
one dreaded.   Happily this dreadful poise between life and
death lasted not long; for, the sagacious animal calmly
picking its way fell into the track by a path, which no
human eye could discern, and the guides gave me great
praise for my self-command; a praise I never desire to
purchase again by a similar trial.   If however anything
could render a stranger easy in crossing the heights, it
would be the amazing skill and celerity which these people
display; the road winds in a zigzag direction; and in the
most acute, and of course, in the most dangerous turns they
leap from crag to crag as if they held their lives on lease,
and might safely run all risks, till the term expired.—The
plain, as it is called, at the top of this mountain is six miles
across: as we proceeded we found " still hills on hills, and

Alps on Alps arise " ; for we continued to be surrounded by snow top mountains, where reigns eternal frost.   The heat of the sun had thawed the passage, so that we met with no inconvenience, but we passed great quantities of ice lodged in the crannies.   There is a very large lake on the plain, said to be unfathomable; that I can tell nothing about, but that it contains excellent, salmon and trout, am well convinced, for we stopped at the Inn according to the laudable custom of all travellers, for the sole purpose of tasting it.   An Inn, say you, at the top of Mont Cenis! Yes, it is really a fact, not that I envy them their situation, but they are not the only inhabitants:. for there are more than twenty farm houses, where they make most excellent butter and cheese.   Every spot around, where it is possible for the hand of cultivation to scatter seeds for the use of man, is treasured with care and nourished by industry; and you see gardens no bigger than a dining table, and fields like a patch of carpet, from time to time, smiling beneath the rugged battlements of rocks, like the violets peeping in the hedges.   Far, among the apparently inaccessible heights of this " cloud capt " region, they pointed out to me a Chapel, vulgarly called notre Dame de Neige; and justly have they named her, for eternal snows designate her dwelling; if however these simple and sequestered beings can there draw near to God, and experience the comfort of religious hope, and providential care, this singular edifice has not been reared in vain, to bless such a region of desolation.

When you read an account of the road, it will readily be perceived that my fellow travellers must have found some difficulty in getting the horses over, as the poor beasts were not accustomed to such a rugged path; for you are to understand that, the people in the neighbouring villages of Lanneburg and Novalese have no other means of subsistence than carrying passengers over the mountain.   It is therefore their interest to render it impassable to any but themselves, so that the whole passage of fifteen miles, is covered with great loose pieces of rock, which must be clambered over: the guides skip from one piece to another like goats, and go at the rate of five or six miles an hour; but my unfortunate companions could not proceed at this pace; so every ten minutes we had to wait for them—As I was carried down in an armed chair, fastened to poles and slung upon straps, in the manner of our sedans, between two men and in which I soon felt tolerably at my ease; I had the pleasure of seeing them continually: sometimes in the clouds, and at others nothing visible but their heads, which was rather amusing to me, knowing they were in no danger, especially as Mr. Fay had affected to make very light of it, and even said " I might walk very well if I chose it," but when we reached the bottom, he told a very different tale, and stormed violently at his own sufferings. The drollest part of our procession was, that of the poor mule which bore our chaise in a kind of machine, on its back; and another with the two wheels placed on each side, in the oddest way imaginable. A good night's rest put us all in good humour, and we proceeded cheerfully forty miles along a very delightful road, for the most part planted with double rows of trees, to Turin, where we remained three days and were much amused; but having crossed the mountain, I must allow myself and you a little rest.

June, 26th.—I was more pleased with the Palace at Turin than any other I have met with during our journey, not for its external appearance certainly, for that is unpromising, but the inside simply atones for the deficiency. The rooms are all in long ranges, opening into each other by doors, which by folding within the pannels become invisible. The furniture is beyond description rich and elegant, but the best part of every finely decorated house must ever be the paintings, and this palace seemed to say, " You are already in Italy: " like a true Englishwoman however, I looked more, I believe, at a picture of our Charles the first, and afterwards at one by Vandyke of that unfortunate monarch's three children, than at any other in the collection. The face of the King is exquisitely done, but his dress struck me as too fine, and withal so stiff, that I could not admire it. Poor Charles! we are tempted to forget the errors of the Prince, in considering the amiable qualities and long sufferings of the man: nor is it possible to contemplate the benevolent melancholy of his counte- nance, and credit every accusation of his enemies. I looked on his mild penetrating eyes, till my own were suffused with tears. As to his children, they are the sweetest creatures I ever beheld; and to see them thus, was perhaps the more pleasant, from a consciousness of its being the only period wherein they could communicate that sensation to a reflecting mind.—There was no tracing the selfish, and eventually, callous libertine in Charles; nor the tyrant and bigot in James; all seems playful grace, and dignified gentleness; and the painter appears to have given a kind of royal polish to the beauty (certainly far beyond nature) which he had so happily depicted in these unfortunate children. Among what I deemed the most curious portraits, were those of Martin Luther, and his wife. I have frequently meditated on this great character, and always felt myself so much obliged to him (especially since my residence in a Catholic country,) that I confess I was disappointed to see him a homely, and rather vulgar looking man. I cannot believe this is a good likeness; at least the one I saw of him in the abbey of St Bertin at St Omers left a very different impression on my mind. The Reformer might not be handsome, in the common accepta- tion of the word, but surely, penetration courage and firm- ness must have stampt their expression on his features.

Here is a terrible representation of another great man, tho'
in my opinion deficient in the first mentioned quality (Sir
Thomas Moore) of his head rather, for it appears just
severed from the body; his daughter has fainted at the
horrible spectacle; and her complexion is so exactly what
it should be, that the whole scene appears natural, and you
feel too much for her, even to offer her restoratives to life
and misery. I would not live in the same room with such
a picture for the world; it would be worse than the cave of
Trophonious.

I was doomed to experience another disappointment in
what is affirmed to be a faithful portrait of Petrarch's Laura,
which I had fancied was like the Venus of Apelles, an
assemblage of all that was lovely and graceful in woman.
You remember my saying, that it was worth all the pains I
took in learning Italian, to read his sonnets in praise of this
idolized being. So no wonder that I ran eagerly to seize
on features that had inspired such verses, and awakened
such tender constancy as Petrarch displayed. Judge then
how disagreeably I was surprised at seeing a little red-
haired, formal looking, old maidish thing, no more like the
beauty in " my mind's eye " than " I to Hercules. . . ."
Petrarch too was as ugly as needs be. Well, well, they are
not the only couple seen to most advantage in their Poetic
dress. What further I have to say about the Palace, must
be very concise. I cannot help informing you though,
that we saw the King of Sardinia at mass with his whole
family but none of them seem to be remarkable for beauty.
Though not esteemed rich, yet he lives in great splendour;
the furniture of his state bed-chamber, even to the frames
of the chairs, is all of massive silver.[3]

The Theatre is a vast building and so magnificent in
every respect, that nothing you have seen can give you any
idea of it; the stage is so extensive, that when they want to
exhibit battles, triumphant entries, or any kind of grand

show they have room enough to produce the finest effect, and really seem to transport you to the scene they would represent.   It is not uncommon to have fifty or sixty horses, at a time upon this stage, with triumphal cars, thrones &c &c.   The King's box, is consistent with his superb Palace; it is as large as a handsome parlour, and lined throughout with mirrors, which have a beautiful effect, as they reflect the stage and thus double the display of its grand processions &c: all the boxes in this Theatre are neat and commodious; furnished with chairs and curtains, so that if the party choose to be retired they are at full liberty; and, as coffee and other refreshments are served, they frequently pay little attention to the Stage, except when some celebrated performer or grand spectacle excites their curiosity.   There is a smaller Theatre, which opens when this is closed, but I did not see it.   I visited the royal gardens, but thought them very uninteresting, as all appear after those that surround the seats of our English Nobility and gentry; and on running thro' another Palace, an academy and various other places, nothing struck me as sufficiently novel to merit your attention; and, I have written such an intolerably long letter, that I must conclude for the present, tho' I mean to bring you on my journey to-morrow, as I have not yet told you half that is on my mind; but there is such an uncertainty in my present movements, that it is desirable not to lose a single day in forwarding a letter.   Believe me however and wherever I may be,

most affectionately yours,

E. F.

In Continuation.

Leghorn, 28*th June*.

I RESUME my journal of yesterday which I shall now inclose in this; I am still waiting a summons for departure, and anxious to say all I can, to my dear friends, before what may probably be a long adieu. From Turin we sat out on the 26th ultimo, to Genoa, a distance of 130 miles; and now I own my courage begun to fail; for having been some days ill, I grew so much worse, from the motion of the chaise, that we were obliged to stop and get Mr. Fay's horse ready for me to ride, which was a great ease to me; but notwithstanding this relief, on the second evening I was seized with every symptom of fever, and that of the most violent kind; " Well," thought I, " it is all over with me for a week at least; " but thank God I was mistaken, for at two o'clock in the morning, I fell into the most profuse perspiration I ever experienced, which, tho' it exceedingly weakened me, yet considerably abated the disorder, and altho' I felt ill, dispirited, and every way unfit to travel, yet I made a sad shift to pursue my journey.

Unfortunately, in coming out of Alessandria the place where I had been so ill, we had a wide river to ford, and there was no way for poor miserable me to get over, but by Mr. Fay's taking me before him across the mare, which was tolerably well accomplished. When he had landed me safe he went back, and with great difficulty whipped the old horse through; he was up to the girth in water, and I expected every moment, he would break the chaise to pieces for he frequently attempted to lie down. When we had overcome this difficulty we continued in tolerable spirits, until our arrival next day at the Buchetta, an appenine mountain, by the side of which Mont Cenis would appear contemptible; it is near twenty miles over, without any plain at the top, so that no sooner do you reach its summit, than you turn short, and descend immediately. Had the weather proved fine, the prospect from this prodigious eminence must have been glorious; but so thick a fog enveloped us, that we could not distinguish any thing of five yards distance, and the cold was as piercing as with us in January. Never shall I forget the sense of wearisome, overbearing desolateness, which seemed to bow down both my body and mind at this juncture. I felt a kind of dejection unknown before through all my peregrinations, and which doubtless tended to increase the unusual fears that operated on my mind, when we arrived at the end of this day's journey. It was nearly dark; the Inn was little better than a large barn or hovel, and the men we found in it, so completely like all we conceive of Banditti, and assassins, that every horrible story I had heard or read of, instantly came into my head; and I perceived that the thoughts of my companions were occupied in the same painful way; our looks were the only medium of communication we could use, for we were afraid of speaking, lest we should accelerate the fate we dreaded. Every thing around us combined to keep alive suspicion and strengthen fear; we were at a distance from every human habitation: various whisperings, and looks directed towards us, continually passed amongst the men, and we fancied they were endeavouring to find whether we had any concealed arms. When we retired for the night worn out as we were, not one dared to sleep and surely never night appeared so long. With the earliest dawn we departed, and as the people saw us set out without offering us any injury, we are now persuaded that we wronged them; but yet the impression made upon our minds will not easily be effaced: we feel as if we had escaped some projected mischief.

We arrived pretty early at Genoa, a grand but gloomy disagreeable city, owing to the houses being very high, and the streets so narrow you might almost shake hands across them out of the window. It abounds with magnificent Churches and Palaces, principally built of the most beautiful marble, at least they are faced and ornamented with it. Their roofs flat, and rendered very agreeable gardens, by flowering shrubs, little arbours, covered with wood-bine and jessamine, elegant verandahs, awnings &c. In these the ladies wander from morning to night.—As far as I can hear or see, they are more remarkable for pride than any thing else. Their dress costly, but heavy and unbecoming, except so far as they manage their veils, which are so contrived as to give very good play to a pair of fine eyes. They wear rouge; but apply it better than the French ladies, who may be said rather to plaster than to paint: when the best however is made of this practice it is still a very hateful one in my opinion.—I went to view the Palaces of Doria, Doraggio, and Pallavicini, where are many fine pictures and statues; but the rooms are so large, and so many of them are only half furnished, that they had on the whole an uncomfortable look. I was much pleased with several of the churches; the Cathedral is completely lined with marble, but I was attracted more by the Jesuits' church on account of the paintings, though, I have neither health nor spirits to enter into a particular description of them. The assumption of the Virgin by Guido, is a most delightful performance to my taste. I always admire his pictures, but being simply an admirer, without knowledge on the subject, I seldom hazard a remark as to the manner in which a piece is executed.—The theatre here is large, but not to be compared with that at Turin. The gardens are every where in the same style, all neat and trim, like a desert Island in a pastry cook's shop, with garnish and frippery enough to please a Dutchman. There are many admirable churches in this city; but its chief boast, in my opinion, consists in being the birth place of Columbus, who was undoubtedly a great man, and from his talents, firmness, wisdom and misfortunes, entitled to inspire admiration and pity. I often thought of him, as I passed these streets and was ready to exclaim, you were not worthy of such a Citizen. The velvets, goldwork, and artificial flowers manufactured

here, are said to be unrivalled; but I made no purchases
for very obvious reasons.

We saw a very grand procession on Corpus Christi
day, at which the Doge assisted, and all the principal
nobility, clothed in their most magnificent habiliments,
and each carrying a lighted taper; several images also,
adorned with jewels (as I was informed) to an almost incredible amount, were borne along to grace the spectacle.
It is to be lamented that, this noble city should disgrace
itself by the encouragement given to assasination, for a
man after committing half a score murders, has only to
take a boat which nobody prevents him from doing, and
claim the protection of any foreign ship, which none dares
to refuse, and there he remains in safety. Mr. Fay saw
five of these wretches on board one vessel. What you have
heard respecting the custom of married women in Italy
being attended by their Cicisbeos, is perfectly true. They
speak of it with all the indifference imaginable. Surely,
after all that has been said, the usage must be an innocent
one, if any thing can be called so which tends to separate
the affections of husband and wife, and *that*, the constant
attendance, the profound respect of another man, must be
likely to effect. Altogether it is a vile fashion, make the
best of it, and I heartily hope never to see such a mode
adopted in old England.

We sold our horses at Genoa, for about three guineas
profit—and no more, as Mr. Fay embraced the first offer
that was made him. You who know me, will be well
aware, that I could not part with these mute but faithful
companions of our journey without a sigh. Far different
were my sensations on bidding adieu to our fellow traveller
Mr. B——r, who left us on our arrival at this place. My
first impression of his character was but too just, and every
day's experience more fully displayed a mind, estranged
from all that was praise worthy, and prone to every species

of vice. He professed himself almost an Atheist, and I am persuaded, had led the life of one; it was perhaps fortunate that his manners were as disgusting as his principles were wicked, and that he constantly reminded one, of that expression of the Psalmist " the *Fool* hath said in his heart there is no God "; as the comment, he was but a fool, rose to remembrance at the same moment.

We took our passage in a Felucca from Genoa, and arrived here in thirty three hours. My first message was to the Post Office, where was only one letter for me, dated 10th May. I am impatient for more, being kept in daily expectation of sailing, and it would be mortifying to leave any behind. I must now conclude; believe me,

Ever most affectionately your's,
E. F.

P. S. I open this to say, our letters and remittances are arrived. Ten thousand thanks for your kindness, but I have not time to add another word.

LETTER V.

Outer Mole, Leghorn,
On board the Hellespont,

My Dear Friends,

July 2nd, 1779.

You may perceive from this date that I have quitted Leghorn, but how I came to take up my quarters *here*, cannot be explained, till after the relation of some particulars which I must first notice, in order to proceed regularly with my journal.

Our letter of introduction from Mr. Baretto [4] of London to his brother, the king of Sardinia's Consul at Leghorn, procured us the kindest attentions from that gentleman and his family, indeed they were so friendly to us in every respect, that I soon felt all the ease of old acquaintance in their society, and shall ever remember them, with sentiments of the most cordial esteem. Through this kind family I saw whatever was worthy of note in Leghorn, and its environs; but my increasing anxiety as to our journey, took from me all power of investigation. When one sees merely with the eye, and the wandering mind is travelling to the friends left far behind, or forward to the unknown clime whither its destiny points, few recollections of places and things will remain on it. But far different will be its recognition of persons. When these have softened an anxious hour by kindness, or relieved its irksomeness, by smiles and gaiety, the heart will register their action and their image, and gratitude engrave their names on the tablet of remembrance. What a romantic flight! methinks I hear you exclaim; but consider, this is the land of Poesy, surely, I may be permitted to evince a little of its spirit. I shall never forget that Leghorn contains the Baretti's, and Franco's. The latter are eminent merchants; the house has been established above a century. The eldest of the present family is above eighty years of age; a most venerable and agreeable old man; with more of active kindness and benevolent politeness, than I ever met with in one, so far advanced in life, and who has seen so much of the world. He not only shewed us every attention during our stay, but has given us a letter recommending us in the strongest terms to a Mr. Abraham, of Grand Cairo; which should Mr. Baldwin, the East India Company's resident, be absent when we arrive there, may prove useful. At all events, we are equally indebted to Mr. Franco's friendly intentions.

We have often boasted of the superiority of the British flag, but alas poor old England! her flag is here humbled in the dust; we have several ships in the mole, but if one dare venture out, so many French Privateers are hovering round, that she must be taken in a few hours. I pity the poor Captains from my heart, but the person for whom I feel most interested, is a Captain Les—r of the Hellespont, (Mr. P—'s relation). I cannot express half what I owe to his civility. From the moment he knew of my probable connection with his family, he has uniformly shown us every possible attention. His situation is very disagreeable, to be forced either to abandon so fine a ship, or incur almost a certainty of being taken prisoner in her, as she must soon venture out; for she has already eaten her head off, by lying here a whole twelvemonth on expence, as such is the deplorable state of our commerce in the Mediterranean, that no one will now underwrite an English ship at any premium. I think the number lying here is seven, and believe they intend soon to make a bold push together; but it will be all in vain; they never can get through the Straits of Gibraltar, unmolested.

4 o'clock p. m. A Hard Gale.

I told you this morning what reason I had to esteem Captain L.— He is now entitled to at least a double portion of my gratitude, if estimated by the service done. As there was no likelihood of meeting with an English vessel, we engaged a passage in a Swedish one, called the *Julius*, Captain Norberg, for Alexandria, at £6 each, (cheap enough you will say); and had all in readiness: so last night I quitted the shores of Europe, God knows for how long: his will be done. Captain L.— as his ship lay next but one to our's, and we were not to sail 'till day break, offered us his cabin, because, as he very considerately observed, we could not sleep confortably in our own, amidst the noise of preparing for Sea. I readily complied, well knowing the advantages of his proposal, having already dined several times on board the Hellespont, which is kept clean and in good order, equal to the nicest house I ever saw. This morning the Julius went out to the Road, and we prepared to follow; but just at that time arose a sudden squall of thunder and lightning, succeeded by a very strong gale of wind; the poor Julius was forced to drop anchor, and there she lies, two miles off, pitching (driving piles Captain L— calls it) and has just struck her lower yards; she slipped one cable two hours ago, but the other brought her up. I see her now and would not exchange cabins for a trifle.

Several vessels have been driven in, in distress; one dashed directly against the Hellespont and snapped her Bowsprit short; we had but just time to secure the poop lanthorn from the stroke of another; the *iron* was torn away, so you may guess it blows smartly, but I feel perfectly easy. I am luckily sheltered now, and no one shall persuade me to leave this ship 'till all is over, and the weather settled again. I doubt we shall not be able to sail this day or two, for the wind is rising; but so that we arrive, time enough to save our season at Suez, all will be well. Tea is waiting, and they are tormenting me to death. Adieu. God bless you all, prays,

Your affectionate
E. F.

LETTER VI.

Ship Julius at sea, 20*th July*, 1779.

I HOPE, my dear friends will safely receive my letter of the 2nd Instant, from Leghorn, wherein I mentioned the kindness of Captain L.— and our situation in his Ship. We remained with him 'till Sunday evening, when we embarked on the Julius, and the following morning, sailed with a fair wind, but it changed in less than six hours, and came on so strong, that we were forced to put back again and cast anchor. The gale lasted 'till Wednesday evening; however we made shift to ride it out, though we were continually paying out cable (as it is called;) and expected every moment to be driven on shore.

When the weather moderated, Mr. Franco sent off a letter to Mr. Fay, stating that he had just heard from Mr. Abraham of Grand Cairo, who was about to proceed to Europe, with his family, by the first ship; therefore to guard against any future disappointment, this kind gentleman inclosed a general letter to the Jewish merchants, Mr. Franco's name being well known throughout the East. Having already seven letters of introduction to persons in Grand Cairo, we shall not, I imagine, have occasion to make use of this.

On Thursday the 8th, we ventured to sail once more, and have hitherto gone on pleasantly enough.

Tuesday, 20th July. Since my last date, I have been a good deal vexed at an accident which, perhaps, will appear very trivial. I had a pair of beautiful pigeons given me at

Leghorn, which furnished me with much amusement. These pretty little creatures, their wings being cut, ranged at liberty about the ship. At length one of them fell, or rather was blown overboard. I saw it a long while struggling for life, and looking towards the vessel, as if to implore assistance; yet, notwithstanding my fondness for the poor bird, and anxious desire to extricate it from its perilous situation, if such a thing were possible, I could not even wish that, a ship running eight knots an hour, should be hove to, and a boat sent out after a Pigeon. The widowed mate lived only three days afterwards, never touching a morsel of food, from the time the other disappeared, and uttering, at intervals, the most plaintive sounds, which I could not avoid hearing, my cabin being upon deck. For you must know, it is a regulation on board Swedish vessels, that the whole ship's company join twice a day, in devotional exercises ; so Capt. Norberg reserved his great Cabin for the purpose, of assembling them together, or we would willingly have engaged it. So much for my little favourites. I shall now advert to a more chearful topic.

My voyage has been rendered very interesting, and instructive, by the conversation of one of our passengers, a Franciscan Friar, from Rome, who is going as a Missionary to Jerusalem; and in my opinion no man can be better calculated for the hazardous office he has undertaken. Figure to yourself, a man in the prime of life (under forty), tall, well made, and athletic in his person; and seemingly of a temperament to brave every danger: add to these advantages a pair of dark eyes, beaming with intelligence, and a most venerable auburn beard, descending nearly to his girdle, and, you cannot fail to pronounce him, irresistible. He appears also to possess, all the enthusiasm and eloquence necessary for pleading the important cause of Christianity; yet one must regret that so noble a mind, should be warped by the belief of such ridiculous superstitions, as disgrace the Romish creed.—He became extremely zealous for my conversion, and anxiously forwarded my endeavours, after improvement in the Italian language, that I might the more readily comprehend the arguments, he adduced to effect that desirable purpose. Like other disputants, we sometimes used to contend very fiercely, and one day on my speaking rather lightly of what he chose to call, a miracle of the Catholic Church, he even went so far as to tell me, that my mouth spouted forth heresies, as water gushes from a fountain.

This morning (the 22nd) at breakfast, he intreated me to give up my coffee, as a libation to the bambino (child) Jesus, and on my declining to do so, urged me with the most impressive earnestness, to spare only a single cup, which he would immediately pour out in honour of the Blessed Infant. Professing my disbelief in the efficacy of such a sacrifice, I again excused myself from complying with his request: upon which declaring that he was equally shocked at my willful incredulity and obstinate heresy he withdrew to another part of the vessel, and I have not seen him since.

23rd A. M. We are now off Alexandria, which makes a fine appearance from the sea on a near approach; but being built on low ground, is, as the seamen say " very difficult to hit." We were two days almost abreast of the Town. There is a handsome Pharos or light-house in the new harbour, and it is in all respects far preferable; but no vessels belonging to Christians can anchor there, so we were forced to go into the old one, of which however we escaped the dangers, if any exist.[5]

My acquaintance with the Reverend Father has terminated rather unpleasantly. A little while ago being upon deck together, and forgetting our quarrel about the libation, I made a remark on the extreme heat of the weather, " Aye " replied he, with a most malignant expression of countenance, such as I could not have thought it possible, for a face benign like his to assume, " aye you will find it ten thousand times hotter in the Devil's House " (Nella Casa di Diavolo). I pitied his bigotry and prayed for his conversion to the genuine principles of that religion, whose doctrines he professed to teach.

Mr. Brandy[6] to whom Mr. Fay sent ashore an introductory letter, came on board to visit us. I rejoice to hear from him, that there are two ships at Suez, yet no time must be lost, lest we miss the season. This gentleman resides here, as Consul for one of the German Courts, and may be of great use to us. We received an invitation to sup with him to-morrow; he has secured a lodging for us, and engaged a Jew and his wife to go with us to Grand Cairo as dragoman, (or interpreter) and attendant: should we proceed by water, which is not yet decided on, Mr. B— will provide a proper boat. I am summoned to an early dinner, immediately after which we shall go on shore with our Dragoman, that we may have time to view whatever is remarkable.

24th July. Having mounted our asses, the use of horses being forbidden to any but musselmans, we sallied forth preceded by a Janizary, with his drawn sword, about three miles over a sandy desert, to see Pompey's Pillar, esteemed to be the finest column in the World. This pillar which is exceedingly lofty, but I have no means of ascertaining its exact height, is composed of three blocks of Granite; (the pedestal, shaft, and capital, each containing one). When we consider the immense weight of the granite, the raising such masses, appear beyond the powers of man. Although quite unadorned, the proportions are so exquisite, that it must strike every beholder with a kind of awe, which softens into melancholy, when one reflects that the renowned Hero whose name it bears, was treacherously murdered on this very Coast, by the boatmen who were conveying him to Alexandria; while his wretched wife stood on the vessel he had just left, watching his departure, as we may naturally suppose, with inexpressible anxiety. What must have been her agonies at the dreadful event! Though this splendid memorial bears the name of Pompey, it is by many supposed to have been erected in memory of the triumph, gained over him at the battle of Pharsalia. Leaving more learned heads than mine to settle this disputed point, let us proceed to ancient Alexandria, about a league from the modern town; which presents to the eye an instructive lesson on the instability of all sublunary objects. This once magnificent City, built by the most famous of all Conquerors, and adorned with the most exquisite productions of art, is now little more than a heap of Ruins; yet the form of the streets can still be discerned; they were regular, and many of the houses (as I recollect to have read of Athens) had fore-courts bounded by dwarf walls, so much in the manner of our Lincoln's-Inn Fields, that the resemblance immediately struck me.

We saw also the *outside* of St. Athanasius's Church, who was Bishop of this Diocese, but it being now a Mosque were forbidden to enter, unless on condition of turning mahometans, or losing our lives, neither of which alternatives exactly suited my ideas, so that I deemed it prudent to repress my curiosity. I could not however resist a desire to visit the Palace of Cleopatra, of which few vestiges remain. The marble walls of the Banqueting room are yet standing, but the roof is long since decayed. Never do I remember being so affected by a like object. I stood in the midst of the ruins, meditating on the awful scene, 'till I could almost have fancied I beheld its former mistress, revelling in Luxury, with her infatuated lover, Marc Anthony, who for her sake lost all.

The houses in the new Town of Alexandria thro' which we returned, are flat roofed, and, in general, have gardens on their tops. These in some measure, in so warm a country, may be called luxuries. As to the bazars (or markets) they are wretched places, and the streets exceedingly narrow. Christians of all denominations live here on paying a tax, but they are frequently ill treated; and if one of them commits even an unintentional offence against a musselman, he is pursued by a most insatiable spirit of revenge and his whole family suffers for it. One cannot help shuddering at the bare idea of being in the hands of such bigotted wretches. I forgot to mention that Mr. Brandy met us near Cleopatra's needles, which are two immense obelisks of Granite. One of them, time has levelled with the ground; the other is intire; they are both covered with hieroglyphic figures, which, on the sides not exposed to the wind and sand from the Desert, remain uninjured; but the key being lost, no one can decypher their meaning. I thought Mr. B— might perhaps have heard something relative to them; he, however, seems to know no more than ourselves. A droll circumstance occurred on our return. He is a stout man of a very athletic make, and above six feet high; so you may judge what a curious figure he must have made, riding on an ass, and with difficulty holding up his long legs to suit the size of the animal; which watched an opportunity of walking away from between them, and left the poor Consul standing, erect, like a Colossus: in truth, it was a most ludicrous scene to behold.

25th July. The weather being intensely hot, we staid at home 'till the evening, when Mr. Brandy called to escort us to his house. We were most graciously received by Mrs. B— who is a native of this place; but as she could speak a little Italian, we managed to carry on something like conversation. She was most curiously bedizened on the occasion, and being short, dark complexioned, and of a complete dumpling shape, appeared altogether the strangest lump of finery I had ever beheld; she had a handkerchief bound round her head, covered with strings composed of thin plates of gold, in the manner of spangles but very large, intermixed with pearls and emeralds; her neck and bosom were ornamented in the same way. Add to all this an embroidered girdle with a pair of gold clasps, I verily think near four inches square, enormous earrings, and a large diamond sprig on the top of her forehead, and you must allow, that altogether she was a most brilliant figure. They have a sweet little girl about seven years of age, who was decked out much in the same style; but she really looked pretty in spite of her incongruous finery. On the whole, though, I was pleased with both mother and child, their looks and behaviour were kind: and to a stranger in a strange land (and this is literally so to us) a little attention is soothing and consolatory; especially when one feels surrounded by hostilities, which every European must do here. Compared with the uncouth beings who govern this country, I felt at home among the natives of France, and I will even say of Italy.

On taking leave, our Host presented a book containing certificates of his great politeness and attention towards travellers; which were signed by many persons of consideration: and at the same time requesting that Mr. Fay and myself would add *our* names to the list, we complied, though not without surprize, that a gentleman in his situation, should have recourse to such an expedient, which cannot but degrade him in the eyes of his Guests.

It being determined that we shall proceed by water, for reasons too tedious to detail at present, I must now prepare to embark. I shall endeavour to keep up my spirits. Be assured that I will omit no opportunity of writing, and comfort yourselves with the idea, that before *this* reaches you, I shall have surmounted all my difficulties.   I certainly deem myself very fortunate in quitting this place so soon. Farewell; all good be with you, my ever *ever* dear Friends prays,

Your *own*,

E. F.

LETTER VII.

GRAND CAIRO, 27*th August,* 1779.

MY DEAR FRIENDS, In coming to this place, we were in
great peril, and bade adieu to the sea at the hazard of our
lives, the Bar of the Nile being exceedingly dangerous.
Fourteen persons were lost there, the day before we crossed
it, a circumstance that of course tended to increase our
anxiety on the subject, and which was told me just before
I closed my last letter; but for the world I would not have
communicated such intelligence. Our only alternative to
this hazardous passage, was crossing a desert, notorious for
the robberies and murders committed on it; where we
could not hope for escape, and from the smallness of our
number, had no chance of superiority in case of attack.
The night after we had congratulated ourselves on being
out of danger from the bar, we were alarmed by perceiving
a boat making after us, as the people said, to plunder, and
perhaps, to murder us. Our Jew interpreter, who, with
his wife, slept in the outer cabin, begged me not to move
our dollars, which I was just attempting to do, lest the
thieves should hear the sound, and kill us all, for the
supposed booty. You may judge in what a situation we
remained, while this dreadful evil seemed impending over
us. Mr. Fay fired two pistols, to give notice of our being
armed. At length, thank God, we out-sailed them; and
nothing of the kind occurred again, during our stay on
board; though we passed several villages, said to be inhabited entirely by thieves.

As morning broke, I was delighted with the appearance of the country, a more charming scene my eyes never beheld. The Nile, that perpetual source of plenty, was just beginning to overflow its banks; so that on every side, we saw such quantities of water drawn up for the use of more distant lands, that it is surprising any remains. The machine chiefly used for that purpose is a wheel with earthen pitchers tied round it, which empty themselves into tubs, from whence numerous canals are supplied. Oxen and Buffaloes are the animals generally employed in this labour. It is curious to see how the latter contrive to keep themselves cool during the intense heat that prevails here; they lie in the River by hundreds, with their heads just above water, for hours together.

Rosetta [7] is a most beautiful place, surrounded by groves of lemon and orange trees; and the flat roofs of the houses have gardens on them, whose fragrance perfumes the air. There is an appearance of cleanliness in it, the more gratifying to an English eye, because seldom met with in any degree, so as to remind us of what we are accustomed to at home. The landscape around, was interesting from its novelty, and became peculiarly so on considering it as the country where, the children of Israel sojourned. The beautiful, I may say, the unparalleled story of Joseph and his brethren, rose to my mind as I surveyed those Banks, on which the Patriarch sought shelter for his old age; and where his self convicted sons bowed down before their younger brother, and I almost felt as if in a dream, so wonderful appeared the circumstance of my being here. You will readily conceive that, as I drew near Grand Cairo, and beheld those prodigies of human labour, the Pyramids of Egypt, these sensations were still more strongly awakened; and I could have fancied myself an inhabitant of a world, long passed away: for who can look on buildings, reared, (moderately computing the time) above *three thousand years ago*, without seeming to step back as it were, in existence, and live through days, now gone by, and sunk in oblivion " like a tale that is told."

Situated as I was, the Pyramids [8] were not all in sight, but I was assured that those which came under my eye, were decidedly the most magnificent. We went out of our way to view them nearer, and by the aid of a telescope, were enabled to form a tolerable idea of their construction. It has been supposed by many that the Israelites built these Pyramids, during their bondage in Egypt, and I rather incline to that opinion; for, altho' it has lately been proved that they were intended to serve as repositories for the dead, yet each, being said to contain only one sarcophagus, this circumstance, and their very form, rendered them of so little comparative use, that most probably, they were raised to furnish employment for multitudes of unfortunate slaves; and who more aptly agree with this description, than the wretched posterity of Jacob? I understand there is a little flat, on the tops of the larger Pyramids, from which it is conjectured that the Egyptians made astronomical observations. The largest, is said to be, above five hundred feet high, perpendicularly. The inclined plane must measure much more: the steps are nearly three feet distant of the Pyramids; though I very anxiously wished to have inspected them, and the sphinx, prudence forbade me from making the attempt, as you will allow, when I proceed farther in my narrative.

On the 29th, we reached Bulac the port of Grand Cairo, and within two miles of that city, to my great joy; for on this river, there is either little wind, or else it comes in squalls, so suddenly, that the boats are often in danger of being overset, as they carry only, what I believe is called, a shoulder-of-Mutton-sail, which turns on a sort of swivel, and is very difficult to manage, when the wind takes it the wrong way. It seems indeed almost miraculous how we escaped.

Mr. Fay sat out almost immediately to Mr. Baldwin's,[9] who received him with much civility, and sent an ass for me, with directions to make all possible haste, as a Caravan was to set off in three hours.

I must now give you a description of my dress,[10] as my Jewess decked me out, preparatory to our entering the Great City. I had, in the first place, a pair of trowsers, with yellow leather half-boots and slippers over them; a long sattin gown, with wide sleeves, open to the elbows; and a girdle round my waist, with large silver clasps; over that another robe with short sleeves: round my head a fine, coloured, muslin handkerchief, closely bound, but so arranged that one corner hung down three quarters of a yard behind. This is the dress for the House; but as I was going out, she next put on a long robe of silk, like a surplice, and then covered my face with a piece of muslin, half a yard wide, which reached from the forehead to the feet, except an opening for the eyes; over all, she threw a piece of black silk, long and wide enough to envelop the whole form; so, thus equipped, stumbling at every step, I sallied forth, and with great difficulty got across my noble beast: but, as it was in the full heat of the day and the veil prevented me from breathing freely, I thought I must have died by the way. However, at last, I was safely housed, but found a great change had taken place; all thoughts of going were now laid aside. I dare not at present enter into particulars, and can only say that, some thing was wrong, and on that account we were kept in suspense, 'till about a week ago, when just as we had determined to proceed, if possible, another way, matters were adjusted: so to-morrow afternoon we are to enter on the Desert, and shall, please God, arrive at Suez, most likely, on Monday, from whence I propose writing again. The season is so far advanced that a good passage cannot be expected: we have no hopes of reaching Calcutta in less than three months, but at any rate, the voyage is preferable to going through the long Desert, from Aleppo to Bassora.

When I write from India I will give a full detail of the affair to which I allude, though as it is very important, you will, most probably, see the whole in the papers. Adieu for the present it is bed time.

28*th*. Again I take up the pen to hold a little further converse with my dear friends, while waiting the summons to depart; and as health is the most important of all earthly subjects, shall begin with that. It will, I know, give you pleasure to hear that I have found scarce any inconvenience from the heat, though all of our Party, who have been in India agree that, they never felt the weather so oppressively hot as here; which proceeds from the terrible sandy deserts, that surround the town, causing the air to smell like hot bricks. This however I could have borne, but just on our arrival, there broke out a severe epidemical disease, with violent symptoms. People are attacked at a moments warning with dreadful pains in the limbs, a burning fever, with delirium and a total stoppage of perspiration. During two days it increases; on the third, there comes on uniformly a profuse sweat (pardon the expression) with vomiting, which carries all off.—The only remedies prescribed, are lying in bed and drinking plentifully, even two gallons a day, of Nile water: no nourishment, and not so much as gruel, is allowed until after the crisis; not one has died of the disease, nor, I believe, scarcely one escaped: even the beasts have been affected. Mr. Fay had it three weeks ago, and among all I conversed with here, I remained the only healthy person, and really hoped to have proved the truth of what is asserted by physicians, that nervous persons are not subject to be attacked by contagious distempers, not even by the Plague itself. However, this day sennight, I was seized with most violent symptoms, so that at the three days end, my strength seemed entirely exhausted; but I have, thanks be to Providence, recovered as surprizingly; and am already nearly well.   It had every sign of the Plague, except that it was not mortal.   Do not be frightened at the name, but I assure you, it is commonly called " la queue de la Peste," and the general opinion is, that had it arrived in the month of February, the living would scarce have been sufficient to bury the dead.

Grand Cairo by no means answers to its name at present, whatever it may have done formerly.—There are certainly many magnificent houses, belonging to the Beys and other rich individuals, but as a city, I can perceive neither order, beauty, nor grandeur; and the contrast between the great, who seem to wallow in splendour and luxury, and the people at large, who appear to want the common necessaries of life, is not more striking, than disgusting; because, those who are raised above their fellows, do not look, as though they merited the distinction, either by talent, manners or even the most ordinary pretentions.   The Christians (who are called Franks) live all together in one street, which is closed at each end every night; a precaution neither unpleasant nor useless.   An agreeable variety is given to the appearance of the town by the Mosques, or I should consider the whole wretchedly stupid.   A wedding, here, is a gay and amusing spectacle, from the procession which accompanies the Bride in all her movements, drums, hautboys and every other kind of noise and parade they can make, seem indispensible: but the circumstance of completely veiling, not only the face, but the whole figure of the woman, in the enveloping mantle of black silk, before described, gives an air of melancholy to these exhibitions. To show the face is considered here, an act of downright indecency; a terrible fashion for one like me, to whom free air seems the great requisite for existence.

I must not conclude without mentioning a disappointment I met with. As the fertility of Egypt depends on the due increase of the Nile, persons are hired to go round Grand Cairo, twice a day, and report how many inches the water has risen; returning solemn thanks to Almighty God for the blessing. This is continued 'till it gain a certain point, when the Dykes are broken down, and the river flows majestically into the Canal, formed for its reception; while the inhabitants hail its approach with every demonstration of joy. Such was the account I heard, and great was my anxiety, lest I should not be permitted to witness this *August* ceremony. At length the period arrived, but never, sure, were highly raised expectations more miserably deceived: For this famous Canal, being dry nine months out of the twelve, and serving during that interval as a receptacle for the filth of a populous, and not *over* cleanly City, I leave you to judge, how beautifully *pellucid* its waters must appear: nor could St. Giles's itself pour forth such an assembly of half naked, wretched creatures, as preceded this so vaunted stream; crying aloud, and making all sorts of frantic gestures, like so many maniacs. Not a decent person could I distinguish amongst the whole group. So much for this grand exhibition, which we have abundant cause to wish, had not taken place, for the vapours arising from such a mass of impurity, have rendered the heat more intolerable than ever. My bed chamber overlooks the Canal, so that I enjoy the full benefit to be derived from its proximity.[11]

I am now compelled, much against my inclination, to bid you adieu; for I have a thousand things to do, and this immense letter has left me little time.

Ever your's most truly,
&c. &c.

P. S. Not being able to enlarge on the only interesting subject, has induced me to be rather diffuse on others, as

I wished to convey *some* information by this, perhaps, *last* opportunity, 'till our arrival in India; for it is doubtful whether I may have any safe channel of conveyance from Suez.

LETTER VIII.

From Mr. Fay[12] to Mr. C.

On Board Ship, in the Red Sea,
Near Suez.
September 1st 1779.

Honoured Sir,

I seize the chance of three minutes, to tell you
that we yesterday arrived at Suez from Grand Cairo,
after a journey of three days, over a most dreadful Desert,
where every night we slept under the great canopy of
Heaven, and where we were every hour in danger of being
destroyed, by troops of Arabian robbers. But having a
little party of English gentlemen, and servants (among
whom I held a principal command) well armed, and under
the orders of Major Baillie, and another military officer,
we marched the whole way in order of battle, and though
we could frequently see superior numbers, they never dared
to molest us.

Your daughter behaved most courageously and is
extremely well, considering the extraordinary fatigue she
has undergone. There is another English lady and her
husband on board, which promises to make it an agreeable voyage. The ship is a very fine one, and we have
a handsome little chamber, and I hope in all things
shall find ourselves well accommodated. We expect to
sail in four hours. The ship is called the Nathalia,
Captain Chenu, a Frenchman, and apparently a very

polite good-natured man, which is a great matter in a long
voyage.

I thank God I was never in better health and spirits,
tho' I never slept during the whole journey on the Desert,
and lived the whole time on bread and water, notwithstanding we had abundance of wine and provisions; but the
heat being excessive, I found no other food agree with me
so well, and Mrs. Fay by adopting the same diet, preserved
her health also; whereas all the rest were knocked up
before we got half way over that confounded Desert, and
some are now very ill; but I stood it, as well as any Arabian
in the Caravan, which consisted at least of five thousand
people. My wife insists on taking the pen out of my hands,
so I can only say God bless you all.

MY DEAR FRIENDS

I have not a moments time, for the boat is
waiting, therefore can only beg that you will unite with me,
in praising our heavenly Protector for our escape from the
various dangers of our journey. I never could have thought
my constitution was so strong. I bore the fatigues of the
desert, like a Lion, though but just recovering from my
illness. We have been pillaged of almost every thing, by
the Arabs. This is the Paradise of thieves, I think the
whole population may be divided into two classes of them;
those who adopt force, and those who effect their purpose
by fraud. I was obliged to purchase a thick cloak, and
veil, proper for the journey, and what was worse, to wear
them all the way hither, which rendered the heat almost
insupportable.—Never was I more happy, than when I came
on board; although the ship having been for six weeks in
the hands of the natives, the reason of which I cannot
enlarge on here, is totally despoiled of every article of
furniture; we have not a chair or a table, but as the carpenter

makes them, for there is no buying such things here.   Our greatest inconvenience is the want of good water; what can be procured here, is so brackish, as to be scarcely drinkable. I have not another moment.   God bless you! pray for me my beloved friends.

LETTER IX.

FROM MRS. FAY.

MOCHA 13*th September* 1779.

THANK GOD MY DEAR FRIENDS, I am once more enabled to date from a place of comparative liberty, and an European Gentleman having promised me a safe conveyance for my packet, I shall proceed to give you a hurried and melancholy detail of circumstances of which it has been my chief consolation to know that you were ignorant. You are of course impatient to be informed to what I allude; take then the particulars: but I must go a good way back in order to elucidate matters, which would otherwise appear mysterious or irrelevant.[13]

The East India Company sent out positive orders some time ago, to prohibit the trade to Suez, as interfering with their privileges; but as there never was a law made, but means might be found to evade it, several English merchants freighted a ship (the Nathalia) from Serampore, a Danish settlement on the Hooghly, fourteen miles above Calcutta, whose commander, Vanderfield, a Dane, passed for owner of the ship and cargo. Mr. O'Donnell one of the persons concerned, and who had property on board to the amount of above £20,000, came as passenger, as did Mr. Barrington the real supercargo, also a freighter, and two Frenchmen, brothers, named Chevalier. They left Bengal on New year's day 1779, and came first to Calicut on the coast of Malabar, where they arrived in February; found English, French, Danish and Portuguese Factors, or Consuls there; and trade in a flourishing state, so not apprehending any danger they entered into a contract with one Isaacs, a rich old Jew, who has great influence with the government, to freight them with pepper for Bengal on their return from Suez; that being the greatest town on the Coast for that commodity.—The price was settled and £700 paid as earnest. This business arranged, they proceeded on their voyage; and having luckily disposed of some part of the cargo at this place, reached Suez with the remainder in the beginning of June, landed their Goods to the amount of at least £40,000, and prepared to cross the Desert on their way to Cairo. The company besides those already mentioned, consisted of Chenu the second mate, with some officers and servants, in all twelve Europeans, strengthened by a numerous body of Arabian guards, camel drivers &c., for the conveyance of their property: more than sufficient in every body's opinion; for no one remembered a Caravan being plundered, for altho' sometimes the wandering Arabs were troublesome, yet a few presents never failed to procure a release from them. Thus were they lulled into a fatal security; each calculating the profits likely to accrue, and extremely willing to compound for the loss of a few bales, should they happen to meet with any strolling depredators, not even once supposing their lives were in danger, or intending to use their firearms should they be molested.

On Monday the 14th June they left Suez, and next morning at day break, had travelled about twenty miles (nearly one third of the way) when suddenly an alarm was given of an Attack, as they, poor souls, were sleeping across their baskets (or panniers.) Capt. Barrington on awaking ordered a dozen bales to be given to them immediately: but alas! they were already in possession of the whole; for the Camel drivers did not defend themselves an instant, but left their beasts at the mercy of the robbers; who after detaching a large body to drive them away with their burthens, advanced towards the passengers. Here I must request you to pause, and reflect whether it be possible even for imagination to conceive a more dreadful scene to those concerned, particularly to Mr. O'Donnell, who from a concurrence of fortunate circumstances, had in less than four years realized a fortune of near £30,000; the bulk of which he laid out in merchandise on the inviting prospect of gaining 50 Per Cent, and as his health was in a very weak state proposed retiring to Europe. What must that man have felt, a helpless spectator of his own ruin. But this was nothing to what followed on their being personally attacked. The inhuman wretches not content with stripping them to the skin, drove away their camels, and left them in a burning sandy Desert, which the feet can scarcely touch, without being blistered, exposed to the scorching rays of the sun and utterly destitute of sustenance of every kind; no house, tree, or even shrub to afford them shelter. My heart sickens, my hand trembles as I retrace this scene. Alas! I can too well conceive their situation: I can paint to myself the hopeless anguish of an eye cast abroad in vain for succour! but I must not indulge in reflections, let me simply relate the facts as they occurred. In this extremity they stopped to deliberate, when each gave his reasons, for preferring the road he determined to pursue. Mr. O'Donnell, Chenu, the cook and two others resolved to retrace their steps back to Suez, which was undoubtedly the most eligible plan; and after encountering many hardships, they at length, arrived there in safety. Of the remaining seven who went towards Cairo, only *one* survived. —Mr. Barrington being corpulent and short breathed, sunk under the fatigue the second day; his servant, soon followed him.—One of the French gentlemen was by this time become very ill, and his brother perceiving a house at some miles distance (for in that flat country, one may see a great way,) prevailed on him to lie down under a stunted tree, with his servant, while he endeavoured to procure some water, for want of which the other was expiring. Hope, anxiety, and affection combined to quicken his pace, and rendered poor Vanderfield, the Danish captain, unable to keep up with him, which he most earnestly strove to do. I wept myself almost blind; as the poor Frenchman related his sufferings from conflicting passions; almost worn out with heat and thirst, he was afraid of not being able to reach the house, though his own life and that of his brother, depended on it. On the other hand the heart piercing cries of his fellow sufferer, that he was a dead man unless assisted by him, and conjuring him for God's sake, not to leave him to perish now they were in view of relief, arrested his steps and agonised every nerve. Unable to resist the solemn appeal, for some time he indulged him, 'till finding that the consequence of longer delay must be inevitable destruction to both, he was compelled to shake him off. A servant belonging to some of the party still kept on, and poor Vanderfield was seen to continue his efforts, 'till at length nature being completely exhausted, he dropped and was soon relieved from his miseries by Death. Nor was the condition of the survivors far more enviable, when having, with difficulty, reached the building after which they had toiled so long, it proved to be an uninhabited shed. Giving himself up for lost, the French gentleman lay down under shelter of the wall, to await his last moment, (the servant walked forward and was found dead a little further on). Now it so happened that an Arabian beggar chanced to pass by the wall, who seeing his condition, kindly ran to procure some water, but did not return for an hour. What an age of torture, of horrible suspense! for if " hope deferred maketh the heart sick," the sensation must cause ten-fold anguish at a moment like this.

The unhappy man was mindful of his brother, but utterly unable to undertake the task himself, he directed the beggar, as well as he could, to the spot where he had left him, with a supply of water. But alas! all his endeavours to find the unfortunate men were ineffectual, nor were their bodies ever discovered: It is supposed that they crept for shelter from the sun, into some unfrequented spot, and there expired. The survivor by the assistance of the beggar, reached the hut of a poor old woman, who kindly received him; and through whose care he was soon restored to strength, and arrived safely at Cairo, after as miraculous an escape, as ever human being experienced.

This melancholy story had been mentioned by Mr. Brandy before I landed at Alexandria, (Oh with what horror did I hear his brief recital) and the particulars I soon learnt at Cairo. The subject was in fact closely connected with my fears and sufferings, at that place, and which I hinted at the impossibility of my then revealing, neither could I, for the same reason, give you any account of the Egyptian Government, lest they should intercept my letter, altho' it is necessary you should know a little of it, for the sake of comprehending what I have further to relate, concerning these unfortunate adventurers.[14]

Egypt, then, is governed by twenty four Beys, of whom one presides over the rest, but this superiority is very precarious; for he holds it no longer than 'till some other of the number thinks himself strong enough to contend with him; and as they have here but two maxims in War, the one to fly, the other to pursue, those contests last not long: the vanquished, should he escape assassination retires up the country, 'till Fortune changes her aspect: while the victor takes his place. Thus do their lives pass in perpetual vicissitudes. To-day a Prince, to-morrow a Fugitive, and next day a prince again. These things are so common, that nobody notices them; since they never disturb the inhabitants or compel them to take part in their disputes. In order to be a check on these gentlemen, the Grand

Signor sends a Bashaw, to reside among them, whom they receive with great respect and compliment with presents of value, pretending the utmost deference for his authority, but at the same time a strict eye is kept over him, and on the least opposition to their will, he is sent in disgrace away—happy if he escape with life, after refunding all his presents and paying enormous sums besides.

By the above statement you will perceive that, the Beys are in reality independent, and likewise discern the hinge on which their politics turn, for as long as under colour of submission, they consent to receive a Bashaw, it is in their power constantly to throw the odium of every disagreeable occurrence on his shoulders, under pretence of Orders from the Porte. Now briefly to proceed with my little history, some time after the fatal robbery, another ship called the St. Helena, arrived at Suez, under Danish colours with the real owner, a Mr. Moore, on board. He justly apprehensive of a similar fate, refused to land his Cargo 'till the *then* Chief Amurath Bey, had accorded him a solemn permission or rather protection, under which he safely reached Cairo, disposed of his effects, and prepared for his return to his ship with a fresh Cargo. But in the interim, Mr. O'Donnell had been advised to present a memorial to the Beys, by which he reclaimed his property as an Englishman, threatened them with the vengeance of his nation if not immediately redressed, and declared himself totally independent of the Danes. This rash procedure alarmed the people in power, who however still continued apparently friendly, in hopes of a larger booty, 'till the 30th July, when they threw off the mask, seized the Caravan even to the passenger's baggage, and made Mr. Moore a prisoner. You may recollect that in my letter from Cairo, I told you what a hurry Mr. Fay was in, to fetch me from Bulac, not having, as he then thought, a moments time to spare. It so happened that I arrived within an hour after the seizure of the Caravan and when all the gentlemen concerned, were in the first transports of that indignation, which such a daring outrage could not fail to excite; at once exasperated by this treacherous behaviour and alarmed, lest some new crime should be committed against them.

Every one is of opinion that their design was to cut us *all* off, had we gone out ignorant of the seizure of the Caravan. I had scarcely sat down in Mr. Baldwin's parlour, when this terrible news, which seemed to involve the fate of every European alike, burst upon me like a stroke of lightning. Never shall I forget the terrors I felt.—: In a few moments the room was filled with Europeans, chiefly English, all speaking together,—calling out for arms, and declaring they would sell their lives dearly; for not one appeared to entertain a doubt of their being immediately attacked. In the midst of this confusion, Mons. Chevalier (the poor man who escaped from the Desert) cast his eyes upon me, exclaiming " Oh Madam how unhappy you are in having come to this wretched place." This drew the attention of the rest,—and " what shall we do with the lady? "—was every one's question— at last they resolved on sending me to the house of an Italian Physician, as a place of safety; thither I was instantly taken by a native, who even in the distress and confusion of the house, and although the Italian's was only a few steps distant across a narrow lane, felt greatly shocked, because my veil chancing to be a little loose, he could see one corner of my eye, and severely reprehended the indecency of such an exposure.

On reaching my expected Asylum a scene of more serious alarm (if possible) than I had left at Mr. Baldwins awaited me. The lady and her daughter were wringing their hands, and crying out in agony, that they were utterly ruined—; that all the Europeans would be murdered; and they even appeared to think, that receiving another of the proscribed race increased their danger. Imprisonment and massacre in every shape, were the sole subjects of their conversation; and so many terrible images did their fears conjure up, and communicate to my already disordered mind, that there were times, when the reality could have been scarcely more appalling. Oh England! dear England! how often did I apostrophise thee, land of liberty and safety—: but I must not review my thoughts—; a simple narrative is all I dare allow myself to write.

For several days we remained in this harrassing state of suspense, and alarm; at length news arrived that the two ships which had brought these ill-fated adventurers to Egypt's inhospitable shores, were seized by the Government, three days before they took possession of the Caravan. Their prisoners indeed, we already virtually were, not being allowed to quit the City. I should have mentioned that the Bashaw was the tool made use of on this occasion; who pretended he had Orders from Constantinople, to seize all English merchandise and confiscate the Vessels, suffering none but the East India Company's packets to touch at Suez. This Firman was said to be obtained of his sublime highness, by the British resident at the Porte, on behalf of the E.I. Company; whether this pretence was true or false, we could never learn. Many other reports were propagated, as must always be the case in a country under arbitrary government: there being no certain rules to judge by, every one pronounces on the event as his hopes or fears dictate. Some times we were all to be sent prisoners to Constantinople, then we were assured that after a general plunder of our effects, we should certainly be released; and once it was confidently reported that, the *Bowstring* would be secretly applied to prevent our telling tales.

What added much to our mortification and justified our fears was, that all the Christians belonging to the two ships, were on the 10th of August dragged to Cairo in the most ignominious manner, having previously suffered, during their imprisonment at Suez, every species of hardship which barbarity and malice could inflict. The people also at whose house we lodged, behaved to us continually with marked disrespect, if asked a question they seldom deigned to reply, and took care to enlarge perpetually on their condescension in suffering themselves to be incommoded with strangers. To be thus treated, at a time when perpetual solicitude and terror had unbraced my nerves and subdued my spirit, seemed so cruel, that I think it absolutely hurt me more than even our detention; a detention which was certainly harder upon us, than any other Europeans in one sense, since we had no connection whatever with the parties, were coming from a different quarter of the globe; not concerned in trade, and unknown to those who had visited their country on that account: no demon of avarice had led *us* into their power, nor could we afford a prey to *theirs*. These considerations however evident, made no impression on our host, they were rather motives of exultation over us, and what enhanced our misfortune, it was irremediable, for we could not change our abode, without going into another street, where we should have been unprotected.

All the Christians live in one part of the town as I before noticed: during the time when the Plague rages, they visit each other by means of bridges thrown across the streets, from the tops of the houses, and this is a convenience they often resort to at other times, as it saves them from insult, which they often meet below. I find I have written myself into such a strange humour, that I cannot proceed method- ically; but I must try to arrange my thoughts and go forward better.

At length the Beys, enchanted by that Deity whose bewitching attractions few mortals can resist, whether on the banks of the Nile or the Thames: in other words, influenced by the promise of three thousand pounds, and an absolute indemnification from Mr. O'Donnell, gave us leave to proceed on our Voyage in defiance of the tremendous order of their master, and thus ended this most disagreeable and distressing business. I will release you from this wearisome letter. I shall have time at Mocha to continue my journal—, Adieu till to-morrow.

Ever most affectionately your's,
E. F.

LETTER X.

Inclosed in the Foregoing.

MY DEAR SISTER,

I resume my pen in order to give you some account of our passing the Desert, which being done by a method of travelling totally different from any thing in England, may afford amusement, and even without the charm of novelty could not fail to interest you, as the narrative of one so nearly and dearly connected.

When a Caravan is about to depart, large tents are pitched on the skirts of the City, whither all who propose joining it repair: there they are drawn up in order, by the persons who undertake to convey them. Strong bodies of Arabian soldiers guard the van and rear; others flank the sides—; so that the female passengers, and the merchandise, are completely surrounded, and, as one would hope, defended in case of attack. Each gentleman of our party had a horse, and it is common to hire a camel between two, with panniers to carry their provisions &c.—: across the panniers, which are of wicker, a kind of mattress is thrown, whereon they take it by turns to lie, and court repose, during their journey. Females who can afford the expence, are more comfortably accommodated—; these travel in a kind of litter, called a Tataravan; with two poles fastened between two camels, one behind, the other before. The litter has a top and is surmounted by shabby, ill contrived Venetian blinds, which in the day, increase the

96

suffocating heat, but are of use during the nights which are cold and piercing.—Every camel carries skins of water, but before you have been many hours on the Desert, it becomes of the colour of coffee. I was warned of this, and recommended to provide small guglets of porous earth, which after filling with *purified* water, I slung to the top of my *Tataravan;* and these with water melons, and *hard* eggs, proved the best refreshments I could have taken. The water by this means was tolerably preserved; but the motion of the camels and the uncouth manner in which the vehicle is fastened to them, made such a constant rumbling sound among my provisions, as to be exceedingly annoying. Once I was saluted by a parcel of hard eggs breaking loose from their net, and pelting me completely: it was fortunate that *they were* boiled, or I should have been in a pretty trim; to this may be added the frequent violent jerks, occasioned by one or other of the poles slipping out of its wretched fastening, so as to bring one end of the litter to the ground; and you may judge how pleasing this mode of travelling must be.

At our first outset, the novelty of the scene, and the consolation I felt, on leaving a place which had been productive of so much chagrin, and so many too well founded apprehensions, wrought an agreeable change on my harrassed feelings—; but when we had proceeded some distance on the Desert; when all traces of human habitation had vanished—; when every sign of cultivation disappeared; and even vegetation was confined to a few low straggling shrubs, that seemed to stand between life and death as hardly belonging to either—; when the immeasurable plain lay around me, a burning sun darted his fierce rays from above, and no asylum was visible in front, my very heart sunk within me.—I am sure you will do justice to my feelings, the late Catastrophe being deeply imprinted on my mind, and indeed never absent from it. For the world, you should not have known what was passing there, when I made so light of the journey in my letter from Grand Cairo.

In the midst of these soul-subduing reflections, the guides gave notice of a body, apparently much larger than our own, being within view of us.—All the sufferings related by the poor French gentleman, my active imagination now pourtrayed, as about to be inflicted on me. My dear Parents, my sisters, cried I, will never see me more!—should they learn my fate what agonies will they not endure! —but never can they conceive half the terrible realities, that I may be doomed to undergo! Happily, for once, my fears outwent the truth; the party so dreaded, turned off in pursuit of some other prey, or perhaps intimidated by our formidable appearance, left us unmolested.

It is impossible even amidst fear and suspense not to be struck with the exquisite beauty of the nights here; a perfectly cloudless sky, and the atmosphere so clear, that the stars shine with a brilliancy, infinitely surpassing any thing I witnessed elsewhere. Well might the ancient Egyptians become expert astronomers, possessing a climate so favourable to that study; nor were we less indebted to those Heavenly luminaries; since, by their refulgent light, and unvarying revolutions, the guides cross these trackless Deserts with certainty, and like the mariner, steer to the desired haven.

You will perceive, that my boast of having crossed the Desert, like a lion, was not literally just;—but then remember, it was his strength, not his courage to which I alluded: for it is true that, considering how much I had suffered in Cairo, I really did perform the journey well, and on the second day being convinced by the behaviour of some around me, how greatly dejection increased the actual evils of our situation,—I rallied my spirits to the utmost, and lifting up my heart in gratitude to the Almighty, for having thus far supported us, I determined to trust in his goodness, and not desert myself.

On this day I was exceedingly affected by the sufferings of one of our party—Mr. Taylor, going out as assistant surgeon on the Bengal establishment. He complained of illness when we sat out, and seemed overwhelmed with melancholy. He had been plundered of all by the Arabs—had sustained various misfortunes, and of late, appeared to be consumptive. The extreme heat of the weather so over-powered him, that he resigned all hope of life, and at length, in a fit of despondency, actually allowed himself to slide down from his horse, that he might die on the ground. Mr. Fay seeing him fall, ran to assist him in regaining his seat, but he earnestly begged to be left alone, and permitted to die in peace. It was impossible to inspire him with hope and as he appeared to have so little strength, I did not believe that, with so strong a predilection for death, he could have been kept alive—: yet to see a fine young man, a countryman and fellow-traveller expiring amongst us, without striving to the last to preserve him, would have been inhuman. Thank God, our cares so far prevailed that he is still with us, though his disorder is now confirmed, and his melancholy but little abated—. He thanks us for life, as if grateful for our attention, but not for the gift. I fear his heart is breaking, as well as his constitution.

When my mind was a little relieved on poor T—'s account, I had leisure to think of the horses;—you recollect how partial I ever was to these noble animals; and we had several with us, of such singular beauty and docility, that they would have attracted the attention, I had almost said the affection, of the most indifferent spectator. The wretched creatures suffered so much from heat and thirst, that their groanings were terrible, and added to this an involuntary rattling in the throat, as if they were on the point of expiring, so that one heard them with a mixture of compassion and horror extremely painful to bear: yet notwithstanding that this continued for many hours, we were so fortunate, as not to lose a single horse in the Caravan.—With the dogs, we were less successful,—three very fine ones sat out with us, but none survived—one of them was the most beautiful Italian greyhound, I ever beheld;—he cost seven guineas at Venice. The first day he got tolerably well forward; but during the second his strength failed, and he appeared to suffer excruciating pain from the heat. When he was in the most frightful state, his tongue hanging out of his mouth, his eyes wildly staring, and altogether presenting the idea of madness, rather than death, his master Mr. T— had the modesty to bring him to me, and request that I would admit him into my Tatara-van. I hope no person will accuse me of inhumanity, for refusing to receive an animal in that condition,—self-preservation forbade my compliance. I felt that it would be weakness, instead of compassion, to subject myself to such a risk; and you may be certain, my sympathy was not increased for its owner, when he solemnly assured me, by way of inforcing his intreaty, that it would cost him a less severe pang, to see his own father thus suffering, than he then felt—I was induced to credit this assertion; knowing that when last in England, he had remained there seventeen months without visiting the old gentleman; though he acknowledged having been within 150 miles of his resid-ence. A very short time after this, the poor creature dropt down gasping, but ere he had breathed his last, a brutal Arab cut him to pieces before his masters face; and on his expressing anger at his cruel behaviour, ran after him with a drawn scymiter—you may judge from this incident, what wretches we were cast amongst.

We found Suez a miserable place,—little better than the Desert which it bounds, and were, as probably I have already told you, impatient to get on board, where we found every portable necessary of life had been carried off. We had been pretty well pillaged ourselves, and could therefore sympathize with the losers, as well as lament our own personal inconvenience, however, thank Heaven that we escaped as we did;—if ever they catch me on their Desert again, I think I shall deserve all they can inflict.

Our passage down the Red Sea was pleasant, the wind being constantly favourable, but afforded no object of interest, save the distant view of Mount Horeb, which again brought the flight of the children of Israel to my mind; and you may be sure, I did not wonder that they sought to quit the land of Egypt, after the various specimens of its *advantages* that I have experienced.

The only vessels we saw, were those built for the conveyance of coffee, for which this port is famous;—they are so bulky, clumsy, and strangely constructed, that one might almost take them for floating mountains. I cannot be expected to say a great deal of my shipmates, having been so short a time together, but to own the truth, I do not look forward to much comfort, where the elements are so discordant;—however, as we are to touch at Calicut on the Coast of Malabar, you shall from thence have the particulars: for, by that time we shall be pretty well familiarized with each other. May the detail be more agreeable than my present ideas will warrant me in supposing.

Let me now proceed to say a few words of Mocha, which is a pretty considerable place, walled round, and guarded by soldiers.—It appears to great advantage after Suez, being plentifully supplied with fruit and vegetables; —the provisions not bad, and the water excellent. The worst I know of it, is the excessive heat, which is even beyond that of Cairo. Our sailors have a proverb, that there is only a sheet of paper between that and another place— too shocking to be mentioned—I should yet say there were many sheets; for we have really met with so much kindness and hospitality here, as to make us almost forget the heat.

The principal trade is carried on by Banians and Rajaputs, (as they are called, tho' I cannot yet tell why) who come here from India—make comfortable little fortunes and return. A family of the former, consisting of three brothers, named George, has shewn us every possible attention ever since we landed, and the Chevalier de St. Lubin, a French gentleman, of elegant manners and superior information, has treated us, in the most sumptuous style. It is whispered among the English here, that Mons De St. L— has been on a mission from the French Court to Hyder Ally, for the express purpose of sowing the seeds of discord between him, and the English; and that he has to a great degree succeeded; how far this is true, we cannot yet say, but so intirely was Mr. Fuller, one of our passengers, persuaded of the fact, that he just now proposed we should arrest the Chevalier, who is about to proceed in a day or two to Europe. How far Mr. F— may be politically right, I cannot tell; but my heart revolted at the idea of receiving every mark of attention from a man one hour, and on bare suspicion, making him a prisoner the next; and most truly did I rejoice when this scheme was overruled. There should be very sufficient reasons for conduct, so despotic and apparently ungrateful, and we certainly were not in possession of documents to authorise such a procedure. I am much better pleased that this gentleman should return peaceably to his native country, and forward my letters to you, which he has promised on his *honour* to do, and to secure them amongst his private papers.—I might have written twice as much if I chose.[15]

And now my dear Friends, I must again bid you adieu. I trust my next accounts will be more pleasant, than this sad detail must prove, and that I shall meet letters at

Calcutta, with good news of you all.   My heart aches with thinking of the distance between us; but after surmounting so many difficulties and happily escaping from so many dangers; I feel inspired with hope for the future.

Ever most affectionately your's
E. F.

LETTER XI.

ON BOARD THE NATHALIA AT SEA.
28th October, 1779.

MY DEAR FRIENDS,

I wrote you from Mocha, in date the 15th
September, by the Chevalier de St. Lubin who has most
solemnly engaged to forward my letter, and I trust will
keep his word.

We have now been six weeks at sea, and in the course
of a few days hope to reach Calicut. Our passage across
the Indian Ocean, we found very pleasant: the Monsoon
being against us, made it tedious, but no boisterous seas
had we to contend with, as in the Mediterranean:—all has
been calm, easy and free from alarm of every kind hitherto;
fortunate indeed may we deem ourselves in having experienced such fine weather; for our ship is not half laden and
has not Cargo enough to keep her steady. You will now
expect me to say some thing of those with whom we are
cooped up, but my account will not be very satisfactory,
although sufficiently interesting to us—to begin then.

The woman, of whom I entertained some suspicion from
the first, is I am now credibly informed, one of the very
lowest creatures taken off the streets in London; she is so
perfectly depraved in disposition, that her supreme delight
consists in rendering everybody around her, miserable.—It
would be doing her too much honour to stain my paper
with a detail of the various artifices she daily practices to
that end.—Her pretended husband having been in India
before, and giving himself many airs, is looked upon as a

person of mighty consequence, whom nobody chooses to offend; therefore Madam has full scope to exercise her mischievous talents, wherein he never controuls her—not but that he perfectly understands how to make himself feared; coercive measures are *some times* resorted to; it is a common expression of the lady. " Lord bless you, if I did such, or such a thing, Tulloh would make no more to do, but knock me down like an ox." I frequently amuse myself with examining their countenances, where ill nature has fixed her Empire so firmly, that I scarcely believe either of them ever smiled unless maliciously. Miss Howe's description of Solmes, in Clarissa Harlowe, recurs to me as admirably suiting this *amiable* pair—to that I refer you.[16]

Chenu, the Captain, is a mere " Jack in office;" being unexpectedly raised to that post from second mate, by the death of poor Capt. Vanderfield and his chief officer on the *fatal* Desert, is become from this circumstance so insolent and overbearing, that every one detests him. Instead of being ready to accommodate every person with the few necessaries left by the plundering Arabs, he constantly appropriates them to himself. " Where's the Captain's silver spoon? God bless my soul. Sir, you have got my chair, must you be seated before the captain? What have you done with the Captain's glass? " and a great deal more of the same kind; but this may serve as a specimen. And altho' the wretch half starves us, he frequently makes comparisons between *his* table, and that of an Indiaman, which we dare not contradict while in his power; tell me now, should you not doat on three such companions for a long voyage?—but I have a fourth who at least, merits to be added to the triumvirate; his name John Hare, Esqr., Barrister at Law, a man of the very first fashion I assure you, and who would faint at the thought of any thing Plebeian. Taylor was one day shewing him a very handsome silver hilted sword, which he greatly admired, till chancing to cast his eye on the scabbard he read " Royal Exchange." " Take your sword " said he, " its surprizing a man of your sense should commit such an error; for fifty guineas I would not have a City name on any article of *my* dress; now St. James's or Bond street, has a *delicious* sound, don't you think so my dear friend?"—Now would any one suppose this fine gentleman's father was in trade, and he himself brought up in that very City, he effects to despise? very true nevertheless—Quadrille he would not be thought to know; it is only played by the wives and daughters of Tradesmen, in country towns: I want to make you see him; figure to yourself a little mortal, his body constantly bent in a rhetorical attitude, as if addressing the Court, and his face covered with scorbutic blotches. Happily from an affectation of singularity, he always wears spectacles. I say happily, as they serve to conceal the most odious pair of little white eyes mine ever beheld. What Butler says of Hudibras—that

> " he could not ope
> His mouth, but out there flew a trope,"

may literally be applied to this Heaven-born Orator, who certainly outdoes all I ever heard, in the use of overstrained compliments and far-fetched allusions. But with all those oddities, were he only a good-natured harmless simpleton, one might pity him. At first he took so much pains to ingratiate himself with us, that he became a sort of favorite; —so many confessions of superior abilities in Mr. Fay— such intreaties to spare him, when they should practise in the Courts together,—a studied attention to me in the *minutest* article—effectually shielded him from suspicion, till his end was answered, of raising a party against us, by means of that vile woman, who was anxious to triumph over me; especially as I have been repeatedly compelled (for the Honour of the Sex) to censure her swearing, and indecent behaviour. I have therefore little comfort to look forward to, for the remainder of the voyage.[17]

It is, however, only justice to name Mr. Taylor as an amiable, tho' melancholy companion, and Mr. Manesty an agreeable young man, under twenty, going out as a writer on the Bombay Establishment, from whom I always receive the most respectful attention. Mr. Fuller, is a middle aged man; it is easy to see, that he has been accustomed to genteel society. How different *his* manners from those of Hare! Poor man he has, it seems, fallen into the hands of sharpers, and been completely pillaged. He has the finest dark eyes, and one of the most intelligent countenances I ever met with. His trip to Bengal is, I doubt, a last resource. May it prove successful. I have no enmity towards him; for though he has joined the other party, it is evidently with reluctance. Mr. Moreau a musician, going out to India to exercise his profession, is very civil and attentive.

Dissentions have run very high on board. The very day after we sailed from Mocha, a sudden quarrel arose between the Captain, and H— the Barrister; on which the ship was ordered about, and they were going ashore in a great hurry to decide it; but by the interposition of friends, they were prevailed upon to curb their wrath, 'till their arrival at Calicut, as in case of an accident, no officer remained to supply Chenu's place. About a month after, they were reconciled; and so ended this doughty affair.

I had almost forgotten to mention Pierot, the purser of the ship—a lively, well informed little Frenchman,—full of anecdotes and always prepared with a repartée; in short, the *soul* of the party. He sings an excellent song, and has as many tricks as a monkey. I cannot help smiling at his sallies, though they are frequently levelled at me; for he is one of my most virulent persecutors. Indeed, such is our general line of conduct; for, having early discovered the confederacy, prudence determined us to go mildly on, seemingly blind to what it was beyond our power to remedy. Never intermeddling in their disputes, all endeavours to draw us into quarrels are vainly exerted——: indeed I despise them too much to be angry.

During the first fortnight of our voyage my foolish complaisance stood in my way at table; but I soon learnt our genteel maxim was " catch as catch can,"—the longest arm fared best; and you cannot imagine what a good scrambler I am become,—a dish once seized, it is my care, to make use of my good fortune: and now provisions running very short, we are grown quite savages; two or three of us perhaps fighting for a bone; for there is no respect of persons. The wretch of a captain wanting our passage money for nothing, refused to lay in a sufficient quantity of stock; and if we do not soon reach our Port, what must be the consequence, Heaven knows.

After meals I generally retire to my cabin, where I find plenty of employment, having made up a dozen shirts for Mr. F— out of some cloth, I purchased at Mocha, to replace part of those stolen by the Arabs—Sometimes I read French and Italian, and study Portugueze. I likewise prevailed on Mr. Fay to teach me short-hand; in consequence of the airs H— gave himself because he was master of this art, and had taught his sisters to correspond *with* him in it. The matter was very easily accomplished—in short I discovered abundant methods of making my time pass usefully, and not disagreeably. How often since, in this situation have I blessed God, that he has been pleased to endow me with a mind, capable of furnishing its own amusement, in despite of every means used to discompose it.

4th November.—We are now in sight of the Malabar hills, and expect to reach Calicut either this evening, or to-morrow; I shall conclude this letter, and send it under charge of Mr. Manesty, to forward it from Bombay. I am in tolerable health, and looking with a longing eye, towards Bengal, from whence I trust my next will be dated. The climate seems likely to agree very well with me, I do not at all mind the heat, nor does it affect either my spirits, or my appetite.

I remain
Ever affectionately your's,
E. F.

LETTER XII.

MY DEAR FRIENDS

It was my determination never to write to you, during the state of dreadful Captivity in which we have long been held, but having hopes of a release, think I may now venture to give you some account of our sufferings, which have been extreme, both in body and mind, for a period of fifteen weeks, which we have spent in wretched confinement, totally in the power of Barbarians.[18]

I must premise that, such is the harrassing confusion of my mind, and the weakness of my nerves, that I can merely offer you a simple statement of facts, and even that must necessarily be incorrect; for incessant anxiety and constant anticipation of more intolerable evils, have totally unhinged my faculties. God knows whether I may ever recover them; at present all is confused and clouded.—Reflections on the importance of our speedy arrival in Bengal, which so many circumstances had contributed to prevent, and the apprehension lest our delay should afford time to raise serious obstacles against Mr. Fay's admission into the Court, as an advocate, had long been as so many daggers, piercing my vitals: add to this the heart-breaking thought what immense tracts lie between me and those dear *dear* friends, whose society alone can render me completely happy. Even were the most brilliant success to crown our future views, never could I know comfort, 'till the blessed moment arrive, when I shall clasp you all to my fond heart, without fear of a future separation; except by that stroke, to which we must all submit; and which has been suspended over my head as by a single hair. I trust that I have been spared, to afford me the means of proving more substantially than by words, how inestimably precious, absence has made you in my sight.—Well may it be said that, the deprivation of a blessing enhances its value; for my affection rises now to a pitch of Enthusiasm, of which I knew not that my heart was capable;—but which has been its consolation, amidst all the horrors of imprisonment and sickness: no congenial mind to which I could declare my feelings, sure of meeting with sympathizing affection, as I so delightfully experienced in the company of my beloved sister—But I forget that all this while you are impatient to hear how we fell into so distressing a situation; take then the particulars.

I told you in my last that we expected to reach Calicut very shortly, and accordingly next day, on the (to me ever memorable) 5th November, we anchored in the Roads, and to our great concern saw no English flag up. In a short time we were surrounded by vessels which approached us with an air of so much hostility that we became seriously alarmed,—with one exception; this was the redoubtable Mrs. Tulloh. She had frequently, in the course of the voyage, expressed a violent desire for some species of adventure,—a passion for some romantic danger, on which she could descant hereafter; and far from congratulating herself on having arrived at Grand Cairo, when the Caravan was setting off in safety, she ever expressed a wish, that *she* had been present during that period of terror and confusion, of which she envied us the participation. On hearing Chenu declare that he feared he must make a *shew* of engaging, notwithstanding the deficiencies under which he laboured, and which evidently rendered the idea of resistance on our part, a *mere* farce; since we had neither arms, ammunition, nor men on board sufficient to abide the contest, she positively insisted on having a chair brought upon deck, in which she was determined to sit, and see the engagement; observing that, it was the next best thing to escaping from shipwreck.—Having no ambition to play the Heroine in this way, I resolved on going below, and exerting, (should it be necessary) my limited abilities in assisting Mr. Taylor, who had agreed to officiate as Surgeon —not feeling myself inclined to brave horrors of this nature, for the mere love of exhibition.   Most probably had the matter become serious, she would not have been permitted to indulge her fancy; but by degrees our suspicious visitants sheered off, without venturing to commence an attack, seeing us apparently so well prepared to resist them; and we flattered ourselves that our fears had been altogether groundless.

The next morning Hare and two others, going on shore to reconnoitre brought back intelligence, that we might all be safe in the Danish Factory, on condition of our passing for Danes;—as a misunderstanding actually subsisted between Hyder Ally and the English.   Mr. Passavant, the Danish Consul, had been on board meanwhile, and given us pretty nearly the same information, and from others we soon learnt a circumstance, which confirmed our apprehension, that some mischief was brewing,—this was the departure of Mr. Freeman, the English Consul, who had left the place some weeks before, taking with him his furniture and effects,—a positive proof that he supposed hostilities were about to commence; as it has been found a common procedure in these cases, for Asiatic Princes to begin a War, by imprisoning the Embassadors or Residents, of course, a wise man will fly when the storm lowers.

Now our most worthy fellow-passengers, had privately agreed to continue their journey by land, and rejoiced in the opportunity of leaving us in the lurch:—they therefore accepted Mr. Passavant's invitation immediately, without

consulting us. At first this behaviour affected me a good
deal and I resolved to follow them;—Mr. Fay concurring
in opinion.—But on calm reflection, we judged it most
prudent to learn what reception *they* met with, before *we*
ventured on such slippery ground. On Sunday Chenu
dined on board; and appeared very earnest for our quitting
the Ship: but we did not attend to his persuasions. The
Gunner who had charge of the vessel was a very respectable
man, and we had lately held many conversations with him;
he had a vile opinion of the Captain, believing that money
would tempt him to commit *any* act, however atrocious;
and had resolved in case an armed force was seen approaching the ship, to cut and run down to Cochin, with all the
sail he could set,—but alas! before Chenu left us this day,
he ordered all the yards to be struck, saying he should stay
six weeks. This was doubtless done to frighten us, and to
induce us to go on shore; but having taken our resolution,
we were not to be moved; especially as he dropped some
dark hints, respecting the situation of those, who *were* there;
in so much that we had reason to think our only chance of
escaping imprisonment, was by remaining where we were.
Meantime intelligence reached us from various quarters,
that disputes ran high between the Captain and passengers,
about the remaining half of their passage money. As they
proposed leaving the ship there, he demanded payment;
which they refused till they should arrive in Bengal.

On the 8th came Lewis, Hare's servant, for his own
clothes;—he brought news that a challenge had again passed
between his master and Chenu, on the occasion of his
master's trunks being stopped for the passage money—he
left them on the point of deciding it when he came off.
You may suppose we became exceedingly anxious to learn
the event, but had soon other matters to engross our
attention.

During the three days we staid here, after every one

else departed, boats full of people, were continually coming on board by permission of our *worthy* Captain, under pretence of viewing the ship,—we thought this rather odd; but John the Gunner being, as I observed before, a prudent steady man, we trusted to his discretion.   About four, on Monday afternoon, I was sitting in the round-house at work, when a large boat came along side, with *more* than twenty *armed men* in her;—one of them shewed a written *chit* as he called it from Chenu; notwithstanding which, John insisted on their leaving their arms behind them— this, they at length complied with, and were then permitted to enter.   I ran down half frightened to Mr. Fay, who was reading in our cabin, and told him the affair.   " Pho," said he, it is impossible they should mean any harm: are we not under the protection of the Danish flag? " this silenced me at once, and he went upon deck to see the issue.   All this while our visitors feigned to be mighty ignorant, and inquisitive, peeping into every hole and corner, as if, they never saw such a sight in their lives—purposely dallying on the time 'till just dark, when to my great joy they departed.   A heavy squall came on, which they sheltered from under the ship's stern, there another boat met them, and after some parley, they both (as I thought) went away.

But in a few minutes down came Mr. Fay " you must not be alarmed, said he, I have news to tell you:—we are to have a hundred and fifty sepoys on board to-night! " Seapoys: for what!   " Why the English are coming to attack Calicut—Chenu has promised Sudder Khan, the Governor, his assistance, who has sent these troops for our defence "—" Oh Mr. F—" replied I, this is a very improbable story, for God's sake suffer not these people to enter the ship, if you can avoid it; otherwise we are ruined. I see plainly this is a second Suez business ; " (for by the same treacherous pretext they gained possession of the ships there) and at *that* instant, all that those unfortunate men suffered, coming fresh into my mind, I really thought I should have fainted—Seeing that I was rendered more uneasy by being kept in suspense, he now acknowledged, that under favour of the night, a large party, headed by a Capt. Ayres, an Englishman in Hyder's service, had already made good their entrance. The Commander had indeed related the above nonsensical tale to our Gunner, as an excuse for his proceeding; but did not seem himself to expect, it would gain belief: however being nearly destitute of Arms and Ammunition (the Arabs had taken care of that) what could we do, but recommend ourselves to the Divine Protection? which I may truly say, was never more earnestly solicited by me.—When the redoubtable Captain Ayres had settled every thing upon Deck, he favoured us with his company below.—As this Gentleman is in great power, and had a large share in the subsequent transactions, I must here devote a few moments to giving you a little sketch of his history.

He was born in London, and at the usual age bound apprentice to a saddler; but being a lad of spirit, and associating with other promising youths of similar talents, and courage, he soon found an employment more suited to his active genius; in a word, he became a Gentleman Collector on the *Highway*. This post he maintained several years, and if we may credit what he relates when in a boasting humour, performed many notable exploits; it is true he sometimes got inclosed within the hard gripe of the Law, but always found means to liberate himself, from it, 'till on one unlucky trial, proofs ran so strong against him, that in spite of money and friends (which in his case were *never* wanting) he was *Capitally convicted*; though, afterwards, pardoned on condition of transportation for life—This induced him to enlist for the East Indies, where he exercised his former profession, and was twice imprisoned at Calcutta on suspicion; but having acted

cautiously, nothing positive appeared against him: so by
way of changing the scene, he was draughted off for Madras,
where finding his favourite business rather slack, and his
pay insufficient to support him without it, our hero determined on deserting to Hyder Ally, which resolution he soon
found means to put in practice,—carrying with him two
horses, arms, accoutrements, wearing apparel, and every
thing else of value he could lay hands on, to a pretty considerable amount. This shew of property, (no matter how
acquired) gave him consequence with Hyder, who immediately promoted him to the rank of Captain. Being a
thorough paced villain, he has during these seven years
taken the lead in every species of barbarity.—He even
advised his General, who is Governor of this Province, to
massacre all the natives by way of quelling a rebellion
which had arisen.—The least punishment inflicted by him
was cutting off the noses and ears of those miserable wretches,
whose hard fate subjected them to his tyranny. In short
a volume would not contain half the enormities perpetrated
by this disgrace to human nature—but to proceed.

At sight of him I shuddered involuntarily, though at
that time ignorant of his real character, such an air of
wickedness and ferocity overspread his features. The
sergeant who accompanied, him was (always excepting his
master) the most horrid looking creature, I verily believe,
in existence: from such another pair the Lord defend me!
Ayres told me, with the utmost indifference that the people
at the Factory had all been fighting duels:—that Mr.
Passavant the Danish Chief, had sent for a guard to separate
them; and that the Governor finding the ship had no
owner, as all these disputes arose about dividing the spoil,
had thought proper to take possession of her in the *Nabob's*
name, until matters were inquired into; after which he
faithfully promised to restore her, without the least embezzle-
ment—the love of *Justice* alone inducing him thus to act.

Though we perceived the fallacy of these pretences, yet as it was useless to argue with the vile instrument of oppression, we only requested to be set free on shore with our effects.   This he engaged for, and even offered to take *charge* of any *valuables* or *money*—You may be sure we pleaded poverty; declaring that except our clothes, (which could be no object in a country where so few are worn) a guinea would purchase all we possessed; in the mean time we requested a guard to protect our persons from insult.— Having pledged his *Honour* for our security, the captain retired.   You will believe that sleep did not visit our eyelids *that* night: The fright had disordered me so much, that a violent retching came on, succeeded by a strong fever, which occasioned dreadful pains in my limbs.   In the midst of these excruciating tortures, I heard Ayres tell his Serjeant, that orders were come to plunder the Ship, and make all the officers prisoners in the Round-house.

Can any thing be imagined more distressing, than my situation without the means of relief,—no possibility of obtaining advice, and no female to whom I could look for succour or assistance.   This was about two in the morning, —these words sounded like the signal of death in my ears. Immediately a party of armed men surrounded our Cabin, and demanded entrance.   I clung round my husband and begged for God's sake that he would not admit them; for what could be expected from such wretches but the most shocking treatment.   All this while there was such a noise without, of breaking and tearing, to come at their plunder, as convinced me that should we once lose sight of our little property, *every thing was lost:* at first they were pacified on being told that I was asleep, but soon grew out of patience, brandished their scymitears and one man who spoke a little English, threatened with horrible execrations to murder us, if we did not *instantly* comply with their demands, and open the door.—Mr. Fay drew his sword on this declara-

tion, swearing solemnly that he would run the first man
through the body, who should presume to enter his wife's
apartment. His air of resolution and menacing actions,
had their effect so far, as to prevent them from breaking
open the door; the top of which being sashed, I beheld
through it, their terrific countenances, and heard them
incessantly calling " *ao, ao*," (in English come). This
word has made an impression on me, which is indescribable.
I can never hear it pronounced on the most common occasion, without trembling: but to return—Mr. Fay now
intreated me to rise if possible, being fearful he could not
keep them much longer at bay. I endeavoured to comply;
but the agonising pains I suffered, and the extreme weakness brought on by fever, rendered it impossible for me to
stand upright; there was however no remedy—so by
degrees I got my clothes on (I recollect now that I must
have been above an hour employed in this business.)
Through the glass door, I could see the villains outside, use
menacing gestures and urge me to make haste,—vowing
vengeance on me if I kept them longer waiting.

Expecting a strict search and being desirous of rescuing
something from the general wreck, Mr. Fay contrived to
conceal our watches in my hair, having first stopped their
going by sticking pins in the wheels; and the little money
we possessed, and what small articles I could take without
exciting suspicion, were concealed about my person. Thus
equipped I crawled out, *bent double*, and in an instant, the
Cabin was filled with Seapoys. I must here pause, and
intreat my dear sister to imagine herself in my situation at
that *dreadful* moment; for no language can I find, that
would do justice to my feelings.

But when I came on deck, the scene which presented
itself would have appalled the stoutest heart;—mine already
weakened by grief and apprehension could not withstand
it. A sudden burst of tears alone saved me from fainting.

The poor sailors were so distracted, that many of them could scarcely be restrained from jumping over board to escape slavery;—sometimes crying for their wages, and asking the Officers to pay them; who incapable of affording any consolation, walked about like men bereft of reason: no wonder, since this fatal event would, to say the least, occasion them the loss of twelve month's pay, exclusive of their private ventures.

We were immediately ordered on shore, together with the carpenter and ship's steward;—we demanded our baggage, but in vain; at length having represented the necessity of a change of linen, a person was sent down with me, in whose presence I put up a few common things, in a handkerchief, not being allowed to take any thing of value; but having laid out a silk gown the day before, to put on in case I went ashore, I begged hard for that, and obtained it; though my husband was not suffered to take a second coat, or even to change that he had on. Our beds were likewise refused, lest they should contain valuables; and upon deck the bundle was again examined in search of hidden treasure,—but finding nothing, they, contrary to my expectations, searched no further; but permitted us to leave the vessel unmolested; except that they had the cruelty to toss several half extinguished *Blue lights* into the boat, the smoke of which, from the rancid oil and abominable rags used in their composition, almost stifled me.— At this time it rained hard, and continued to do so the whole day, which forced me to creep under the shelter of a kind of half deck, where I sat, bent double, for two long *long* hours, and then a remarkably high surf, prevented large boats from landing,—we had no remedy but to go into a canoe, scarcely bigger than a butcher's tray, half full of water,—so that we reached the shore dripping wet— Compare this account with the many chearful and flattering conversations we have held together on the subject of my

arrival in *India*. What a striking difference! It is true
we were in the hands of the natives; but little did I imagine
that, any power on this Continent, however independent,
would have dared to treat *English* subjects with such
cruelty, as we experienced from them.

As if to aggravate our miseries by every species of
insult, they compelled us to walk above a mile thro' a heavy
sand, surrounded by all the mob of Calicut, who seemed
to take pleasure in beholding the distress of white people,
those constant objects of their envy and detestation.—When
we had proceeded about half way, our Guards detained us
nearly an hour, in an open Square, till the Governor's
pleasure should be known. He sat all the while smoking
his Hooka, and looking down upon us; when having
sufficiently feasted his eyes, he ordered us to be taken to
the English Factory—How I dragged on my weary aching
limbs, I know not. The rain still poured and as we went,
a lad who had deserted from Madras, and was then a
serjeant in Hyder's service, seeing a country-woman in such
distress, offered to procure me an umbrella, but could not
prevail on the barbarians to stop, while he ran for it, though
he was their officer. I thanked the poor lad for his kind
intention and Mr. Fay insisted that I should take his hat,
while he walked on bare-headed to the place of our confinement.—But here I cannot describe the horror which
seized me on finding, we were totally in the power of
wretches, who, for, aught I knew, intended to strip and
murder us: why else were we sent to an empty house?
not a single chair to sit on, or any other bed than the floor.
These were my heart-breaking reflections, as I threw
myself in despair on a window seat, worn out with fatigue
and want of nourishment; without means of procuring
even a draught of water to assuage my thirst, which grew
excessive; for the offer of a bribe would have been dangerous.

In this miserable condition we remained till two o'clock,

when Mr. Passavant having heard of our misfortune, sent us a dinner; but his messenger had very great difficulty in obtaining admittance, with even this temporary relief. From him we learnt that, the other passengers were hitherto unconfined, but expected every moment to be made prisoners. After Mr. Fay had dined, (for my anxiety continued so great, that exhausted as I was, I could not touch a morsel of what was brought) I besought him to look round for some place into which I might crawl, and lie down unseen by the Seapoys, that guarded us. He was averse to this, lest they should imagine that we were seeking to escape, and make that a pretext for ill usage:—but perceiving that the sight of them prevented me from taking that repose, so necessary to recruit my poor worn out frame, he complied with my request, and having discovered a lumber-room leading out of the Veranda which surrounded the house, he assisted me into it—Here with my little bundle for a pillow, I stretched myself on the floor, amidst dirt and rubbish, and enjoyed a fine sleep of more than three hours, when I awoke completely refreshed and entirely free from the dreadful tortures, which had racked me the whole night.—I did not even feel any symptoms of fever.

Surprized and thankful for the change, I joyfully went down to Mr. Fay, declaring that I would continue to make use of the lumber-room to sleep in, and as Mr. Passavant had, during my nap, sent me a rattan couch, tho' by the bye without either mattress, pillow, or musquito curtains, I was just going to have it conveyed there, when the place was found to be swarming with venomous reptiles; perhaps a hundred scorpions and centipedes—happily I slept too soundly to feel them, and I remained unmolested; but had I moved hand or foot, what might have been the consequence!

The next morning we had a visit from Mr. Hare; less,

it appeared, to condole with us on such unexampled suffering, than to embrace the occasion of displaying his own eloquence; for which having a very strong passion, it was no wonder, if he thought the misfortunes of others proper subjects to expatiate on.   Mounting his rhetorical hobby-horse, the Orator harangued a long while, though to little purpose, endeavouring to turn our situation into ridicule;—offered to convey letters for us to Bengal;—pretended to be in raptures with the fine view of the Sea from our Veranda, which I hinted to him he might still have time to admire at his leisure, though he affected to be certain of leaving Calicut in a few hours.   At length he concluded, by advising me to address a *tender* memorial to Hyder Ally, whose general character for gallantry, would not admit of his refusing any request made by a *fair* Lady.   This was wonderfully witty in the speaker's opinion, as you may conceive, how *fair* the Lady in question looked.   How a man could break a jest on a creature so bowed down by affliction, I know not: but I envy not his feelings.

I forgot to tell you that, the duel between the *Captain*, and the *Orator*, was prevented by the guard, doubtless to the regret of these heroes.   It seems the day they went on shore, Ayres accompanied by another Captain of a pretty similar description, named West, made Mr. Passavant a visit, to look at the strangers.   Now as it was of the utmost importance, that they should remain undiscovered by such dangerous people, and as their visitants, though illiterate, were sufficiently acute, all perceived immediately the necessity of being guarded;—accordingly they, every one spoke French, and this, together with their long wide coats, and *preposterous* hats, which had just then become fashionable in England, effectually shielded them from suspicion; when behold, a sudden fit of Patriotism, aided by an irresistible fondness for exhibition, rendered the great Mr. H— incapable of persevering in deception.   " What " exclaimed he, "shall *Englishmen* harbour distrust of each other! perish the ignoble idea!—be the consequences what they may, I will no longer restrain myself from embracing my beloved country-men." At the conclusion of this heroic speech, "Suiting the action to the words" advancing theatrically, he grasped the hand of Ayres, and shook it, with such violence as if he meant to demonstrate the excess of his joy and confidence, by dislocating the shoulder of his newly acquired friend.

The most unreserved intimacy, immediately took place between these congenial souls, and it is asserted that unable to keep any secret from his bosom confidant, H— was really so mad, (I may say, so cruel) as absolutely to acknowledge the ship to be English property. I could not have believed that his folly and imprudence would carry him so far; thus much is, however, undoubtedly fact, that the man in the spectacles is constantly pointed out, as the author of every mischief which followed.—It is surprizing how often we find weakness and malignity united, or rather let us say, that providence has thus ordained it, for the benefit of mankind. Probably the former induced H— to injure the party to which he had attached himself:—the latter undoubtedly led him to visit us, for he could not conceal his exultation at the circumstance of our accidental capture in the Vessel, seeming to involve us *exclusively* in her fate. The unfeeling wretch availed himself of this to lay a scheme, that had it been adequately seconded, must have brought on our destruction.

Ayres was first prevailed on by large presents, to dissuade the Governor from confining *them*, and that point gained, he pushed their interest forward thus, "These gentlemen" said he, "have no concern here of any kind; besides, as they are people of the highest consequence, their detention would bring half India on our back, so take my advice and let them go." "Well, but replies Sudder Khan,

" what must I do with my prisoners? " " Oh keep them by all means " replies *Beelzebub*, " the man is a stout fellow, and after a little breaking in, will make a most excellent soldier: send him and his wife up the country, there feed them on dry rice, he will soon be glad to enlist I warrant you. The chief of the other party Mr. H— is a brother lawyer, so you need not fear, but he will be happy enough to get rid of him; indeed he owned as much to me privately, and pledged his honour that no ill consequence could possibly arise from the transaction;—the person in question not being of sufficient importance for the English to reclaim him solemnly; especially as he came out without leave." You will wonder how I came by all this information; have patience, you shall know in time.[19]

The Governor heard this argument calmly, promised fair, and acted so far agreeably to his professions that, while *we* were closely confined and miserably situated, our worthy fellow passengers enjoyed full liberty to walk about, and amuse themselves as they pleased.—This procedure could not fail to vex us excessively, though we were then ignorant of its real cause, and whenever we ventured to expostulate on our unreasonably harsh treatment with Ayres or any other, who chanced to call, the only answer we could obtain was, with a shrug of affected compassion, " why did you stay on board! nothing can be done for you *now*, you must abide the event." These insinuations created fears, that a distinction would really be made in our eventual disposal, as much to our disadvantage, as the present state of things, but we had no remedy—all avenues to relief were closed.

I think I told you that, our watches were concealed in my hair, being secured with pins to prevent them from going; one of the pins however came out, at the very time I was set on shore. Never shall I forget what a terrible sensation the ticking of the watch caused! I think had it

continued long, I must completely have lost my senses; for
I dared not remove it, from a fear of worse consequences;
but happily it stopped of itself. When we were fixed in
our prison Mr. Fay took these watches, (we had three you
know) and all the money we had power to secure in chequins,
which are of easy conveyance (about twenty-five pounds)
and putting them into his glove, hid them in a snug place,
as he thought, about the Verandah. The day after we were
taken prisoners, a most dreadful hurricane of rain and wind
came in, (it was the breaking up of the monsoon) and next
morning we found to our extreme grief, that the place
where Mr. Fay had concealed our treasure, to which alone
we could look for the means of escape, was entirely blown
down; and no vestige of our little property remaining.
Mr. Fay was in despair from the first; but after he had
told me, I searched diligently all round, but in vain. At
length it struck me, from the direction in which the wind
blew, that if I could make my way into an inclosure, at the
back of the house, it might possibly be found there. The
seapoys guarded the front, but there being only one door
backwards, they seldom took the trouble of going round.
I did not tell Mr. Fay of my scheme, as there was nothing
he opposed so strongly, as the appearance of seeking to
escape; but when he was completely absorbed in contemplating this new misfortune, I stole to the back door.
There was a large lock and key inside and to my surprize,
when I had turned this, my passage was clear to the stairs,
leading to the inclosure; and not a soul in sight. The
grass was excessively high and wet, but I struggled to make
my way through it and waded about, determined at least
not to leave an inch unexplored. Imagine my joy, when in
the midst of a deep tuft I found the old glove, with all its
contents safe, and uninjured. What a treasure it seemed!
how many are there who never felt so much true delight on
receiving a magnificent fortune, as we experienced in again

beholding this sheet anchor of our hopes, thus unexpectedly restored.

But alas! the little unlooked for liberty I had regained, was too tempting *not* to be enjoyed again; and a day or two afterwards as I was walking about in the grass, I espied a seapoy coming round. I was not certain that he saw me, so I endeavoured to reach the house unobserved. At the moment I turned round to fasten the heavy door, he ran to it, pushing it against me, with such violence that the large key which had unfortunately a very long shank, was by this means struck directly against my right breast, and gave me the most excruciating pain. I fainted through excessive agony, and was with difficulty recovered. Much I fear the consequences of this accident will embitter my future life. Having no other nurse than my poor husband, who was not only ignorant of what ought to be done, but totally without the necessaries for any kind of emollient application,—my case was truly distressing; so that even Ayres who chanced to call, expressed some concern for me, and sent plenty of milk which I used as an embrocation with success. I believe he punished the seapoy for his insolence, but this could not repair the mischief.

At the very time when this painful variety took place in the cheerless monotony of our prison days, the cruel designers who had assisted in dooming us to this wretched abode, fell completely into the pit which they had digged for us.—The evening before Ayres Tulloh and Hare had called on us together, the former was (according to his *general* policy) endeavouring to discover whether we had any concealed property; on which I exclaimed "Captain Ayres how should we have any thing left, except the baggage in the vessel, which is of little value? as the Arabs pillaged us to the utmost of their power; we were altogether a set of poor creatures when we came to Calicut; and you are well aware we have received nothing since." "Answer for yourself Mrs. Fay " cried Hare, " for my *own* part I feel happy in saying, that, I am *not* poor, I have property, *valuable* property and shall not shrink from avowing that I possess it." I marked the eye of Ayres during this bombastic speech, and have since found, that I was not deceived in its expression.

Sudder Khan induced by this and other similar stories, which the passengers had told of their own consequence, determined to frighten them into the payment of a large sum of money. Accordingly next morning (the 13th) he sent a large party of seapoys to the Danish Factory, who peremptorily demanded them as the Nabob's prisoners. Mr. Passavant at first refused, but on their threatening to fire into his house, was constrained to yield to this outrageous violation of the most sacred rights, and delivered his guests to slavery. God forbid that I should, generally speaking, be capable of rejoicing in the miseries of my fellow creatures, even where they merit punishment, but I must own, (blame me if you will) that for a short time I *did* feel satisfaction in this stroke of retributive justice, in as far as regarded the Tulloh, and Hare, for the vile conduct of these people, and the malevolence of their dispositions, had steeled my heart against them.

It was certainly a curious sight to behold them, after all their airs of superiority reduced to take up their residence with us, whose situation, while singular, was the object of their ridicule and contempt. The scene was however now changed; although *they*, like many others in the world, were able to support their neighbour's misfortunes with stoical firmness, and even render them a source of amusement, each readily discovered when personally attacked by a similar calamity, that close imprisonment is by no means a proper subject on which to exercise wit, and that people when in distress are not precisely in the humour for relishing the pleasantry of others on their troubles. Tulloh

fortunately understood Moors, which is the general
language among the military throughout India;—by this
means he got his trunks on shore the day after the seizure,
and saved them from the violent storm, which came on next
morning, wherein every one imagined the ship must have
been wrecked.   How we wished to see her drive on shore!
especially when Sudder Khan the Governor who is Hyder's
brother-in-law, was seen walking about in great perturba-
tion on the beach anxiously watching the vessel, praying to
Mahomet, and from time to time, casting up the sand
towards Heaven with earnest invocation and entreaties,
that she might be spared, as a present to the great Hyder;
very probably fearing that some blame might attach to
him in case she were lost.

As it happened, however, all things went wrong for
us—The cabin and steerage where our trunks had been
placed were soon filled with water, and every thing, such as
books, wearing apparel, beds, with laces, buckles, rings &c.
was either stolen or totally spoiled.   These latter I might
have saved, when we were brought on shore, but unfortunately the trunk, which contained my clothes, was
just *without* the cabin-door, and two of the wretches who
watched us sat on it, so that I could not remove an article.
This disaster left us nothing except our lives to be anxious
about—why do I say anxious! since life itself on the terms
we held it, was hardly worth preserving.   The other
passenger's baggage was injured but not like our's; for
we, not being favorites, had been forced to keep *our*
packages at hand, during the voyage, as we had no one
to get them up when wanted, whereas the rest had theirs
stowed away in the hold and consequently little damage
befel them.

Many ships perished in this terrible hurricane.   The
St. Helena which left Mocha a week after us, met with it,
and suffered so much that she was forced to put into Cochin,

(a Danish settlement in Latitude 10) with the loss of her
masts; and so greatly shattered besides, as to be compelled
to undergo a thorough repair.—If this happened to a fine
new vessel, one of the best sailors in India, what must have
become of us, had we continued five days longer at Sea?—
badly found in all respects, and worse manned; not half
people enough to work the ship properly, even in good
weather, was not this another hairsbreadth escape think
you, though by a dreadful alternative? The ways of
providence are inscrutable! But to revert to my main
subject,—glad shall I be when it is concluded; for I detest
matter of fact *writing*, almost as much as matter of fact
conversation:—yet this story must be told in my own way,
or not at all.

When the gale ceased, the whole cargo was landed and
deposited in the Governor's warehouses, where he caused
the Gentlemen's baggage to be opened, and like a child
pleased with gewgaws, every article which struck the eye,
was instantly condemned as his booty. Poor Hare's trunks
were stuffed with knickknacks like a Pedlar's box: judge
then what agonies he appeared in, when the fatal moment
of examination approached, lest they should become, as
might be expected, objects of desire to the Governor.—
Not a single tooth pick case, knife, or knee-buckle was
produced, but what he declared had been received as a
pledge of friendship from different relations; parents,
brothers, sisters, male and female cousins, to the utmost
verge of propinquity, all put in their claims with success.
Tulloh serving as interpreter, until he was perfectly weary
of the office; ashamed of pleading such trifling causes, and
only deterred from throwing up his post, by the earnest
entreaties of Hare, who continued stamping, exclaiming
and fretting, as if his life depended on the issue. At last
a small paper bundle fell into the searcher's hands, he then
became outrageous. "For Heaven's sake, cried he my

dear friend, (almost breathless with apprehension) Oh for Heaven's sake endeavour to preserve *this* parcel for me; should it be taken I am an *undone man*, for I shall never be able to replace the contents; let them take my clothes, my Law books, *every* thing, except my music books—all that I can yield without a sigh." Tulloh imagining that the contents must be of immense value to him from his extreme agitation, earnestly interceded for the parcel; but obtained it with great difficulty, as curiosity and avarice were awakened by perceiving the convulsive eagerness with which the owner petitioned for it.—The former was soon gratified and the latter consoled; for Hare tearing open the parcel discovered to the astonished spectators neither more, nor less, than an exquisite assortment of VENETIAN FIDDLE STRINGS!! But, ah! dire mischance! the remorseless waves, (which are neither respectors of persons or things) had pervaded this invaluable treasure and rendered it wholly useless; and to complete his misery the next thing that presented itself to the sad owner's eyes, was a most expensive and finely toned *Tenor violin*, purchased at Venice, and for which the precious strings were intended,—broken all to pieces! I leave you to form any ideas you may think proper on the subject of that extravagant sorrow, such a character was likely to exhibit—and pass on to matters more interesting.

The general introductory letter which, as you may recollect, Mr. Franco gave us at Leghorn, had remained in Mr. F—'s pocket book from that time, 'till we reached Calicut. We had been told that Isaac, the Jewish merchant, who agreed to freight the Nathalia, and received £700 as earnest on that account, was *immensely* rich, and had great credit with Government, of which he held several large contracts for building ships &c. besides being a great favourite with Sudder Khan. Every one also, even Ayres, spoke highly of his general character. But our introduction to Mr. Baldwin had been productive of, or at least connected with so many misfortunes, that my confidence was lost, and I dreaded making further applications, lest similar events should ensue. This was very foolish reasoning you will say, and I am ready to acknowledge it, the only excuse to be made is, that my mind was weakened by calamity. However after Tulloh and the rest of these people joined us, our situation became, if possible, still more distressing and we anxiously sought every practicable mode of relief. Mr. F— therefore petitioned the Governor for leave to go out under a guard, which being granted, he immediately delivered his letter to Isaac, who seemed highly gratified at hearing from Mr. Franco whom he had personally known at Constantinople, when they were both young men, *above sixty* years ago: for Isaac is also considerably turned of eighty, and like him, enjoys full possession of his faculties, both bodily and mental, being equally remarkable for temperance and sobriety. Mr. F— could not speak to our strangely acquired friend except by an interpreter; so that no confidential conversation could take place. He was apparently touched with pity for our sufferings, especially on hearing how much I was afflicted with illness. My spirits were raised by the account my husband gave of his visit, and soon after his favourable report was confirmed, by my receiving a present brought to the Factory, by a servant, belonging to the benevolent Jew, and which in our situation was truly valuable, consisting of a catty of fine tea, a tea-pot, and a tea-kettle. Although these things were expressly sent to me, yet Mrs. Tulloh and her party seized the last mentioned article, and forcibly kept it; so that I was forced to make my tea, by boiling it in my tea-pot. Ah my dear sister, I was at this time ill enough to be laid up on a sick bed, and carefully nursed, yet was I thankful for such food as I should once have loathed, and I still continued to lie on my rattan couch, without a pillow or any covering except my clothes, and surrounded by people whom my very heart sickened to behold.

I will here by way of relaxation transcribe a few passages from my Journal, as nothing happened for some time worthy of a particular recital; reserving to myself, however, the option of resuming the narrative style, whenever I shall deem it necessary.

14th November, 1779.

Mr. Fay was sent for, this morning, to the Governor, who asked him what he wanted? he replied, *Liberty*:—there was no observation made on this answer, nor can we conceive what Sudder Khan can mean by the detention of so many persons, who never bore arms. They gave Mr. Tulloh 30 rupees for our support. All we are able to procure is tough, lean, old beef, goat's flesh, and a not unpleasant rice cake, but too sweet to be palatable with meat; we preserve either with difficulty from our perpetual visitors the crows, having no cup-board or place to put our victuals in.—Of all existing creatures crows are surely the most voracious, and the most persevering—I have seen one with his eye fixed for a full half hour on a person, and the instant that person's eye was averted, pounce on the bread, or whatever had been prepared and bear away the prize. Mem.—Ayres is remarkably like these crows, he has exactly their *thievish* expression of countenance, and the form of his head resembles their's.

15th November, 1779.

The Gentlemen waited all day at the Governor's house, being promised their baggage, but he thought proper to disappoint them—received 10 rupees subsistence money.

18th November.

A most impudent message brought from the Governor, requiring all the gentlemen to enter into the Nabob's service; which they unanimously refused, with every mark of contempt, and were in consequence ordered to be more closely confined—One of Mr. Fay's trunks brought on shore containing wearing apparel, and law books, probably much damaged, yet certainly valuable to him, as he has *none* remaining. Made application for it but without success. Tulloh received 20 rupees.

20th November.

Received notice to prepare immediately to set off for Seringapatam, a large City about three hundred miles distant, where Hyder Ally usually resides—How can I support this journey over the mountains!—Mr. F— is about drawing up a petition, representing the bad state of my health, and entreating permission for me to proceed to Cochin. We hope to prevail on Isaac to present it.

21st November.

Discover that the journey to Seringapatam was merely a vile plot of the Governor's to put us off our guard, and thereby gain possession of what property had hitherto been concealed; thank God this feint miscarried. A letter reached us from Mr. O'Donnell, stating the arrival of the St. Helena at Cochin. He laments our misfortune and promises to take such methods as shall compel the Nabob to do us speedy and effectual justice. Heaven speed his endeavours; this life is horrible.

22nd November.

The gentlemen waited five hours at the Governor's for their effects, but returned without them. He takes evident satisfaction in seeing them like slaves attendant on his *nod* —Five ships supposed to be English passed in front of our prison. How peculiarly distressing did I feel this sight!

23rd November, 1779.

Mrs. Tulloh being taken ill of a fever, application was made to the Governor for medicines; but this happening to be a high festival, he, like the Pharisees in Scripture, refused to profane it by doing good—Should the woman die in the interim what cares he?

24th November, 1779.

This morning got some medicines from the ship's chest —many flying reports of hostilities having actually commenced between Hyder Ally, and the English—should this really prove true, our fate will be sealed *for life*.   Little did I think when pleading the cause of the Chevalier de St. Lubin at Mocha, that he had been raising a storm whose effects would so materially involve us.   Mem.—The lady is well again.

28th November, 1779.

It is now certain that the Nayhirs [20] have laid siege to Tellicherry; a settlement of our's about a degree to the northward; seven miles nearer lies Mahey which the French held, 'till we took it from them in March last; but not finding it worth keeping, have since evacuated it, after dismantling the fortifications.

29th November, 1779.

Sudder Khan is about to march a thousand troops into Mahey, under pretence of resuming it in the Nabob's name, but every one guesses this to be merely a feint to cover his real intentions of privately assisting the Nayhirs;—should they succeed in their attack, Hyder will then throw off the mask and declare war; but if the English conquer, he will disavow the whole affair.

30th November.

I have now a lamentable tale to relate. We were this morning hurried away at a moments warning to the fort, crouded together in a horrid dark place scarcely twenty feet square, swarming with rats, and almost suffocating for want of air. Mr. and Mrs. Tulloh secured a small room to themselves; but my husband and I, were obliged to pass the night among our companions in misery—rats continually gnawing the feet of my couch, whose perpetual squeaking would have prevented sleep, had our harrassing reflections permitted us to court its approach.

1st December, 1779.

Luckily discovered a trap-door, which led to some rooms, or rather lofts, where no human foot had trod for many *many* years. These had been the store rooms of Angria the Pirate,[21] and they certainly contain " a remnant of all things "—Broken chairs—tables—looking-glasses—books, even a spinnet was among, the articles, but beyond all repair, and vast quantities of broken bottles, which had been filled with liquors of all kinds: but the rats in their gambols had made havoc among them. I remember when I should have shuddered at the thoughts of sleeping in such a wretched place; but now privacy gave it irresistible charms; so having with difficulty obtained leave to occupy it, we exerted every nerve to get a spot cleared out before dark, for my couch; likewise so to arrange some bolts of canvas which were among the spoils, as to form a sort of mattress for Mr. F—; here we lay down, comparatively happy in the hope of enjoying a tolerable nights rest; my husband being provided with a long pole to keep off the rats; but surely never were poor mortals so completely disappointed and for my own part I may add, terrified.—No sooner was the light extinguished, than we heard a fluttering noise, attended at intervals with squeaking—by degrees it approached the *beds*, and we felt that several creatures were hovering over us, but of what description we were totally ignorant—sometimes their wings swept our faces, seeming to fly heavily—then again they would remove farther off, but still continued squeaking.—Good God! what horrors I felt. Mr. F— protested that whole legions of evil spirits had taken possession of our apartment, and were determined to expel the intruders. The rats also acted their part in the Comedy; every now and then jumping towards the beds, as we could hear; however Mr. F— on these occasions laid about him stoutly with his pole, and thus kept *them* at bay; but our winged adversaries were not so easily foiled;—they persisted in their assaults 'till day-break, when what should we find had caused all this disturbance, but a parcel of poor harmless bats! whose " ancient solitary reign we had molested." To any one accustomed to see or hear these creatures our terror must appear ridiculous, but to me who had never chanced to meet with any such, the idea never occurred, nor did even Mr. Fay suggest any probable or natural cause of alarm. We cannot help laughing very heartily at it ourselves now, and you are at full liberty to do the same.

2d December.

Ayres called to tell us that two ships of the line, and a frigate had just passed towards Tellicherry.—We shall soon hear news from thence; Oh! that it may change our hard destiny!—The Governor marched at the head of his troops towards Tellicherry.

10th December.

Application was made this morning to the Lieutenant Governor by Mr. Isaac, who I am now convinced is our true friend, representing that this air disagreeing with me I requested permission to remove to Cochin, and that my husband, on account of my extreme ill health, might accompany me. He promised to consult Sudder Khan upon it. The Quelladar or Governor of the Fort, spent some time with us this morning;—he is a fine old man, with a long red beard, and has altogether a most interesting appearance:—and here I may as well give a short description of this place.

Calicut then, is situated on the coast of Malabar in 11° north latitude and 75° east longitude.[22] It was formerly a very considerable town governed by a Zamorin, who also held the adjoining country; but has been some years in the possession of Hyder Ally, of whom you must have heard on occasion of his war with the English in 1770. They would certainly have put an end to the reign of this Usurper, had he not discovered a *method* of influencing the principal persons in power, in consequence of which he obtained a peace, much more honourable and advantageous to himself than to those who granted it. Having acquired by his genius and intrepidity every thing that he enjoys, he makes his name both feared and respected; so that nobody chooses to quarrel with him. I have indeed heard a comparison drawn between him and the King of Prussia, though I think much to the disadvantage of the latter; as supposing their *natural* abilities to be equal,—the great Frederick ought *infinitely* to surpass a man who can neither write nor read, which is the case with Hyder. The lawful Prince of the country of which he has usurped the Government is held by him in actual confinement, though with every outward shew of respect, by which means he prevents the people from rising, lest their legitimate sovereign should fall a sacrifice to his resentment.

The fort must have been formerly a strong place, but is now in a dilapidated state—the walls are very thick, and they mount guard regularly; which was one inducement for sending us here; as Ayres told the Governor it was not worth while to keep a hundred seapoys watching us, when they were wanted elsewhere and that the fort was quite good enough for us to live in;—these arguments prevailed and here we were sent.   When I first arrived I was so extremely ill, as to be scarcely sensible of what passed for some hours; but I remember Hare burst into a violent flood of tears, declaring that we were all doomed to death by our removal to this wretched spot, which being completely surrounded by stagnant water, could not fail to produce some of those disorders so fatal to Europeans.   We have not however hitherto experienced any complaint.   The loft we sleep in is indeed disgusting beyond belief, and the Quelladar, I suppose at the suggestion of Ayres, has ordered the easier of the two ways of entrance, that discovered by Mr. F— to be blocked up; so that there is no way left but by means of a ladder placed almost in a perpendicular direction:—there is a rope by which to hold, or it would be impossible for any person to descend, but even with this assistance, I have great difficulty to reach the bottom.

11th December, 1779.

Peremptorily ordered to make ready for a journey to Seringapatnam.   By the Governor's desire delivered an Inventory of our losses: he promises full restitution, but has given no answer to my request.   I am full of solicitude on this subject; but would submit to any thing rather than remain in this wretched place.

12th December, 1779.

Mr. F— waited twice on the Lieut. Governor but without effect.   What can he mean by thus trifling with us? is it merely a wanton exercise of power, or intended to hide some dark design? these perpetual surmises distract me. Mem. Tulloh received 144 rupees to pay *all* our debts but took especial care not to let us have a single rupee, what wretches we are cast among! my very soul rises at them.

13th December, 1779.

Mr. F— was sent for by the Governor, who told him, that we might both have permission to go to Cochin whenever we thought proper; that he would furnish a boat and pay every incidental expense, besides making entire satisfaction for damages sustained,—Can all this good news be true? How suspicious I grow? what a change from being credulous—yet where is the wonder after being so frequently deceived?

14th December, 1779.

Preparations are going on briskly all day with our fellow passengers, who are eager for their departure, as well they may. Every thing which was taken from them on shore, has been this day restored, but those left in the ship are irrecoverable; of course we benefit nothing by this restitution—Mr. F— could not obtain our promised licence to-day.—These delays, weigh down my spirits, and increase all my complaints. I have still much pain in my breast; Oh that I fear, will prove a fatal blow—I shall have a great loss in Mr. Taylor.

15th December, 1779.

The Governor still withholding our licence under pretence of business, I advised Mr. F— to insist on being *immediately* dispatched, or in case of refusal, by all means to declare himself ready to accompany the others; for I saw clearly that should they once leave us, it must then be entirely at this fellow's option, whether we went all or not, and who would not rather run the risk of even *dying* of fatigue on the journey, than hazard remaining at the mercy of such wretches! I dread, lest this should be part of the old plan of which I have since never heard, and had almost forgotten it. It is much easier to practise against two individuals than a whole company.

16th December.

The Doolies (a kind of shabby Palanquin in which a person sits upright and is carried between two men) arrived this morning about ten. The gentlemen went to take leave, when Tulloh earnestly represented our case, to which the Governor replied, that he could not possibly attend to other matters till they were gone, but pledged his word that nothing should arise on his part to detain us a single hour afterwards; every one agreed with me how dangerous it was to trust such fallacious promises. On my knees I intreated Mr. F— to pursue the method I had before pointed out, but my advice was despised. At nine in the evening the party commenced their journey, having first stripped the place of provisions and every thing else, which having been bought out of the general purse we had an undoubted right to share. They even took my tea kettle, but luckily the man who had it in charge forgot it amidst the hurry of departure, by which means I recovered it. My heart sunk within me at seeing them quit the fort, not from motives of personal esteem or regret you may suppose, for it was impossible to grieve for the loss of some of the company; we parted with as much indifference as absolute strangers; after a fellowship in misfortune sufficient to have united almost any other society more closely than an intercourse of *years* under common circumstances. I went to bed, but in spite of every endeavour to calm the agitation of my mind, passed a *sleepless* night.

17th December.

Rose in extreme anxiety which was far from being diminished by a message from the Governor, ordering Mr. F— not to attend him 'till the evening; accordingly at four o'clock he sat out, and as I felt extremely ill, the certain consequence of fretting and want of rest, I lay down and had just sunk into a doze, when my poor husband flew into the room like a madman, uttering a thousand extravagant expressions. Starting up in new and indescribable terror, and wringing my hands, I begged only to know what had happened. " Happened! " cried he " why we are betrayed, ruined, utterly undone; you must leave this place instantly, or you may be made a prisoner here for ever." Where are we to go? I very naturally asked! I *heard* not the answer, my head swam, and I dropped on the floor completely overpowered.—Whatever happened at that *fearful* moment I forget and endeavour to banish from my mind, as the effect of insanity.—How he accomplished it I know not, but Mr. F— actually carried me in his arms down that almost perpendicular ladder which I have described and placed me on a kind of bier: I was in this manner conveyed to my former habitation—I opened my eyes and became for a few moments sensible of the motion, but soon fainted again, and did not recover 'till I found myself once more entering the English Factory as a prisoner.

I now inquired, what was the cause of this change in our abode: and learnt that Mr. F— being refused leave to depart, had became so exasperated as wholly to lose all self-command; and rushing up to the musnud (throne) of the Lieutenant Governor had actually seized him, peremptorily insisting on the immediate fulfilment of his promise. Such conduct might have been expected to bring down *instant* destruction; but fortunately every one present was persuaded that grief and vexation had literally turned his brain; and they are not only much terrified at every species of madness, but from their religious prejudices, regard the sufferers under these complaints with a superstitious awe. Swayed by these mingled emotions the wicked Governor condescended to temporize with my husband, acknowledg-

ing that he had no *power* to release us without the Nabob's
order which in consideration of my ill health he would
endeavour to procure; and to pacify him further, he permitted our return to this place, where we are certainly in
every respect more comfortably situated.　But these con-
cessions went little towards allaying that fever of passion,
which his continual and cruel delays had excited: thence
arose the alarm I experienced and which for a time so
materially affected my health.

19th December, 1779.

Received five rupees subsistence money which we were
informed were the last we should ever have.　I cannot
conceive what they mean to do with us or what will be our
fate at last.

21st December, 1779.

The Governor sent for Mr. F— to offer him a commission in the Nabob's service and on his absolute refusal,
swore that he might subsist how he could; that his masters
money should no longer be lavished on idlers, then in a rage
ordered palanquins.　" you shall go to Seringapatam " said
he " they will soon teach you better manners there "　Mr.
F— joyfully acquiesced in this mandate,—we provided
necessaries for our journey which was fixed for the 24th;
but the other knew better than to keep his word, so this
like all our former views, and expectations of liberty ends
in smoke, shall I say?

26th December, 1779.

A very melancholy Christmas-day passed yesterday.
My dear friends little imagined they were drinking the
health of a poor prisoner, (for I know you did not forget
us) neither were we forgotten here, if empty compliments
can be styled remembrance.　All the Europeans and several

of the natives attended our Levée. But alas! what relief
can mere ceremonious visits afford to misfortune! say rather
that *aided by recollection*, such shadowy comforts add *keen-
ness* to afflictions sting. I feel my mind insensibly raised
whenever I attempt to expatiate on any subject which tends
to revive the ideas of our separation. Even now I tread
forbidden ground; for your sakes as well as my own, let
me hasten to escape by skipping over this dangerous season
of Christmas. I therefore pass on.

10th January, 1780.

The little money saved was nearly expended, and we
must soon have been reduced to our last mite had not
providence sent us relief from a quarter little dreamed of.
Mr. F— wrote about a week ago to Mr. Church, Governor
of Tellicherry inclosing a memorial of our case, which he
requested might be translated into the language of the
country and proper methods used for its safe delivery to
Hyder Ally himself. This morning brought in reply, a
most generous humane letter from Mr. Church; which,
after acknowledging himself honoured by our application,
and promising his utmost concurrence in every measure
we may think necessary, concludes thus " my heart bleeds
for your distresses, and those of Mrs. F— she in particular
must have suffered greatly. I have taken the liberty to
accompany this letter by an order for two hundred rupees
to serve *present* occasions: Any sum you may in future
require a line to me shall always command it, as I know
the difficulty of procuring remittances where you are.
Englishmen ought to feel for each other; we are not without
our share of troubles *here*; and I verily believe Hyder is at
the bottom of all." Now pray does not this letter deserve
more than I have said of it! just thus would my dear father
have treated a distressed countryman—Methinks I see his
benevolent heart venting itself in tears of sympathy at the

recital.   Precious tears! why am I not permitted to mingle mine with them! for they will flow in spite of my endeavours to restrain their course.

11*th January.*

Having now money to bribe with, we began to think of attempting an escape; for besides the silence observed on the fate of our companions, though near a month has elapsed since their departure, we live in continual dread of being forced up the country and perhaps massacred there: Every one who leaves this place must first obtain permission from the Governor, but as these passes only mention generally *so many people* and are granted indiscriminately to whoever applies for them, provided they be not suspected persons, one may easily be procured under feigned pretences (it is a matter frequently done.)   A Friar belonging to the Portuguese convent, usually manages these affairs when properly instructed.   This information we have from a Native Portuguese named Pereira, an officer in Hyder's service, with whom Mr. F— commenced an intimacy while we were in the Fort, and who is now quartered here at his special request.   Tho' I must confess I cannot like this man, yet am I obliged to trust him.   The visits we receive from Ayres are terrible trials to one who loathes dissimulation as I do.   This wretch has once or twice mentioned a cow that annoyed him by entering the little garden, or paddock, in which it appears his house is placed; this morning he entered the factory with his scymitar in his hand unsheathed, and bloody, and with an expression of diabolical joy informed me that he had just caught the animal entering and being armed had completely chined her.   You cannot imagine said he, how *sweetly* the sword did the business; my very heart shuddered with horror and indignation, yet I dared not give vent to those feelings.   I doubt not he would murder me with as much pleasure as he killed the cow with; and have no reason to suppose he would be punished for the act.

12th January, 1780.

Some quarrel unknown to me has certainly taken place between Pereira and Mr. F— the looks of the former alarm me; his dark scowling eye is frequently directed towards him, with an expression of dreadful import; yet he appears desirous of forwarding our escape.—He has introduced us to father Ricardo, who engages to provide us all things for our departure to Cochin.

13th January, 1780.

The priest breakfasted with us, and promised to set about the business without loss of time; he is to receive twenty rupees, on our setting off from hence, and twenty more on our arrival at Cochin or Tellichery, through the medium of Isaac, on whom the order from Mr. Church was drawn, by which means we received it without suspicion.

14th January, 1780.

A Licence or Passport is procured for us as two Frenchmen going to Mahey. We have paid twenty rupees boat-hire to a smuggler; these are commonly very courageous men; which is some comfort to me: under Mr. F—'s protection and his, I will endeavour to think myself secure. His house is admirably situated for our purpose, close by the sea side; this is to be our place of rendezvous. The precise time is not yet fixed upon: the intervening hours how anxiously will they pass!

15th January, 1780.

The boatman called to desire we would be at his house at six this evening;—gave him our little baggage (we had

been obliged to purchase many necessaries) and four rupees
to buy provisions. When it grew dark, Mr. F— put on
a sailor's dress and I equipped myself in a nankeen jacket—
a pair of long striped trowsers—a man's night cap, and over
that a *mighty* smart hat,—with a pair of Mr. F—'s shoes
tied on my feet, and a stick in my hand. In this dress
Mr. F— declared that I was the very image of my dear
father, which highly gratified me. I had tied the clothes
we took off, in a handkerchief; with that in one hand and
brandishing my stick in the other, I boldly sallied forth,—
taking care, however, to secure a retreat in case of accidents,
a most fortunate precaution as the event proved.—Father
Ricardo met us at the smuggler's according to appointment
and we paid him twenty rupees, and gave him security for
the other twenty; when this was settled, nothing remained
as we supposed, but to step into the boat,—when behold!
news was brought that the sailors had made their escape
no one knew whither! after waiting two hours in that
dangerous situation to see if they would return, and raving
in all the folly of angry disappointment against those who
had misled me, we made a virtue of necessity and trudged
back to our prison, where we luckily effected an entrance
without exciting suspicion.

17th January, 1780.

Had all arranged for our escape last night but so many
people were about us, that we dared not make the attempt.

19th January, 1780.

Father Ricardo has once more arranged all things for
to-night,—we must give more money, but that is no
object. Once free and we shall doubtless find means of
proceeding on our journey.

5th February, 1780.

Every day has this wicked priest contrived some scheme, to amuse us with false hopes of escaping; every *night* have we lain down in the full persuasion that it was the last we should pass in confinement; and as constantly have we awoke to meet bitter disappointments.—This continued alternation of hope and fear preys on my spirits and prevents me from gaining strength, but yesterday I received a *serious* shock from the behaviour of Pereira, and which excited more alarm than almost any circumstance that has occurred to me—I had long marked his hatred to Mr. F— and dreaded his revenge—I was setting at work when he entered the room—naked from the middle—just as Mr. F— was going into the next room. His strange appearance and the quick step with which he followed my husband caught my attention; and I perceived that he held a short dagger close under his arm, nearly all concealed by his handkerchief and the exigency of the moment gave me courage.—I sprung between him and the door through which Mr. F— had just passed, drawing it close and securing it to prevent his return, and then gently expostulated with P— on the oddness of his conduct and appearance; he slunk away, and I hope, will never trouble us again, especially as he has adopted another mode of revenge which may perhaps be equally effectual, though more slow in its operation. He went to Ayres and informed him that we had endeavoured to escape, mentioning every particular of our scheme, and, as far as I can learn, telling the whole truth; but fortunately naming a different evening from the one on which our unsuccessful attempt really was made on which Ayres exclaimed, " well Pereira you have made up a very fine story, but without a word of truth, for on the very night you mention, F— was setting with me over a bottle of wine; I'll take my oath of that for it was my birth night " this was true likewise, so we were saved for that time; but as Ayres knows that escape is in our heads he will, I fear, guard us with redoubled vigilance, and so far Pereira's design has taken effect.

6th February, 1780.

Mr. F— has completely detected the pious father Ricardo, and his worthy colleague the smuggler, and sorely against their will compelled them to refund his money all to about twenty three rupees, which they pretend has been disbursed. We now discovered, that although our offers might tempt their avarice and lead them to deceive us, yet they dared not persevere in assisting our escape; as the consequence of detection would to them be inevitable death.

10th February, 1780.

At length I begin to cherish hopes of our speedy release, as Sudder Khan returned last night from Seringapatnam; but is encamped without the Town, waiting for a lucky day, till when he dares not enter his own house.—So how long we may still be detained, Heaven knows—Mr. F— and our friend Isaac propose paying him a visit to-morrow.

13th February, 1780.

They went out on Friday and again to-day, but have not yet been able to obtain an audience; and thus we may perhaps be led on a fortnight longer, by his ridiculous superstitions. Mr. Isaac, however, assures my husband, that from all he can learn it is really intended to release us, which makes me comparatively easy; yet it is impossible not to feel severely this delay, at such a critical period; for should Hyder commence hostilities against the English, whilst we remain in his power, not all Isaac's influence will be sufficient to extricate us from it; our doom must be sealed for life.

14th February.

Our indefatigable advocate walked out with Mr. F—(I should have mentioned that the distance is about three miles) but they were again disappointed, Sudder Khan being still closely shut up at his devotions, which are to continue two days longer at least.—How very distressing to be kept in this horrible suspense! But our friend still comforts us with the assurance, that *all* will be well.—He really behaves to me like a father, and as I have now acquired some knowledge of Portuguese, we are enabled to converse tolerably well. I do not recollect having described his person, and will therefore endeavour to give you some, though a very inadequate idea of it.

Isaac then is a fine venerable old man, about eighty-five with a long white beard; his complexion by no means dark, and his countenance benign yet majestic; I could look at him, till I almost fancied that he resembled exactly the Patriarch whose name he bears, were it not for his eye, which is still brilliant. His family I find according to ancient custom in the East, consists of two wives, to whom I am to have an introduction.

15th February.

Saw a letter to-day from Mr. Tulloh, to Mr. Passavant the Danish Factor, dated 19th January, which mentions, that they were fifteen days on their journey to Seringapatam and twelve more confined in a shed, half starved to death, as no one was permitted to assist them except with the coarsest food in small quantities; at length the Nabob granted them an audience, when having listened to their complaint, he sent for Sudder Khan, to answer the charge. " Three successive days " says Tulloh " we were all sent for, and confronted with him, when Hyder commanded him to make instant restitution, however, we have as yet received nothing except that yesterday on taking leave his highness presented us with five hundred rupees for our journey to Madras, besides ordering Palanquins, carriages for our baggage, and every other convenience, likewise a guard of a hundred seapoys to conduct us into the English bounds. I spoke to him for Mr. and Mrs. F— and obtained an order for their release also. Whether the ship will be returned or not, *God Knows*, we are just going to set off." Thus far Tulloh. Now the man who brought this letter, saw them all go and remained at Seringapatam ten days afterward, without hearing further; so I hope we may conclude they are out of *their* troubles. Mrs. Tulloh has now seen enough poor woman to satisfy her taste for adventures. From all I can learn, it would have been utterly impossible for me to have supported the various hardships of their journey, in my precarious state of health; poor Mr. Taylor how sincerely do I pity him.

17th February, 1780.

Mr. Isaac called by appointment about two o'clock and took my husband with him, to wait *once more* on the Governor. He seems to entertain no doubt of bringing back the order for our release. I endeavour to be calm and to rest with confidence on his assurance; but when I contemplate the dreadful alternative, should he meet a peremptory refusal, and recollect the deep machinations that have been practised to keep us here, my heart recoils at the idea. It is now eight in the evening; every thing is packed up and ready for our departure yet they return not. Some obstacle I fear must have been thrown in the way by that vile Sudder Khan to prevent our liberation, and we are destined to remain his wretched prisoners. How shall I support the intelligence? Heaven inspire me with forti-tude! I can neither write, nor attend to any thing!

LETTER XIII.

Cochin, 19*th February*, 1780.

THANKS be to Providence that I am at length permitted to address my beloved friends from this land of liberty towards which my wishes have so long pointed. After wading through my melancholy journal, you will be enabled in some measure to form an idea of the joy that fills my breast on contemplating the contrast between my present situation, and that from which I have so recently escaped—I will not however indulge in reflections, but hasten to proceed with my narrative, which broke off at a most interesting period in my last letter, when I was every instant expecting the news of our release.

I was not relieved from suspense till near twelve on Thursday night, when the gentlemen returned bringing with them the so anxiously desired passports for ourselves, and such trifling articles as remained in our possession; more than this I find they could not obtain for us, though absolute promises of restitution and remuneration had been frequently held out. This however seemed a slight evil compared with what even *one* days detention might produce; we therefore abandoned all thought of farther application on the subject, and on *Friday* 18th February, at 5 A.M. joyfully quitted our detested prison, and repaired to the house of our steady friend and benefactor Isaac, when we found one of his own sloops prepared to convey us to Cochin, with every necessary refreshment on board.

Thus by the indefatigable exertions of this most excellent

man, we are at last released from a situation of which it is impossible for you to appreciate the horrors. To him we are indebted for the inestimable gift of liberty. No words can I find adequate to the expression of my gratitude. In whatever part of the world and under whatever circumstances my lot may be cast; whether we shall have the happiness to reach in safety the place to which all our hopes and wishes tend, or are doomed to experience again the anxieties and sufferings of captivity; whether I shall pass the remainder of my days in the sunshine of prosperity, or exposed to the chilling blasts of adversity; the name of *Isaac the Jew* will ever be associated with the happiest recollections of my life; and while my heart continues to beat, and warm blood animates my mortal frame, no distance of time or space can efface from my mind, the grateful remembrance of what we owe to this most worthy of men. When we were plundered and held in bondage by the Mahometan robbers amongst whom we had fallen; when there was no sympathizing friend to soothe us among our Christian fellow captives; when there was no hand to help us, and the last ray of hope gradually forsook the darkening scene of our distress; kind Providence sent a good Samaritan to our relief in the person of this benevolent Jew, who proved himself an Israelite indeed. Oh my dear sister! how can I in the overflowing of a grateful heart do otherwise than lament, that the name of this once distinguished people should have become a term of reproach! Exiled from the land promised to the seed of Abraham; scattered over the face of the earth, yet adhering with firmness to the religion of their fathers, this race once the boasted favourites of Heaven, are despised and rejected by every nation in the world. The land that affords shelter, denies them a participation in the rights of citizenship. Under such circumstances of mortifying contempt, and invidious segregation, it is no wonder that many of the children of

Israel in the present day evince more acuteness than delicacy in their transactions, and are too well disposed to take advantage of those, from whom they have endured so much scorn and persecution.   It gives me therefore peculiar pleasure to record their good deeds, and to proclaim in *my* limited circle, that such men as a FRANCO and an ISAAC, are to be found among the posterity of Jacob.   These sentiments are not overstrained but the genuine effusions of a thankful heart: as such receive them.

19th February, 1780.

This morning about eleven we arrived at our long wished for Port, and were landed close to the house of our good friend ISAAC which is pleasantly situated by the river side about a mile from Cochin, and rendered in every respect a most delightful residence.   Here we were welcomed by the two wives of ISAAC who were most splendidly dressed to receive us, rather overloaded with ornaments yet not inelegant.   Indeed I think the Eastern dresses have infinitely the advantage over ours; they are much more easy and graceful; besides affording greater scope for the display of taste, than our strange unnatural modes.   They were extremely hospitable and very fond of talking.

I mentioned before, having learned a little Portuguese during my imprisonment, which was of great advantage to me here, for except Malabars, it is the only language they speak, and a miserable jargon indeed is what they call Portuguese here.—However we contrived to make ourselves mutually understood so far as to be convinced that each was kindly disposed towards the other.   Had I been differently circumstanced, it would have given me great pleasure to have accepted the pressing invitations of these ladies to pass some time with them—the entire novelty of the scene would have amused me.   Novel I may *well* call it, in more respects than one; we were entertained with all the profusion that wealth can command, and generosity display. Though religious prejudices banished us from *their* table, ours was loaded with every delicacy,—all served on massive plate; among many other articles of luxury which I had never seen before, were numbers of solid silver *Peekdanees*, which served the purpose of spitting boxes (excuse the term.) They stood at each end of the couches in the principal room: some of them were nearly three feet high, with broad bottoms; the middle of the tube twisted and open at the top, with a wide mouth, for the convenience of such as had occasion to expectorate. These are not what *we* should call delicate indulgences in England; but in a country where smoking tobacco and chewing betel are universally practised, they must be allowed to be necessary ones.

You will judge what a change these apartments were to me when contrasted, not with our prison in the Fort of Calicut, for our residence there was undoubtedly the *acme* of wretchness, but even with the house in which I had so long lived, without any furniture at all, save my unmattressed couch, an old table and three broken chairs; and where many a time the poor Portuguese lad who served us, had entered at the hour of dinner empty handed, exclaiming that the dogs had carried off all that had been provided. My own face I never saw during the whole period, there not being so much as the fragment of a looking-glass to be obtained.

The younger wife of ISAAC attached herself to me in such a manner as I never before experienced, and really appeared as if she could not bear to part with me, even when I went with my husband to see the town of Cochin, which is truly a very pretty romantic place; but what was far more to my satisfaction, we luckily found Mr. Moore there, who proposed sailing the next day, and kindly offered us a passage on the St. Helena, which you may be sure we gratefully accepted. On our way back we were accosted by a Captain Richardson, whose ship is under repair here, and will be ready in about six weeks. He shook hands with us as country folks, and directly offered us both a passage to Bengal with every accommodation in his house during our stay here,—a most liberal proposal; was it not? and which would have been very fortunate for us, had we missed the St. Helena; in the present case his offer was of course declined, but I shall ever recollect the kindness which dictated it, and trust opportunities will be afforded to evince my gratitude.

On the 21st, at 5 A.M. Mr. F— left me with my new friends, promising to return for me in half an hour, to the great grief of the fair Jewess who was become so fond of me—but alas! I waited hour after hour, and no husband returned. I was in the greatest anxiety and consternation imaginable, dreading lest some new disaster had overtaken us, and that our ill starred journey was again stopped short in its course—It is impossible for you to conceive what I suffered during his absence and how my mind was harrassed by various tormenting conjectures,—those only, who have been subject to such cross accidents as I have so frequently experienced, can judge of my feelings—At length about noon he made his appearance, and very calmly began unpacking the chest as if to replace the things at his leisure —I asked of course what had occurred and if Mr. Moore had changed his intention? " Why, answered he, Moore and all the rest are gone on board, but somehow I dont think he will sail to-day for all that." This reply almost bereft me of my senses, knowing the consequence of being left behind would be a journey by land to Madras, (for he would never have had patience to wait till Captain Richardson's ship was ready) the expense of which alone must amount to eight or nine hundred rupees, not to mention the intolerable fatigue of travelling in this Country. Aware that if I did not exert myself all was lost, I took a hasty leave of our kind friends, and we immediately proceeded to Cochin with our little baggage, and sent out for a boat, but by this time the afternoon breeze had set in and the sea ran so high, that none would venture over the Bar; at last a man agreed to provide a large boat and take us off for sixteen rupees. When we came to the water side, what should this mighty boat prove, but a narrow Canoe with paddles, scarcely big enough to contain us and our four rowers. I hesitated—the people ran round me on all sides, intreating me not to venture, and assuring us both by words and gestures that the danger was imminent. Captain Richardson who was among them declared that, it would be next to a miracle if we escaped: indeed every moment evidently increased the risk; but Mr. F— now seeing the error of his delay, swore to run all hazards, rather than stop any longer at Cochin: a common practice with most people who have brought themselves into difficulties by their imprudence and who seek to regain by obstinacy, what they have lost through folly. Pity such cannot always suffer alone. Finding him positive I commended myself to the protection of the Almighty and stepped in; all the spectators seeming to look upon me as a *self* devoted victim: yet how was it possible to avoid going! had I refused Mr. F— would constantly have upbraided me with whatever ill consequence might have resulted from the delay, and who could wish for life on such terms! " No " thought I at the moment, " rather let me brave death in the line of my duty, than have my future days embittered by reproach, however unmerited." As we proceeded the waves gradually rose higher, and began to break over us: one man was continually employed in baling out the water, though his only utensil was a bamboo, which hardly held a quart. Never shall I forget what I felt on looking round in this situation; every wave rising many feet higher than the boat, and threatening to overwhelm us with instant destruction. I sat at first with my face to the stern, but afterwards moved to the front, and when I saw a wave coming, bowed my head to receive it. We were a mile from the shore, and at least *two* from the ship; was not this sufficient to appal the stoutest heart! yet I can truly say that my mind was perfectly composed, conscious of the rectitude of my intentions,—I could look up boldly to Heaven for protection. Mr. F— will tell you how frequently I begged him not to entertain the least doubt of our safety. " We have never " said I, " been conducted thus far by the hand of Providence to perish; remember my dear parents; is not *their* happiness involved in *our* safety? depend upon it we shall be preserved to become the humble instruments of rendering their declining years happy."

While I was speaking a tremendous wave broke over us, and half filled the boat with water, on which, thinking it would be presumptuous to proceed, we ordered the men to make for the nearest land, but this the wind would not permit, so we were obliged to keep on, and had reached within a mile of the ship, when she began to spread her sails, and in a few minutes got under weigh with a fair wind.— Our people now wanted to quit the pursuit, as she gained ground considerably, but we kept them in good humour by promising more money, and putting a white handkerchief on a stick, waved it in the air. After some time we had the pleasure to see her tack about and lye to so in another half hour we came up with her, having been three hours in the condition I have described,—wet through and nearly frightened to death, being every moment in the most imminent danger. To describe my joy is impossible or my impatience to quit the boat; without waiting for the chair to be lowered I scrambled on board, and had I not been relieved by a violent burst of tears, must have fainted.

Every one in the vessel blamed Mr. F— exceedingly for running such a risk by his delay as the other passengers who went on board in the morning, did not experience the slightest inconvenience. Mr. Moore luckily came in the provision boat, which was six hours in getting on board. This circumstance was the means of saving our passage.

When we reached Ceylon the wind became contrary, which together with a strong current, kept us upwards of three weeks beating off the Island, before we could weather Point de Galle. This will account to you for my letter being scarcely legible.—I am at this moment writing on my knees in bed, and if I had not been contented with this method all the way, I could not have written at all. My father well knows, a vessel has not a very agreeable motion, when beating up in the winds eye.

4th April, 1780.

At length thank Heaven! we are at anchor in Madras Roads, having been six weeks making a passage that with a fair wind we could almost have performed in as many days. Happily for me our society has been very different from the last I was condemned to mix with on shipboard;—of those Mr. Moore, and Mr. O'Donnell are of the most importance to us, our acquaintance with them commenced in Egypt, and as they were indeed (though innocently) the cause of all we suffered there, a very agreeable fellow-feeling has naturally taken place between us. The latter is now obliged to return to India to begin life again, (his losses on the Desert having been followed by many unavoidable expenses, as you will learn from my narrative), and seek a competence under all the disadvantages that an injured constitution added to a deep sense of disappointment and injustice, subject him to.—You may be sure we have had many conversations concerning the sad story of the Desert, and the last moments of those who perished there.—A boat is just come to take us on shore, so adieu for the present. The Roads are very full, there are eight ships of the line and above sixty other vessels, which form a magnificent spectacle.

6th April, 1780.

I was exceedingly alarmed yesterday by the surf. We got safe over it, but another boat upset just afterwards; however, fortunately no lives were lost.—Sir Thomas Rumbold is hourly expected to embark, which is all that detains the fleet; so that perhaps I may not be able to write ten lines more—

6 P.M. As far as I can judge I feel pleased with Madras, and gratified by the reception I have hitherto met with. I shall of course write to you again from thence, being likely to remain here a week or two; at present I must close my letter; but as a matter of curiosity shall just mention the astonishing celerity of the Indian tailors.—Yesterday evening Mr. Fay, not being *overstocked* with clothes to appear in, ordered a complete suit of black silk, with waistcoat sleeves, which they brought home *before nine* this morning, very neatly made though the whole must have been done by candle-light.

I cannot conclude without saying, that although I feel rather weak, my health is improving, and that the pain I suffer from the accident *which* befel me at the Factory, is not so violent as formerly—God grant I may soon be relieved from apprehension on *that* score.

The Governor is gone on board.—Captain Richardson of the *Ganges* under whose especial charge this packet (containing the whole of my narrative from Mocha) will be placed, as I had no safe opportunity of forwarding any letter from Calicut or Cochin, has sent for it. The perusal will cost you many tears but recollect that all is *over*, and my future communications will I trust, be of a very different complexion. May this reach you safely and meet you all well and comfortable. Adieu—God Almighty preserve you prays your own,

E.F.

LETTER XIV.

MY DEAR FRIENDS,

Agreeably to my promise I take up the pen to
give you some account of this settlement, which has proved
to me a pleasant resting-place after the many hardships and
distresses it has lately been my lot to encounter; and where
in the kind attentions and agreeable society of some of my
own sex, I have found myself soothed and consoled for the
long want of that comfort; while my health has in general
reaped great advantages from the same source.

There is something uncommonly striking and grand in
this town, and its whole appearance charms you from
novelty, as well as beauty. Many of the houses and public
buildings are very extensive and elegant—they are covered
with a sort of shell-lime which takes a polish like marble,
and produces a wonderful effect.—I could have fancied
myself transported into Italy, so magnificently are they
decorated, yet with the utmost taste. People here say that
the *chunam* as it is called, loses its properties when transported to Bengal, where the dampness of the atmosphere,
prevents it from receiving that exquisite polish so much
admired by all who visit Madras. This may very likely be
the case.

The free exercise of all religions being allowed; the
different sects seem to vie with each other in ornamenting
their places of worship, which are in general well built, and
from their great variety, and novel forms afford much

gratification, particularly when viewed from the country, as the beautiful groups of trees intermingle their tall forms and majestic foliage, with the white chunam and rising spires, communicating such harmony softness and elegance to the scene, as to be altogether delightful; and rather resembling the images that float on the imagination after reading fairy tales, or the Arabian nights entertainment, than any thing in real life; in fact Madras *is* what I conceived Grand Cairo to be, before I was so unlucky as to be undeceived. This idea is still further heightened by the intermixture of inhabitants; by seeing Asiatic splendour, combined with European taste exhibited around you on every side, under the forms of flowing drapery, stately palanquins, elegant carriages, innumerable servants, and all the pomp and circumstance of luxurious ease, and unbounded wealth. It is true this glittering surface is here, and there tinged with the sombre hue that more or less colours every condition of life; —you behold Europeans, languishing under various complaints which they call incidental to the climate, an assertion it would ill become a stranger like myself to controvert, but respecting which I am a little sceptical; because I see very plainly that the same mode of living, would produce the same effects, even "in the hardy regions of the North." You may likewise perceive that human nature has its faults and follies every where, and that *black* rogues are to the full as common as white ones, but in my opinion more impudent. On your arrival you are pestered with Dubashees, and servants of all kinds who crouch to you as if they were already your slaves, but who will cheat you in every possible way; though in fact there is no living without one of the former to manage your affairs as a kind of steward, and you may deem yourself very fortunate if you procure one in this land of pillagers, who will let nobody cheat you but himself. I wish these people would not vex one by their tricks; for there is something in the mild countenances and gentle manners of the Hindoos that interests me exceedingly.

We are at present with Mr. and Mrs. Popham from whom we have received every possible civility. He is a brother lawyer, and a countryman of my husbands, and she is a lively woman, her spirits have in some measure restored mine to the standard from which those amiable gentlemen, the Beys of Egypt, and Sudder Khan with his coadjutors Ayres and my worthy ship mates, had so cruelly chased them.

We have made several excursions in the neighbourhood of Madras which is every where delightful, the whole vicinity being ornamented with gentlemen's houses built in a shewy style of architecture, and covered with that beautiful chunam. As they are almost surrounded by trees, when you see one of these superb dwellings incompassed by a grove, a distant view of Madras with the sea and shipping, so disposed as to form a perfect landscape, it is beyond comparison the most charming picture I ever beheld or could have imagined. Wonder not at my enthusiasm; so long shut up from every pleasing object, it is natural that my feelings should be powerfully excited when such are presented to me.

Nothing is more terrible at Madras than the surf which as I hinted before, is not only alarming but dangerous. They have here two kinds of boats to guard against this great evil, but yet, notwithstanding every care, many lives are lost. One of these conveyances called the Massulah boat, is large, but remarkably light, and the planks of which it is constructed are actually sewed together by the fibres of the Cocoa-nut. It is well calculated to stem the violence of the surf but for greater safety it requires to be attended by the other, called a Catamaran, which is merely composed of bamboos fastened together and paddled by one man. Two or three of these attend the Massulah boat, and in case of its being overset usually pick up the drowning passengers. The dexterity with which they manage these things is inconceivable;—but no dexterity can entirely ward off the danger. The beach is remarkably fine.

The ladies here are very fashionable I assure you: I found several novelties in dress since I quitted England, which a good deal surprised me, as I had no idea that fashions travelled so fast. It is customary to take the air in carriages every evening in the environs of Madras: for excursions in the country these are commonly used; but in town they have Palanquins carried by four bearers, which I prefer. They are often beautifully ornamented, and appear in character with the country, and with the languid air of those who use them, which, though very different from any thing I have been accustomed to admire in a woman as you well know, yet is not unpleasing in a country the charms of which are heightened by exhibiting a view of society entirely new to me.

Mr. Popham is one of the most eccentric beings I ever met with.—Poor man he is a perpetual projector, a race whose exertions have frequently benefitted society, but seldom I believe been productive of much advantage to themselves or their families. He is at present laying plans for building what is called the black town, to a great extent, and confidently expects to realize an immense fortune, but others foresee such difficulties in the way, that they fear he may be ruined by the undertaking. The pleasure he takes in his visionary scheme should not be omitted in the account as of some value, for it really seems to be an uncommon source of enjoyment.[23]

The Black town is that part of Madras, which was formerly inhabited wholly by the natives, but of late many Europeans have taken houses there, rents being considerably lower than in Fort St. George, which is a very strong Garrison, built by the English, and where since have been constructed many fine houses, &c.—this is considered of course a more fashionable place to reside in. Between the Black town and the Fort, lies Choultry Plain which being covered entirely with a whitish sand, reflects such a dazzling light, and intolerable heat, as to render it a terrible annoyance especially to strangers. MR. FAY has been exceedingly pressed to take up his abode here, and really many substantial inducements have been held out to him; but as his views have been all directed to Calcutta, where knowledge and talents are most likely to meet encouragement he cannot be persuaded to remain. Besides, a capital objection is, that no Supreme Court being as yet established he could be only admitted to practise as an attorney, no advocates being allowed in the Mayors Court: so that his rank as a Barrister would avail nothing here: I most cordially acquiesce in this determination. But I must suspend my scribbling; MR. P— is waiting to take me to ST. THOMAS'S MOUNT.

17th April, 1780.

I resume my pen, resolved to devote this day to my dear friends, as it is likely to be the last I shall spend in Madras. I found ST. THOMAS' MOUNT a very beautiful place, it is a high hill of a conical form, crowned at the top with white houses, and a Church built by the Portuguese in memory of some ST. THOMAS, who they say, was murdered on this spot by a Brahmin.—The road to this place is delightful, being a complete avenue of the finest trees I ever saw, whose intermingling branches are absolutely impervious to the sun. Not far from hence I was shewn a prodigiously fine Banian tree, the singular nature of which is, that its branches bend down to the ground, take root and thence spring out anew; thus forming innumerable arches. I call it a vegetable Cathedral, and could not help fancying that Banian groves were formerly appropriated to idolatrous worship, since they are admirably calculated for the celebration of any mysterious and solemn rites from which the uninitiated are excluded; and may be properly called " Temples not made with hands." On the whole I felt highly gratified by my little excursion, which was, I believe, not more than seven miles from Madras.[24]

I must now assure you that I have actually seen several of those things with my own eyes which we girls used to think poor Captain S—— took traveller's liberty in relating, such as dancing snakes, Jugglers swallowing swords &c. The snakes were to me somewhat alarming, the other a very disgusting spectacle; when they are become familiar I may be amused with the one, since the various forms, the prismatic colours, and graceful motions of the snakes may give pleasure which the other exhibitions never can. When you have seen a man thrust a sword down his throat and are fully convinced that there is no deception, you feel that you have beheld a wonder, and there the gratification ends, for the sight is unnatural and disgusting. With some other tricks of the Juggler, I was however much pleased; his power of balancing was astonishing, and he had a method of throwing four brass balls up and catching them with such amazing rapidity, that they perpetually encircled his head, forming a kind of hat around it; he likewise threaded small beads with his tongue, and performed a number of very curious slights of hand. Dancing girls are a constant source of amusement here, but I was much disappointed in them, they wrap such a quantity of muslin round them by way of petticoat, that they almost appear to have hoops;—and their motions are so slow, formal and little varied, that you see the whole dance as it were at once; they are very inferior to those of the same profession at Grand Cairo though I never saw any there but in the streets, however their dancing is certainly less indecent, at least so far as I could witness it.

There seems to be a strange inconsistency in the character of the natives; they appear the most pusillanimous creatures in existence, except those employed on the water, whose activity and exertions are inconceivable. They will encounter every danger for the sake of reward, with all the eagerness of avarice, and all the heroism of courage; so that if you have occasion to send off a note to a ship, no matter how high the surf may run, you will always find some one ready to convey it for you, and generally without being damaged, as their turbans are curiously folded with waxed cloth for that purpose; so off they skip to their Catamarans,—for the prospect of gain renders them as brisk as the most lively Europeans.

The Hindoos have generally their heads shaved but they preserve a single lock and a pair of small whiskers with the greatest care. Their manner of writing is curious; they write with iron needles, on palm-leaves which are afterwards strung together and form books. Boys are taught to write on the sand; a very good plan as it saves materials and a number can be instructed at the same time. For teaching arithmetic, great numbers of pebbles are used; so that every part of the apparatus is cheap.

The natives of India are immoderately fond of an intoxicating liquor called *Toddy* which is the unfermented juice of the Cocoa-nut or Palmyra tree;—sugar and water is also a favourite beverage. Butter is very scarce and not good; what they call *Ghee* is butter boiled or clarified, in order to preserve it, and is very useful for many purposes, such as frying &c. On the whole one may live very well at Madras,—to me it appears a land of luxury as you may suppose, when you recollect, how I had been accustomed to fare. We may think ourselves very well off in escaping from the paws of that fell tyger Hyder Ally as we did, for I am assured that the threat of sending us up the country to be fed on dry rice, was not likely to be a vain one; it is thought that several of our countrymen are at this very time suffering in that way: if so, I heartily wish that the War he has provoked, may go forward 'till those unhappy beings are released and the usurping tyrant is effectually humbled.

MR. O'DONNELL has just called and desired me to prepare for an early summons to-morrow. I have ever found him friendly and attentive and must always deem myself highly obliged to him, as he certainly had but too much occasion to feel hurt by the behaviour of MR. FAY, whose temper, you know, is not the most placid in the world. He quarrelled with both him and MR. MOORE during the passage about the *merest* trifles (wherein too he was palpably in the wrong) and challenged them both: Judge what I must have suffered during these altercations, vainly endeavouring to conciliate, and in agonies lest things should proceed to extremities.—On our arrival here, I prevailed on MR. POPHAM to act as a mediator between the parties; who at length, though with great difficulty, convinced MR. F— that he had been to blame, and induced him to make a proper apology to both gentlemen: thus ended the affair but I have reason to think, that had I not been with him, he would not have been invited to proceed farther on the ship; nor am I free from apprehension at present, yet MR. O'D— has proved himself so true a friend and has so materially served my husband, that I trust our short trip from hence to Calcutta, will prove a pleasant one. I understand that several additional passengers are to join us, which may operate as a check on *fiery spirits*.

18th *April*.

MR. & MRS. P— have completed their hospitable kindness by insisting that we should partake of an *early* dinner (at one o'clock) after which we immediately proceed on board; and heartily rejoiced shall I be, when once over the terrific surf.   I leave Madras with some regret having met with much civility and even sympathy here.   I must now bid you adieu; in my next I hope to announce that my long pilgrimage is ended.   I likewise shall expect to find letters from you, waiting my arrival at Calcutta.   My anxiety at times arises to impatience, lest any evil should have befallen you, during the long period in which all communication has been suspended between us: my heart however yet retains its power of conversing with you. Whenever I see any thing new or entertaining I directly imagine how *you* would have looked, and what *you* would have said on the occasion; and thus cheat myself into a pleasing dream of social intercourse with those most dear to me.

Our stay at Madras has been the means of procuring us some respectable recommendations to persons in Calcutta; for we have made several desirable connections here.   Hope again smiles on us and I endeavour to cherish her suggestions; for it is as much my *duty* as my *interest* to keep up my spirits, since in my present state of health, without them, I must wholly sink; and now more than ever I feel the necessity of using exertion.

The hot winds prevail here at present, which renders the *weather* peculiarly oppressive, but a few hours will change the scene.   Adieu: remember me in your prayers, my beloved parents, my dear sisters, and rest assured of the unalterable affection of your own

ELIZA.

LETTER XV.

My Dear Friends,

I may now indeed call for your congratulations
since after an eventful period of twelve months and eighteen
days, I have at length reached the place for which I have
so long sighed, to which I have looked with innumerable
hopes and fears, and where I have long rested my most
rational expectations of future prosperity and comfort. I
must now in order to keep up the connection of my story
return to Madras, and from thence conduct you here
regularly.

Mr. F— and Mr. Popham both assured me that a
massulah boat was engaged, but on arriving at the beach
none could be had; so there being no remedy, I went off
in a common cargo boat which had no accommodations
whatever for passengers, and where my only seat was one
of the cross beams. How I saved myself from falling
Heaven knows, Mr. F— was under the necessity of
exerting his whole strength to keep me up, so he suffered
a little for his negligence. It was what is called a black
surf and deemed very dangerous; there were some moments
when I really thought we were nearly gone; for how could
I in my weak state have buffetted the waves had the boat
overset? When once on board our voyage passed comfortably enough; our society was pleasant; indeed Mr.
O'Donnell is ever a host to us in kindness; Mr. Moore
our supercargo was however more strict in his enforcement

of rules than was agreeable to most of us; we were kept more orderly than so many children at school; for if we were in the midst of a rubber at whist, he would make us give over at nine precisely, and we were obliged to keep our score 'till the following evening. But this was of little moment, for as we advanced towards the place of our destination, we were too much interested to think of any thing else. We had a distant view of the pagodas of *Jaggernauth*,—three large pyramidical buildings very famous temples among the Hindoos, who there worship the images of *Jaggernauth* and keep a splendid establishment of the Priesthood attendant on the Idols in the manner of the ancient heathens. I am credibly assured that at stated intervals the principal figure is taken out in an enormous car, with a great number of wheels beneath which his votaries prostrate themselves with the most undaunted resolution; firmly persuaded that by thus sacrificing their lives, they shall pass immediately after death into a state of everlasting felicity. Well may we say that, " life and immortality were brought to light by the Gospel " since in regions where its sacred influence is unknown or unattended to, we see such gross acts of folly and superstition as these, sanctioned by authority: may it please the Almighty disposer of events to hasten the period of their emancipation, that all mankind may hail each other as brothers, and we may be brought together as " one fold, under one shepherd."

Calcutta, you know is on the Hoogly, a branch of the Ganges, and as you enter Garden - reach which extends about nine miles below the town, the most interesting views that can possibly be imagined greet the eye. The banks of the river are as one may say absolutely studded with elegant mansions, called here as at Madras, garden-houses. These houses are surrounded by groves and lawns, which descend to the waters edge, and present a constant succession of whatever can delight the eye, or bespeak wealth and elegance in the owners. The noble appearance of the river also, which is much wider than the Thames at London bridge, together with the amazing variety of vessels continually passing on its surface, add to the beauty of the scene. Some of these are so whimsically constructed as to charm by their novelty. I was much pleased with the snake boat in particular. Budgerows somewhat resembling our city barges, are very common,—many of these are spacious enough to accommodate a large family. Besides these the different kinds of pleasure boats intermixed with mercantile vessels, and ships of war, render the whole a magnificent and beautiful moving picture; at once exhilarating the heart, and charming the senses: for every object of sight is viewed through a medium that heightens its attraction in this brilliant climate.

The town of Calcutta reaches along the eastern bank of the Hoogly; as you come up past Fort William and the Esplanade it has a beautiful appearance. Esplanade-row, as it is called, which fronts the Fort, seems to be composed of palaces; the whole range, except what is taken up by the Government and Council houses, is occupied by the principal gentlemen in the settlement—no person being allowed to reside in Fort William, but such as are attached to the Army, gives it greatly the advantage over FORT ST. GEORGE, which is so incumbered with buildings of one kind or other, that it has more the look of a town than of a military Garrison. *Our* Fort is also so well kept and every thing in such excellent order, that it is quite a curiosity to see it—all the slopes, banks, and ramparts, are covered with the richest verdure, which completes the enchantment of the scene. Indeed the general aspect of the country is astonishing; notwithstanding the extreme heat (the thermometer seldom standing below ninety in the afternoon) I never saw a more vivid green than adorns the surrounding fields—not that parched miserable look our lands have

during the summer heats;—large fissures opening in the
earth, as if all vegetation were suspended; in fact the
copious dews which fall at night, restore moisture to the
ground, and cause a short thick grass to spring up, which
makes the finest food imaginable for the cattle. Bengal
mutton, always good, is at this period excellent—I must
not forget to tell you that there is a very good race ground
at a short distance from Calcutta, which is a place of fashionable resort, for morning and evening airings.

Through Mr. O'Donnell's kindness we were introduced
to a very respectable Portuguese family who received us
with the greatest civility, inviting us to take up our abode
with them until we could provide ourselves with a house—
Mr. Da C— was a widower, but his late wife's sisters, who
resided with him, were born at Chandernagore, (a French
settlement between twenty and thirty miles higher up the
river;) but from long disuse they had lost the habit of
speaking their native language, though they *understood* it
perfectly; so I was forced to make out their Portuguese in
the best manner I could, constantly answering in French.
In this way we frequently conversed, and I gained much
information respecting the customs of the place—the price
of provisions, and many other useful matters.

Fortunately, throughout all our difficulties we had preserved our letters of introduction, by keeping them always
concealed about us, together with Mr. F—'s admission
to the Bar and other credentials, which were essentially
necessary to his establishment here: so that my husband
became immediately known to Sir Robert Chambers, who
behaved to him with the utmost attention; and whose lady
after hearing a little of my melancholy story, and finding
I was too much indisposed to admit of my paying my
respects to her, had the goodness to wave all ceremony,
and accompanied by her husband, to visit me at the house
of the Portuguese merchant, which was a condescension

that I certainly had no right to expect. She is the most beautiful woman I ever beheld,—in the bloom of youth; and there is an agreeable frankness in her manners, that enhances her loveliness, and renders her truly fascinating. Her kindness towards me daily increases; and she seems never weary of listening to my sad story. " She loves me for the dangers I have passed, and I love her that she does pity them." [25]

29th May.

I have delivered my letter of introduction to Mrs. Hastings, on whom I should have waited long ago, had the state of my health admitted of the exertion. She resides at Belvidere-house about, I believe, five miles from Calcutta, which is a great distance at this season and for an invalid. The lady was fortunately at home and had three of her most intimate friends with her on a visit, one of them, Mrs. Motte, a most charming woman. Mrs. H— herself, it is easy to perceive at the first glance, is far superior to the generality of her sex; though her appearance is rather eccentric, owing to the circumstance of her beautiful auburn hair being disposed in ringlets, throwing an air of elegant, nay almost infantine simplicity over the countenance, most admirably adapted to heighten the effect intended to be produced. Her whole dress too, though studiously becoming being at variance with our present modes which are certainly not so, perhaps for that reason, she has chosen to depart from them—as a foreigner you know, she may be excused for not strictly conforming to our fashions; besides her rank in the settlement sets her above the necessity of studying any thing but the whim of the moment. It is easy to perceive how fully sensible she is of her own conse-quence. She is indeed raised to a " giddy height " and expects to be treated with the most profound respect and deference. She received me civilly and insisted on my staying dinner, which I had no inclination to refuse, but she seemed not to evince much sympathy when I slightly touched on the misfortunes which had befallen me; nay she even hinted that I had brought them on myself, by imprudently venturing on such an expedition out of mere curiosity. Alas! Mrs. H— could not know what you are well acquainted with, that I undertook the journey with a view of preserving my husband from destruction, for had I not accompanied him, and in many instances restrained his extravagance and dissipated habits, he would never, never, I am convinced, have reached Bengal, but have fallen a wretched sacrifice to them on the way, or perhaps through the violence of his temper been involved in some dispute, which he was too ready to provoke—but to return I could not help feeling vexed at Mrs. H—s observation, to say the best of it, it was unfeeling;—but I excuse her. Those basking in the lap of prosperity can little appreciate the sufferings or make allowance for the errors of the unfortunate; whom they regard as almost beings of another order."

You will expect me to say something of the house, which is a perfect *bijou*; most superbly fitted up with all that unbounded affluence can display; but still deficient in that simple elegance which the wealthy so seldom attain, from the circumstance of not being obliged to search for effect without much cost, which those but moderately rich, find to be indispensable. The gardens are said to be very tastefully laid out, but how far this report is accurate I had no opportunity of judging; the windows being all as it were hermetically closed; sashes, blinds, and every opening, except where tatties were placed to exclude the hot wind. This surprized me very much: but I understand no method is so effectual for that purpose. I was not permitted to take my departure till the evening, when the fair lady of the mansion, dismissed me with many general professions of kindness, of which I knew how to estimate the value.

Next morning we received an invitation to the ball given annually on the King's birthday. This however I was under the necessity of declining on the plea of ill health and Mr. F— could hardly ever be persuaded to attend such formal assemblies.

When my husband waited on Sir Elijah Impey, the Chief Justice, to shew his credentials, he met with a most flattering reception. It so happened that he was called to the Bar from Lincoln's Inn himself, and seemed quite at home while perusing the papers, being acquainted with the hand-writing of the officers who prepared them; and perhaps that circumstance might render him more partial. On Mr. Fay's expressing some apprehensions lest his having come out without leave of the E. I. Company might throw obstacles in the way of his admission to the Bar here, Sir Elijah indignantly exclaimed " No Sir, had you dropped from the clouds with such documents, we would admit you. The Supreme Court is independent and will never endure to be dictated to, by any body of men whose claims are not enforced by superior authority. It is nothing to us whether you *had* or *had not* permission from the Court of Directors, to proceed to this settlement; you come to us as an authen-ticated English Barrister, and as such, we shall on the first day of the next Term, admit you to *our Bar*." Sir E— also offered to introduce him to Mr. Hyde which Mr. F— thankfully accepted. Do you not admire the high tone in which Sir E— delivers his sentiments? There exists, it seems, a strong jealousy between the Government and the Supreme Court, lest either should encroach on the preroga-tives of the other. The latter not long since committed Mr. Naylor the Company's Attorney for some breach of privi-lege, who being in a weak state of health at the time, died in confinement—this has increased the difference.[27] I merely mention this *en passant*, for it regards not us, let them quarrel, or agree; so the business of the Court be not impeded we cannot suffer. Mr. F— is already retained in several causes. His whole mind will now, I trust, be occupied with his profession, and as his abilities have never been questioned, I flatter myself that he has every reason to look forward to ultimate success.

20th July.

Hyder Ally has at length thrown off the mask, and commenced hostilities in good earnest. How providential was our liberation at that critical juncture! and my gratitude to Heaven was lately called forth in another instance—I recently conversed with a gentleman who crossed the Great Desert by way of Aleppo.——He assures me that besides the danger from the Arabs, there is so much more from other causes than in going over *that* to Suez, that he is quite confident, *I* never could have survived, the journey; "or he added any European woman"—therefore on the whole we seem to have experienced the lesser evil, though the alternative of falling into the hands of the enemy was horrible! I am concerned to say that dreadful reports are in circulation respecting the excesses committed by Hyder's troops in the Carnatic, but the particulars are too shocking to be repeated.

You have no idea how busy I am. Lady Chambers has been kind enough to lend me some of her dresses, for mine to be made by—I have commenced house-keeping, and am arranging my establishment, which is no little trouble in a country where the servants will not do a single thing, but that for which you expressly engage them nor even that willingly. I just now asked a man to place a small table near me; he began to bawl as loud as he could for the bearers to come and help him. "Why dont you do it yourself" said I? rising as I spoke to assist. *Oh I no*

English. I Bengal man. I no estrong like English; one, two, three Bengal men cannot do like one Englishman.—Adieu remember you must write me long letters. you see even the heat has not reduced mine to a single sheet. I trust that I shall never be found incapable of addressing *you.* Mr. F— unites with me in kind remembrances.

I am ever most affectionately your's
&c. &c.

LETTER XVI.

CALCUTTA, 29*th August*.

MY DEAR FRIENDS,

Ten thousand thanks for the precious packet of
letters I yesterday received: you can form no idea of the
eagerness with which I flew from my dressing room; and
Mr. Fay from his study—at the joyful sound of " letters
from England." But my very eagerness wrought for a
while its own disappointment; for when I laid my hands
on the prize, I fell into a kind of hysteric, and it was some
time before I could break the seals, and yet would not suffer
Mr. F— to deprive me of the gratification for which I had
so long panted—over such treasures who would not be a
miser—I would not permit a single scrap to escape me till
I had devoured the whole. Those only know what that
impatient hunger of the heart is after information, and the
intercourse of affection, who have been debarred as long
as I had been from objects so dear.

I rejoice to find that the Chevalier de St. Lubin performed his promise and that you now are in possession of
every event that occurred to us till our arrival at Mocha.
To know that we had passed the desert, that object of my
dear mother's dread and apprehension, must have set her
mind comparatively at ease; Alas! little did she suppose,
how far more horrible were the miseries that we had still
to undergo! thank Heaven, they are past.—I will quit the
subject which agitates me too much.

I am happy to say that our house is a very comfortable

one, but we are surrounded by a set of thieves. In England, if servants are dishonest we punish them, or turn them away in disgrace, and their fate proves, it may be hoped, a warning to others; but these wretches have no sense of shame. I will give you an instance or two of their conduct, that you may perceive how enviably I am situated. My Khansaman (or house steward) brought in a charge of a gallon of milk and thirteen eggs, for making scarcely a pint and half of custard; this was so barefaced a cheat, that I refused to allow it, on which he gave me warning. I sent for another, and, after I had hired him, " now said I, take notice friend, I have enquired into the market price of every article that enters my house and will submit to no imposition; you must therefore agree to deliver in a just account to me every morning "—what reply do you think he made? why he demanded double wages; you may be sure I dismissed him, and have since forgiven the first but not till he had *salaamed* to my foot, that is placed his right hand under my foot,—this is the most abject token of submission (alas! how much better should I like a little common honesty.) I know him to be a rogue, and so are they all, but as he understands me now, he will perhaps be induced to use rather more moderation in his attempts to defraud.— At first he used to charge me with twelve ounces of butter a day, for each person; now he grants that the consumption is only four ounces. As if these people were aware that I am writing about them, they have very obligingly furnished me with another anecdote. It seems my comprodore (or market man) is gone away; he says poor servants have no profit by staying with *me*; at other gentlemen's houses he always made a rupee a day at least! besides his wages; but here if he only charges an anna or two more, it is sure to be taken off—So you see what a terrible creature I am! I dare say you never gave me credit for being so close.—I find I was imposed on, in taking a comprodore at all; the Khansaman ought to do that business. Judge whether I have not sufficient employment among these harpies? feeling as I do the necessity of a reasonable economy. It is astonishing, and would be amusing if one did not suffer by it, to see the various arts they will practice to keep a few annas in their hands, for though the lawful interest of money is but 12 per Cent (enough you will say), yet twenty four is given by the shop-keepers, who will lend or borrow the smallest sums for a single day, and ascertain the precise interest to the greatest exactitude, having the advantage of cowrees, 5,120 of which go to make one rupee. The foolish custom which subsists here of keeping Banians, gives rise to a thousand deceptions, as no one pays or receives money but through the medium of these people who have their profit on every thing that comes into the house.

In order to give you an idea of my houshold expenses and the price of living here, I must inform you that, our house costs only 200 rupees per month, because it is not in a part of the town much esteemed; otherwise we must pay 3 or 400 rupees; we are now seeking for a better situation. We were very frequently told in England you know, that the heat in Bengal destroyed the appetite, I must own that I never yet saw any proof of that; on the contrary I cannot help thinking that I never saw an equal quantity of victuals consumed.[28] We dine too at two o'clock, in the very heat of the day. At this moment Mr. F— is looking out with an hawk's eye, for his dinner; and though still much of an invalid, I have no doubt of being able to pick a bit myself. I will give you our bill of fare, and the general prices of things. A soup, a roast fowl, curry and rice, a mutton pie, a fore quarter of lamb, a rice pudding, tarts, very good cheese, fresh churned butter, fine bread, excellent Madeira (that is expensive but eatables are very cheap,)—a whole sheep costs but two rupees: a lamb one rupee, six good fowls or ducks ditto—twelve pigeons ditto— twelve pounds of bread ditto—two pounds butter ditto; and a joint of veal ditto—good cheese two months ago sold at the enormous price of three or four rupees per pound, but now you may buy it for one and a half—English claret sells at this time for sixty rupees a dozen. There's a price for you! I need not say that much of it will not be seen at our table; now and then we are forced to produce it, but very seldom. I assure you much caution is requisite to avoid running deeply in debt—the facility of obtaining credit is beyond what I could have imagined; the Europe shop keepers are always ready to send in goods; and the Banians are so anxious to get into employment, that they out bid each other. One says " master better take me, I will advance five thousand rupees "—another offers seven, and perhaps a third ten thousand: a Company's servant particularly will always find numbers ready to support his extravagance. It is not uncommon to see *writers* within a few months after their arrivals dashing away on the course *four in hand*: allowing for the inconsiderateness of youth, is it surprising if many become deeply embarrassed? —Several have been pointed out to me, who in the course of two or three years, have involved themselves almost beyond hope of redemption. The interest of money here being twelve per Cent, and the Banian taking care to secure bonds for whatever he advances, making up the account yearly and adding the sum due for interest, his thoughtless *master*, (as he calls him, but in fact his slave) soon finds his debt doubled, and dares not complain unless he has the means of release which alas! are denied him.

I should have told you before that Mr. F— was admitted an advocate in the Supreme Court, on the 16th June,— has been engaged in several causes, wherein he acquitted himself to general satisfaction and is at present as busy as can be desired. Every one seems willing to encourage him and if he continue but his own friend, all will, I feel persuaded, go well with us, and we shall collect our share of gold mohurs, as well as our neighbours.—I like to see the briefs come in well enough. The fees are much higher here than in England, so you will say " they ought " and I perfectly agree with you.

Sir R. Chambers met with an accident some weeks ago (by jumping out of a carriage when the horses were restive) which confined him to his house a long while but he is now recovering; I was a good deal vexed both on his own account poor man, and because Mr. F— was deprived of his friendly aid. I have seen little of my kind patroness since, for she goes scarce any where without her husband— we were to dine with them the very day the circumstance happened. They are gone up the country and will not return for some months.

31 *August*.

I have received another packet and rejoice to hear you are all going on so well. They talk of a frigate being soon to sail, in which case I shall close and dispatch this.—As I propose sending you a regular supply of Calcutta Gazettes,[29] there can be no necessity to fill my letters with political information. I trust that in a short time Hyder will be effectually humbled.

Mr. Hare has visited us several times; and is now quite complaisant to Mr. Fay. This is the way of the world you know, and of course to be expected from such a slave to outward circumstance, such a mere " summer friend " as this man ever evinced himself.—By his account the hardships they underwent would very soon have destroyed so poor a creature as I was at that time: so that the difficulties we fell into, though at the moment of suffering so deplored, proved eventually our safe guard in more respects than one. Had we not touched at Calicut, I am fully persuaded we should have been shipwrecked, and had not my illness furnished a pretext for detaining us there after the rest, I should have died among those cruel people in the most shocking way imaginable, since they were for a long while absolutely destitute of every necessary. What short-sighted beings we are! how futile, how defective our best formed calculations! I have sometimes pleased myself (I hope not improperly) with the idea, that the power of discerning clearly the beneficent designs of providence during our earthly pilgrimage, and of perceiving that in a thousand instances like these, a rough and stony path has led to safety and ultimate happiness, may be intended to form part of our enjoyment in a future state, wherein we are taught that to contemplate the Supreme Being in his perfections will constitute the height of bliss.—Let me have your sentiments on the subject; its discussion can do neither of us harm and may lead to improvement.

8th September.

I have nothing particular to add—my health continues very good considering all things. This is a dull time: vacations are always so to professional people. God bless you and grant us a happy meeting—our prospects are good; nothing but the grossest misconduct can prevent our success. Adieu

Yours most affectionately

E. F.

LETTER XVII.

CALCUTTA, 27th September.

MY DEAR FRIENDS,

The bad news I hinted at some time ago is already avenged; and a much more serious affair has happened since, but for the present I must relate what has occupied a great deal of attention for some days past: no less than a duel between the Governor General and the first in Council, Mr. Francis; there were two shots fired, and the Governor's second fire took place; he immediately ran up to his antagonist and expressed his sorrow for what had happened, which I dare say was sincere, for he is said to be a very amiable man. Happily the ball was soon extracted; and if he escape fever, there is no doubt of his speedy recovery. What gave occasion to the quarrel is said to have been an offensive Minute entered on the Council books by Mr. Francis, which he refused to rescind; but being unacquainted with the particulars, I have as little right as inclination to make any comments on the subject—It always vexes me to hear of such things. What a shocking custom is that of duelling! yet there are times when men may be so situated that, as the world goes, one knows not how they could act otherwise; much may be effected by the judicious interference of friends, but those qualified for the task are rarely to be met with. Mr. Francis is highly respected here, and being now at the head of what is called the opposition party, his death would be severely felt by many who affect great indifference about the event.[30]

Since I wrote last we have had a good deal of trouble with out Mohametan servants, on account of an old custom; not one of them would touch a plate on which pork had been laid—so that whenever we had any at table our plates remained, till the cook or his mate came up to change them. This being represented as a religious prejedice, I felt it right to give way, however ridiculous it might appear, in fact it was an inconvenience we felt in common with the whole settlement, except the gentlemen of the Army who had long before emancipated themselves from any such restraint; finding this to be really the case the whole of the European inhabitants agreed to insist upon their servants doing the same as those of the officers at the Fort, or quitting their places. They chose the latter alternative, and as their prejudices run very high in all religious matters, we were in doubt whether they would not prefer suffering the greatest extremity rather, than touch the very vessels which contained this abhorred food,—but behold in about four days they came back again requesting to be reinstated; and acknowledging that the only penalty incurred by touching the plates was the necessity of bathing afterwards: from this you may judge of their excessive idleness; however all now goes on well and we hear no more of their objection—

The serious affair at which I hinted in the beginning of this letter, was the cutting off Col. Baillie's detachment with dreadful slaughter. I trust we shall soon have ample revenge, for that fine old veteran Sir Eyre Coote is about to take the field and his very name will strike those undisciplined hordes with terror—Oh how I feel interested in the event! [31]

Nothing surely can be more disagreeable than the weather here at present, it is very hot with scarcely a breath of air stirring; and such swarms of insects buzzing about, but beyond all the bug fly is disgusting—one of them will scent a room; they are in form like a ladybird but their

smell is a thousand times more offensive than that of our
bugs. A good breeze would disperse them all, but that we
must not expect till the monsoon changes, that is, about the
middle of next month.

I never told you that one of the Captains who had charge
of us at Calicut made his escape some months ago, and came
to ask our assistance till he could get employment up the
country. Mr. F— gave him a lower room, and he remained
with us several weeks: his name is West. This was the
man from whom we collected intelligence of the plots laid
against us there, and which had nearly proved successful.
West is a stout fellow accustomed in his early days to labour,
and seasoned to the climate;—he is gone up to Patna, in
charge of some boats and is to remain there. Ayres used
to treat him very ill at times, and *he* says attemped more than
once to assassinate him, because he refused to concur with a
party that Ayres headed, consisting of six or eight abandoned
wretches whose intention it was to cut off several of the more
opulent natives *secretly*, and possess themselves of their
effects; while they should contrive to fix the guilt of the
transaction on some persons who were obnoxious to them.
West threatened to reveal the whole plot, on which they
pretended to abandon it, but he soon found their object was
to rid themselves of him; and he effected his escape in a
canoe (at the utmost risk of perishing in the attempt) to
Cochin, from whence he easily got a passage to Bengal.
What a horrible fellow is that Ayres! surely he will meet
his deserts: should the English take him he will be shot
instantly as a deserter.

We have found out a nephew of Isaac's named Daniel,
he is a man of no great consequence here, either in point of
situation or circumstances though not absolutely poor:—
we asked him to dinner, and endeavoured by every means
in our power to evince the grateful sense we entertain of
his worthy uncle's kindness and beneficence.

3rd November.

Since my last date I have the pleasure to acknowledge the receipt of another packet from England, with the gratifying intelligence that you were all well on the 7th of April. My time has passed very stupidly for some months, but the town is now beginning to fill,—people are returning for the cold season. Term has commenced, and Mr. F— has no reason to complain of business falling off; if *he* fall not from it, all will be well. My first Patroness Lady Chambers is returned from her tour but Sir Robert having purchased an elegant mansion in Calcutta, (for which he is to pay £6,000, in England) her Ladyship has full employment in arranging and fitting up her new abode; so that I see but little of her; she is however always kind and full of condescension towards me when we do meet.

19th December.

Mr. Fay has met with a gentleman here, a Dr. Jackson who comes from the same part of Ireland, and knows many of his connections; they soon became intimate. Dr. J— is physician to the Company, and in very high practice besides; I have been visited by the whole family. The eldest son a fine noble looking young man, is a Lieutenant in the Army, and has lately married a very pretty little woman, who came out in the same ship under the protection of his mother; as did Miss Chantry a most amiable and interesting young Lady, who now resides with them. They have not been long arrived.[32] The Doctor's Lady is a native of Jamaica and like those " children of the sun," frank and hospitable to a degree—fond of social parties in the old style " where the song and merry jest circulate round the festive board " particularly after supper. Dinner parties they seldom give; but I have been present at several elsewhere since the commencement of the cold season. The dinner hour as I mentioned before is two, and it is customary to sit a long while at table; particularly during the cold season; for people here are mighty fond of grills and stews, which they season themselves, and generally make very hot. The Burdwan stew takes a deal of time; it is composed of every thing at table, fish, flesh and fowl;—somewhat like the Spanish Olla Podrida,—Many suppose that unless prepared in a silver saucepan it cannot be good; on this point I must not presume to give an opinion, being satisfied with plain food; and never tasting any of these incentives to luxurious indulgence. During dinner a good deal of wine is drank, but a very little after the cloth is removed; except in Bachelors parties, as they are called; for the custom of reposing, if not of sleeping after dinner is so general that the streets of Calcutta are from four to five in the afternoon almost as empty of Europeans as if it were midnight—Next come the evening airings to the Course, every one goes, though sure of being half suffocated with dust. On returning from thence, tea is served, and universally drank here, even during the extreme heats. After tea, either cards or music fill up the space, 'till ten, when supper is generally announced. Five card loo is the usual game and they play a rupee a fish limited to ten. This will strike you as being enormously high but it is thought nothing of here. Tré dille and Whist are much in fashion but ladies seldom join in the latter; for though the stakes are moderate, bets frequently run high among the gentlemen which renders those anxious who sit down for amusement, lest others should lose by their blunders.

Formal visits are paid in the evening; they are generally very short, as perhaps each lady has a dozen to make and a party waiting for her at home besides. Gentlemen also call to offer their respects and if asked to put down their hat, it is considered as an invitation to supper. Many a hat have I seen vainly dangling in its owner's hand for half an hour, who at last has been compelled to withdraw without any one's offering to relieve him from the burthen.

Great preparations are making for the Christmas, and New year's public balls;—of course you will not expect me to write much till they are over; nor to own the truth am I in spirits, having great reason to be dissatisfied with Mr. Fay's conduct. Instead of cultivating the intimacy of those who might be serviceable or paying the necessary attention to persons in power; I can scarcely ever prevail on him to accompany me even to Dr. Jackson's who is generally visited by the first people; but he cannot endure being subjected to the forms of society—some times he has called on Sir Robert Chambers, but the other Judges he has never *seen*, except on the bench since his admission: he did not even accept Sir Elijah Impey's obliging offer to introduce him to Mr. Hyde, but suffered Mr. Sealy to perform that ceremony, and when the Chief Justice advanced to accompany him, he was forced to acknowledge that he had been already introduced,—upon which the great man turned on his heel and hardly ever noticed him afterwards. This happened on the day Mr. Fay was admitted to the bar at Mr. Hyde's public breakfast at whose house the professional gentlemen all meet on the first day of every Term and go from thence in procession to the Court House.[33] I will now close this letter in the hope of having better accounts to give you in my next.

Your's affectionately

E. F.

LETTER XVIII.

MY DEAR SISTER,

     Since my last we have been engaged in a per-
petual round of gaiety—keeping Christmas, as it is called,
though sinking into disuse at home, prevails here with all
its ancient festivity. The external appearance of the English gentlemen's houses on Christmas-day, is really pleasing
from its novelty. Large plantain trees are placed on each
side of the principal entrances, and the gates and pillars
being ornamented with wreaths of flowers fancifully disposed, enliven the scene.

     All the servants bring presents of fish and fruit from
the Banian down to the lowest menial; for these it is true
we are obliged in many instances to make a return, perhaps
beyond the real value, but still it is considered as a compliment to our *burrah din* (great day). A public dinner is
given at the Government house to the gentlemen of the
Presidency, and the evening concludes with an elegant Ball
& Supper for the Ladies. These are repeated on New
year's day and again on the King's birth day. I should
say have been, for that grand festival happening at the
hottest season, and every one being obliged to appear full
dressed, so much inconvenience resulted from the immense
croud, even in some cases severe fits of illness being the
consequence, that it has been determined to change the day
of celebration to the 8th of December which arrangement
gives general satisfaction.—I shall not attempt to describe

these splendid entertainments farther than by saying that they were in the highest style of magnificence: in fact such grand parties so much resemble each other, that a particular detail would be unnecessary and even tiresome.

I felt far more gratified some time ago, when Mrs. Jackson procured me a ticket for the Harmonic[34] which was supported by a select number of gentlemen who each in alphabetical rotation gave a concert, ball, and supper, during the cold season; I believe once a fortnight—that I attended was given by a Mr. Taylor, which closed the subscription and I understand it will not be renewed, a circumstance generally regretted as it was an elegant amusement and conducted on a very eligible plan.   We had a great deal of delightful music, and Lady Chambers, who is a capital performer on the harpsichord played amongst other pieces a Sonata of Nicolai's in a most brilliant style.   A gentleman who was present and who seemed to be quite charmed with her execution, asked me the next evening, if I did not think that *jig* Lady C— played the night before, was the prettiest thing I ever heard?   He meant the rondo which is remarkably lively; but I dare say " Over the water to Charley " would have pleased him equally well.

Mrs. Hastings was of the party; she came in late, and happened to place herself on the opposite side of the room, beyond a speaking distance, so strange to tell, I quite forgot she was there!   After some time had elapsed, my observant friend Mrs. Jackson, who had been impatiently watching my looks, asked if I had paid my respects to the Lady Governess?   I answered in the negative, having had no opportunity, as she had not chanced to look towards me when I was prepared to do so.   " Oh, replied the kind old lady, you must fix your eyes on her, and never take them off 'till she notices you; Miss Chantry has done this, and so have I; it is absolutely necessary to avoid giving offence."   I followed her prudent advice and was soon honoured with a complacent glance, which I returned as became me by a most respectful bend. Not long after she walked over to our side and conversed very affably with me, for we are now through Mrs. Jackson's interference on good terms together.

She also introduced me to Lady Coote [35] and her inseparable friend Miss Molly Bazett.   It was agreed between them when they were both girls that, whichever married first the other was to live with her, and accordingly when Sir Eyre took his lady from St. Helena, of which place her father was governor, Miss Molly who is a native of the island accompanied them to England and from thence to India, where she has remained ever since;—thus giving a proof of steady attachment not often equalled and never perhaps excelled.

19th February.

Yesterday being the Anniversary of our release from imprisonment, we invited Dr. Jackson's family, Mr. O'Donnell and some friends to assist in its celebration; I call it my ' Jubilee Day ' and trust my dear friends at home did not forget the occasion.

This reminds me to tell you that Sudder Khan and Ayres our chief enemies have both closed their career of wickedness.   The former died of wounds received before Tellicherry;   and the latter having repeatedly advanced close to the lines of that place, holding the most contemptuous language and indecent gestures towards the Officers; setting every one at defiance and daring them to fire at him, (I suppose in a state of intoxication, miserable wretch!) was at length picked off, to use a military phrase.—Too honourable a death for such a monster of iniquity.   My hope was, that he would have been taken prisoner, and afterwards recognised and shot as a deserter.

Poor West is also dead; he never reached his destination—the boat he went up in, by some accident struck on a sand bank and nearly all on board perished.

26th March.

A Frigate being ordered to sail for Europe with dispatches from Government, I shall avail myself of the occasion, and close this letter with a few remarks on our theatrical amusements.

The house was built by subscription; it is very neatly fitted up, and the scenery and decorations quite equal to what could be expected here. The parts are entirely represented by amateurs in the drama—no hired performers being allowed to act. I assure you I have seen characters supported in a manner that would not disgrace *any* European stage. *Venice Preserved* was exhibited some time ago, when Captain Call (of the Army) Mr. Droz (a member of the Board of Trade) and Lieutenant Norfar, in Jaffier, Pierre, and Belvidera shewed very superior theatrical talents. The latter has rather an effeminate appearance off the stage, yet I am told he is a very brave Officer when on service; and though always dressed as if for a ball, when he makes his appearance, is among the most alert in a moment of danger. I cannot imagine how he contrives it, for the present mode of arranging the hair requires a great deal of time to make it look tolerable; however this is said to be the case.[36]—One of the chief inconveniences in establishments of this kind, is that the performers being independent of any controul, will some times persist in taking parts to which their abilities are by no means adequate;—this throws an air of ridicule over the whole, as the spectators are too apt to indulge their mirth on the least opening of that kind: in fact many go to see a tragedy for the express purpose of enjoying a laugh, which is certainly very illiberal and must prove detrimental to the hopes of an enfant institution like the one in question:

—for my own part I think such a mode of passing an evening highly rational; and were I not debarred by the expence should seldom miss a representation—but a gold mohur is really too much to bestow on such a temporary gratification. Adieu—I shall write again soon.

Your's most affectionately
E. F.

LETTER XIX.

My Dear Sister,

      You must have perceived that the style of my letters for some months past has been constrained, nor could it possibly be otherwise; for not wishing to grieve your affectionate heart by a recital of the melancholy change in my prospects, occasioned by Mr. Fay's imprudent behaviour, I was reduced to enlarge on less important subjects. Some hints however escaped me which must have led you to suspect that all was not going on properly; but his conduct of late has been such that no hope remains of his *ever* being able to prosecute his profession here.

      Ever since our arrival he has acted in every respect directly contrary to my advice—By constantly associating with persons who had distinguished themselves by thwarting the measures of Government,—he soon became equally obnoxious. On one occasion when a tax was proposed to be levied on houses, several meetings were held at our house, wherein he openly insisted on the illegality of such a procedure, and encouraged his *new* friends to assert their independence. I remonstrated in the strongest terms against measures so pregnant with evil, and which must terminate in utter ruin, if not speedily abandoned; the character of our *chief ruler* being well known;—he will never *desert* a friend or *forgive* an enemy; what chance then has an individual who rashly incurs his resentment of escaping its baneful effects? all this and more I repeatedly but alas *vainly* urged——my representations were as heretofore treated with contempt: he still persevered, giving himself entirely up to low and unworthy pursuits, while his professional duties were wholly neglected and his best friends slighted.

We were frequently invited to parties which he as constantly evaded, leaving me to make what excuses I could for his absence.——My dear kind Patroness Lady Chambers, still continues on my account to shew him attention as do the Jacksons and some few others: she has lately added a son to her family;——I was with her at the time, and the sweet infant seems to have formed closer ties between us. On a late occasion however she was compelled to speak plainly. The christening is to take place in a few days; Sir Elijah and Lady Impey have offered to stand for the child, and Lady C— wishes me to be present, but Sir E— positively refuses to meet Mr. F— who of course cannot be included; so unless I can reconcile him to the omission I must remain at home also.

3rd June.

The grand ceremony is over. I had no difficulty with Mr. F— he declared himself pre-engaged the instant I mentioned the subject, and insisted that I should make some apology for him which was readily promised——You may suppose that I could not under such circumstances enjoy much pleasure though Sir E— and his Lady behaved very graciously. But the idea that my husband was so totally proscribed where he might have figured among the foremost pierced my very soul; yet was I forced to put on the appearance of cheerfulness, that I might seem to receive as a compliment what was certainly so intended. The public countenance of Lady C— and being admitted to such a select party cannot but operate favourably for me at this crisis, when I shall stand so much in need of support.

24th June.

Though term is now far advanced, Mr. Fay has scarcely a brief. The attorneys are positively afraid to employ him; and causes have actually come on with two advocates on one side and one on the other, rather than permit him to appear in them. What a noble opportunity of making an ample fortune is thus wantonly thrown away! Heaven grant me patience. I have only this reflection to console me, that every effort in my power has been made to ward off the blow which is now inevitable.

I yesterday confided to Lady C— my real situation: who (on my stating that Mr. F— must certainly be obliged to quit the Settlement very shortly,) with the utmost kindness insisted on my making her house, my home whenever that event should take place; and Sir R— has in the most cordial way inforced the invitation.—Thus through the goodness of Providence am I provided with a secure and highly respectable asylum, till a passage to Europe can be obtained on moderate terms, a difficult matter to accomplish.

17th July.

On the last day of the present month we must quit our house; and when my husband and I may reside under the same roof together again, Heaven alone can tell. It is astonishing to see with what apparent unconcern he supports the shock: but the acquisition of a new Patron has raised his spirits. Colonel Watson, a man of superior abilities and immense fortune has been long a determined opposer of Government, and the *bitter* enemy of Sir Elijah Impey, against whom he has set an impeachment on foot, to prosecute which it is requisite that a confidential agent should serve the process on the defendant here, and proceed to England with the necessary documents.[37] Mr. F— has contrived to get himself appointed to this office: he has drawn up a set of articles many copies of which are preparing by Bengalee writers, who though they profess to understand English and are tolerably correct in copying what is put before them, know not the meaning of any thing they write; a great convenience this to such as conduct affairs that require secrecy, since the persons employed, cannot, if they were so disposed, betray their trust. Colonel Watson never comes here; all is carried on with an air of profound mystery—I like not such proceedings and doubt if any good can come of them, but I dare not interfere nor drop even a hint which might lead to suspicion that any thing extraordinary is going forward. The duty of a wife which is paramount to all other civil obligations, compels me silently to witness what is beyond my power to counteract; although the character of a highly revered friend is obliquely glanced at, and may be in future more seriously implicated in the business—you will guess to whom I allude. Adieu you shall hear from me again when I change my abode.

Your's affectionately

E. F.

LETTER XX.

My Dear Sister,

Since I wrote last, my feelings have been harrassed in various ways almost beyond endurance—Mr. Fay quitted me on the 31st ultimo, and the rest of that day was devoted to the distressing (however just and necessary) task of delivering back such articles of furniture as had not been paid for, to the persons who supplied us with them; and also returning what had been borrowed of different friends for our convenience; what remained was taken possession of next morning, by a man to whom my unfortunate husband had given a bond for money advanced on the most exorbitant terms, to support his extravagance. Thus am I left destitute of every thing but my clothes, to endure the wretched effects of his imprudence, with a constitution weakened by the sufferings and privations, I underwent during my eventful journey, added to the dread which I cannot avoid feeling lest that unlucky blow I received in Calicut should be productive of serious consequences.

Lady Chambers welcomed me as a sister, she wishes me to accompany her every where but time alone can reconcile me to general society:—The very day of my removal here, a circumstance was disclosed that determined me no longer to bind my destiny with that of a man who could thus set at defiance all ties divine and human. After consulting my legal friends I demanded a separation, to which he having consented, a deed was drawn up by Mr. S—— under the inspection of Sir Robert Chambers, in the fullest manner possible rendering me wholly independent of Mr. F——'s authority, with power, to make a will &c. in short conceived in the strongest terms our language could supply. I have appointed Mr. G. Jones Solicitor of Lincoln's Inn and Mr. Mc Veagh one of the masters in Chancery here to act as my Trustees. Two more respectable men I could not have chosen. You my dear sister, who know better than any one, what exertions I have used, and what sacrifices I have *vainly* made for this most ungrateful of beings, will not be surprised to find that even *my* patience was not proof against this last outrage.

But let me dismiss the hateful subject merely stating that the deeds were signed on the 11th instant. His secret is safe with me, though when we met on that occasion he had the insolence to hint his belief that out of *revenge* I should divulge it. So let him *still* think, for I deigned no reply except by a look; when I with secret triumph beheld his hitherto undaunted eye sink beneath the indignant glance of mine.

" Tis Conscience that makes cowards of us all."

5th September.

Sir Robert being appointed President of the Court at Chinsurah, is gone up to take possession of his charge, accompanied by Lady Chambers and the family.[38] So here am I left alone to ramble over this great house and meditate on irreparable evils. Sir R—— has however kindly entrusted me with the keys of his immense library, which will furnish a rich treat when my mind acquires sufficient calmness to look beyond itself in search of amusement.

The acquaintance of Mrs. Wheler I have found a most valuable acquisition.[39] I went with Lady C—— to pass a day with her at the gardens, and have been treated with the utmost attention ever since. She has authorised me to look up to her as a steady patroness on all occasions. Mr. Hastings being gone up the country on political business Mr. Wheler of course takes the chair during his absence so you may judge what influence Mrs. W— possesses; but " she bears her honors so meekly " and contrives to soften the refusals which she is frequently compelled to give by so much affability and sympathy, as to conciliate all parties and render herself generally beloved.

I have never mentioned yet how indifferently we are provided with respect to a place of worship; divine service being performed, in a room, (not a very large one) at the Old Fort; which is a great disgrace to the settlement. They talk of building a Church and have fixed on a very eligible spot whereon to erect it but no further progress has been made in the business.[40]

I now propose, having full leisure to give you some account of the East Indian customs and ceremonies, such as I have been able to collect, but it must be considered as a mere sketch, to point your further researches. And first for that horrible custom of widows burning themselves with the dead bodies of their husbands; the fact is indubitable, but I have never had an opportunity of witnessing the various incidental ceremonies, nor have I ever seen any European who had been present at them. I cannot suppose that the usage originated in the superior tenderness, and ardent attachment of Indian wives towards their spouses, since the same tenderness and ardour would doubtless extend to his offspring and prevent them from exposing the innocent survivors to the miseries attendant on an orphan state, and they would see clearly that to live and cherish these pledges of affection would be the most rational and natural way of shewing their regard for both husband and children. I apprehend that as personal fondness can have no part here at all, since all matches are made between the parents of the parties who are betrothed to each other at too early a period for choice to be consulted, this practice is entirely a political scheme intended to insure the care and good offices of wives to their husbands, who have not failed in most countries to invent a sufficient number of rules to render the weaker sex totally subservient to their authority. I cannot avoid smiling when I hear gentlemen bring forward the conduct of the Hindoo women, as a test of superior character, since I am well aware that so much are we the slaves of habit *every where* that were it necessary for a woman's reputation to burn herself in England, many a one who has *accepted* a husband merely for the sake of an establishment, who has lived with him without affection; perhaps thwarted his views, dissipated his fortune and rendered his life uncomfortable to its close, would yet mount the funeral pile with all imaginable decency and die with heroic fortitude. The most specious sacrifices are not always the greatest, she who wages war with a naturally petulant temper, who practises a rigid self-denial, endures without complaining the unkindness, infidelity, extravagance, meanness or scorn, of the man to whom she has given a tender and confiding heart, and for whose happiness and well being in life all the powers of her mind are engaged; —is ten times more of a heroine than the slave of bigotry and superstition, who affects to scorn the life demanded of her by the laws of her country or at least that country's custom; and many such we have in England, and I doubt not in India likewise: so indeed we ought, have we not a religion infinitely more pure than that of India? The Hindoos, or gentoos are divided into four castes or tribes called the Brahmin, the Khutree, the Buesho, and the Shodor: their rank in the land, declines gradually to the last named, and if any of them commit an offence which deprives them of the privileges that belong to their respective castes, they become Parias, which may therefore be

called a filthy tribe formed as it were of the refuse of the rest.
Those are indeed considered the very dregs of the people,
and supply all the lowest offices of human life.   They all
profess what is called the religion of Brahma, from the
caste which bears his name all the priests are chosen, who
are treated in every respect with distinguished honour and
reverence.   Their religious Code is contained in a book
called the Veda, which only the Brahmins are allowed to
read; it is written in a dead language called the Sanscrit.
They worship three Deities, Brahma, the creator, Vistnoo
the preserver, and Sheevah the destroyer.   But they profess
to believe them only the representations or types of the
great spirit Brahma (the Supreme God) whom they also call
the spirit of wisdom, and the principle of Truth: none but
Hindoos are allowed to enter temples, but I am told the
Idols worshipped there are of the very ugliest forms that
imagination can conceive; and to whom Pope's description
of the heathen deities may, in other respects, be strictly
applied.

> " Gods changeful, partial, passionate unjust.
> Whose attributes *are* rage, revenge, or lust."

I lament to add to such wretched objects as these,
numbers of the deluded natives are devoted in the strongest
and most absolute manner possible.   A certain sect named
Pundarams live in continual beggary; extreme hunger alone
induces them to ask for food, which when granted, they only
take just what will preserve life, and spend all their days
in singing songs in praise of Sheevah; another sect add a
tabor, and hollow brass rings about their ancles to increase
the noise with which they extol *their* deity.   I consider both
these as a species of monks but believe the holy fathers fall
far short of the Jogees and Seniases of India, in their
religious austerities.   These not only endure all possible
privations with apparent indifference, but invent for themselves various kinds of tortures which they carry to an

astonishing length; such as keeping their hands clenched 'till the nails grow into them,—standing on one foot for days and even weeks together—and hiring people to support their hands in a perpendicular position.

Their expiatory punishments are some of them dreadful. I myself saw a man running in the streets with a piece of iron thrust through his tongue which was bleeding profusely. On the Churruk Poojah (swinging feast) hundreds I have heard, are suspended at an amazing height by means of hooks, firmly fixed in the flesh of the back, to which sometimes a cloth is added round the body to afford the miserable victim a chance of escape, should the hook give way. I, by accident, (for voluntarily nothing should have tempted me to witness such a spectacle) saw one of these wretches, who was whirling round with surprizing rapidity, and at that distance scarcely appeared to retain the semblance of a human form. They firmly expect by this infliction to obtain pardon of all their offences, and should death be the consequence, they go straight to heaven—thus changing the horrid state of privation and misery in which they exist here, for one of bliss: if such be their real persuasion, who can condemn the result.

Indeed under other circumstances it is found that, notwithstanding their apparent gentleness and timidity, the Hindoos will meet death with intrepid firmness—they are also invincibly obstinate, and will *die* rather than concede a point: of this a very painful instance has lately occurred.— A Hindoo beggar of the Brahmin caste went to the house of a very rich man, but of an inferior tribe, requesting alms; he was either rejected, or considered himself inadequately relieved, and refused to quit the place. As his lying before the door and thus obstructing the passage was unpleasant, one of the servants first intreated, then insisted on his retiring, and in speaking pushed him gently away; he chose to call this push a blow, and cried aloud for redress, declaring that he would never stir from the spot 'till he had obtained justice against the man: who now endeavoured to sooth him but in vain; like a true Hindoo he sat down, and never moved again, but thirty-eight hours afterwards expired, demanding justice with his latest breath; being well aware that in the event of this, the master would have an enormous fine to pay, which accordingly happened. I am assured that such evidences of the surprizing indifference to life, the inflexible stubbornness, and vindictive dispositions of these people are by no means rare; it seems extraordinary though, that sentiments and feelings apparently so contrary to each other should operate on the same minds; seeing them so quiet and supine, so (if it may be so expressed) only half alive, as they generally shew themselves, one is prepared for their sinking, without an effort to avert any impending danger; but that they should at the same time nourish so violent and active a passion as revenge, and brave even death so intrepidly as they often do in pursuit of it, is very singular:—but enough of these silly enthusiasts.

I had lately the opportunity of witnessing the marriage procession of a rich Hindoo. The bride (as I was told) sat in the same palanquin with the bridegroom, which was splendidly ornamented;—they were accompanied by all the relations on both sides, dressed in the most superb manner; —some on horse back, some in palanquins, and several on elephants;—bands of dancing girls and musicians I understood preceded them;—and in the evening there were fireworks at the bride's father's house and the appearance of much feasting &c. but no Europeans were present. This wedding was of a nature by no means uncommon here; a rich man had an only daughter, and he bargained to dispose of her, or rather to take for her a husband out of a poor man's family, but of his own *Caste*: for this is indispensable. In this case the bridegroom is brought home to his father-in-law's house and becomes a member of the family; so that although the law prohibits a man from giving a dowry with his daughter, yet you see he does it in effect, since he gives a house to a man who wants one; gives in fact, a fortune but saddled with an encumbrance;—perhaps in a few years the old man may die, and the young one having fulfilled the wishes of his parents, and provided for his own wants, may employ some of his female relations to look round among the poorer families of his caste for a pretty girl, whom he will take as a second wife, tho' the first always retains the pre-eminence, and governs the house; nor can the husband devote more of his time to one than the other,—the law compelling him to live with them alternately, you may be sure the account is strictly kept. My Banian Dattaram Chuckerbutty has been married between twenty and thirty years, without taking a second lady, and he boasts of being much happier with his old wife (as he calls her) than the generality of his friends are amidst the charms of variety. For my own part, I have not a doubt but he is in the right.

The Hindoo ladies are never seen abroad; when they go out their carriages are closely covered with curtains, so that one has little chance of satisfying curiosity. I once saw two apparently very beautiful women: they use so much art however, as renders it difficult to judge what claim they *really* have to that appellation—Their whole time is taken up in decorating their persons:—the hair—eye-lids—eye-brows—teeth—hands and nails, all undergo certain processes to render them more completely fascinating; nor can one seriously blame their having recourse to these, or the like artifices—the motive being to secure the affections of a husband, or to counteract the plans of a rival.

27th September.

The Hindoos who can afford to purchase wood for a funeral pile, burn their dead; one cannot go on the river without seeing numbers of these exhibitions, especially at night, and most disgusting spectacles they are. I will not enlarge on the subject. This mode however is far superior to that of throwing them into the river as practised by the poor; where they offend more senses than one. I have been frequently obliged to return precipitately from a walk along the river side, by the noisome exhalations which arose from these wretched objects.

Some of the Hindoo customs respecting the sick are really shocking—When a person is given over by the Brahmins, (who are physicians as well as priests) the relations immediately carry him, if within a reasonable distance, to the banks of the Ganges, where he is smeared with the mud, quantities of which I am told are thrust into his mouth, nose, and ears. This treatment soon reduces him to a dying state; nor is it desirable that he should recover, since he must in that case lose caste; for it is an established rule, that whoever removes from the spot where the sacred rites have been performed, becomes an outcast. Dr. Jackson was once fortunate enough to be called in to attend the wife of a Hindoo Rajah whom they were on the point of taking to the river when he arrived—he assured the Rajah that he perceived no dangerous symptoms and would answer for her doing well.—Luckily the tremendous ceremonies had not commenced: The event justified our good Doctor's predictions—the lady is still living and his success in this instance, has led to several others, highly gratifying to the best feelings of humanity and certainly beneficial to his fortune.

This letter has run to such an enormous length that I must now conclude, with wishing that I may soon hear good news of you. I remain,

Your's most affectionately

E. F.

LETTER XXI.

My Dear Sister.

Sir R— and Lady C— have been down since I wrote last, and remained here during term, but are now gone up again, though much distressed. Mrs. C— prefers staying here.—A melancholy event has occurred in the family; the sweet little boy just turned of six months old, to whom I was so fondly attached, died a few weeks ago. Dear interesting child! I shall *long* lament his loss. He was not ill more than three days; so rapid is the progress of disease in this country.

Mr. and Mrs. Hosea are arrived in Town and have taken accommodations on the *Grosvenor*, Captain Coxon. I was in hopes of being able to take my passage with them but am disappointed.[41]

Mr. H— was Resident at one of the upper stations; he is a man of high character and generally esteemed; and his wife one of the most amiable women I ever knew; it is impossible to do otherwise than love her. As she daily looks to be confined, her leaving Calcutta till after that period, is out of the question, so they must suffer the *Grosvenor* to proceed to Madras without them, where she is expected to remain a month at least, and the family and baggage of Mr. H— are to follow in a Country ship at the risk of arriving too late.

The agreement is that, if she sail from thence before a certain day a small sum is to be forfeited; but *after* that day, should Captain Coxon be compelled to proceed on his voyage without them, he is still to receive ten thousand rupees, that is half the passage money by way of compensation. I state these particulars to shew what large sums are exacted of passengers.

The society of Mrs. Chambers, who is a fine looking respectable old lady, well informed and chearful, with that of Mrs. Hosea, who has charming spirits, enables me to pass the time far more pleasantly than when I was left here during the rains. Besides I often visit at Dr. Jacksons, and have made acquaintance with several agreeable families, who allow me to call on them without formality; the very idea of which is hateful to me at present: so cruelly fallen are my once highly and justly raised expectations. For what place do I now hold in the Society with which I am permitted to mix? Alas, none except by sufferance: but most ardently do I wish to escape from this fatal spot the scene of so many severe afflictions, and seek comfort with those who have never failed to afford it. There I shall not be constantly reminded of past hopes, now alas! sunk in disappointment. Think not these observations proceed from a repining spirit, or unmindfulness of favors received; I have been most beneficently treated and my views have been furthered in a way which I had no right whatever to expect. Can attentions like those be forgotten? No! it forms my proudest boast that *I have* such friends, and while life remains I must ever cherish the remembrance of their generous exertions. The approaching season always inspires melancholy reflections—I will therefore pass it over, and look forward to the next, when by the blessing of Providence I hope to be with my beloved family.

27th January, 1782.

My dear Mrs. Hosea has thank heaven, got happily over her confinement, which took place three weeks ago;

and all is now bustle and preparation for their departure.——
Sir Robert's eldest son, Thomas, goes under their care;
he is a charming boy, nearly seven years of age, which is
rather late; but no good opportunity has occurred 'till
now;—a Miss Shore (the daughter of an intimate friend)
about the age of Thomas, also proceeds with them. Mrs.
H— takes one little girl of her own, sixteen months old;
the baby is to be left with Lady C—: she promises to be a
lovely child.

We are to have the christening to-morrow when I shall
take my leave of large parties; except one, which I must
attend. Mrs. H—s infant daughter is to be christened
early next month and Sir R—s whole family is invited. At
present I devote myself entirely to Mrs. H— who I really
think has a friendship for me. Would it were in my power
to accompany her, but that for many reasons is impossible.

Another Indiaman (The Dartmouth Captain Thompson)
has just sailed, but *she* too is absolutely *crowded* with passengers; so I must have patience—It is almost incredible
what quantities of baggage, people of consequence invariably take with them; I myself counted twenty-nine trunks
that were sent on board, for Mr. and Mrs. H— exclusive
of chests of drawers and other packages, with cabin stores
&c. and more still remain to be shipped. This separate
passage to Madras will add greatly to the expense; for
Captain Coxon would not have charged a rupee more, had
they embarked with him at Bengal; even removing so much
baggage from one ship to another will occasion no small
inconvenience.

CHINSURAH, 10*th February*.

My time has been too much taken up for this fortnight
past to afford leisure for writing. I have another melancholy
event to record; but let me proceed regularly.

Our friends left us on the second Instant. Poor Mrs.

H— was dreadfully affected at parting with her infant; it seemed cruel for a mother to abandon her child only twenty-five days old; but it must in all probability have fallen a sacrifice. Her anxiety in other respects was great. Admiral Suffren is said to keep a sharp look out after English ships going down the Bay; but, I trust, Sir E. Hughes will find the French fleet better employment than cruizing about after our vessels.[42]

Sir R— and Lady C— felt severely the shock of their son's departure but poor Mrs. C— whose very soul seemed treasured up, if I may so express myself, in her grandson, sunk under the blow. On the fifth she was seized with a violent illness, of which on the seventh she expired. Sir R— is deeply afflicted, and I should be surprised if he were not, for, to him she was ever an exemplary parent; and gave an irrefragable proof of strong maternal affection, by accompanying him to this country at her advanced period of life. Her death is generally lamented, as a most charitable humane good woman. " Let her works praise her." She was in her seventieth year. We came up here immediately after the funeral which took place the next day, and was most numerously attended; I may say by almost the whole settlement—gentlemen as well as ladies. Her character demanded this testimony of respect and that it was paid, affords me pleasure.

You will expect me to give you some account of this place; but after having told you that it contains many very fine houses,—is regularly built,—and kept remarkably clean; nothing more remains to be said. One cannot expect much chearfulness among the inhabitants, though they are treated with the utmost kindness, and all private property is held sacred.

A strange circumstance occurred at the time of its capture, which will probably become a subject of litigation. A King's ship, either a frigate or a sloop of war, was lying

off Calcutta, when news arrived that the Dutch had commenced hostilities.—The Captain accompanied by a party
of his officers and seamen, proceeded with all expedition to
Chinsurah, which he reached about 2 A. M. next day, and
summoned the place to surrender to *His Majesty's* Arms.
The Governor being totally unprovided with the means of
resistance complied; so that when a detachment of the
Company's troops marched in at seven o'clock to take possession they found the business already settled, and had the
laugh most completely against them. The Captain was
soon induced to relinquish his capture, but insisted that his
people were entitled to prize money, and has put in his
claim accordingly—Is it not an odd affair?

21st February.

Sir R— is going to dispatch some letters for England
and I will profit by the occasion, having at present nothing
further to communicate. All remains in uncertainty.

I am,
Your affectionate
E. F.

LETTER XXII.

CALCUTTA, 17*th March*.

My Dear Sister,

This is in all probability the last letter I shall
write from Bengal.   Mrs. Wheler has been indefatigable
in her exertions; and has at length secured a passage for
me on the Valentine, Captain Lewis; a fine new ship—this
is her first voyage.   I shall have a female companion too,
which is certainly desirable.   Colonel and Mrs. Tottingham with their family accompany us, besides these we shall
have seven military gentlemen, two of the company's civil
servants, and thirteen children, under Captain Lewis's
immediate protection.   The ship is expected to sail in the
beginning of next month.   I dined in company with Captain
Lewis yesterday at Mrs. W——s, and we were both much
pleased with his behaviour.—When we retired after dinner
my good friend congratulated me on the prospect of sailing
with such a commander, for many of them assume airs of
consequence, but Captain Lewis does not seem at all that
way disposed; and should the passengers prove agreeable,
I really think we may promise ourselves a comfortable
voyage.

I am using every effort in preparing my baggage, and
Lady C—— with her usual kindness renders me every
assistance; nor have my other friends been neglectful of
any thing that can contribute to my comfort both on the
passage and after my arrival in England; till my health
shall, with the blessing of Providence, be restored, when

I may be enabled to seek out some decent means of support.

I had a very eligible proposal made me of entering into partnership with a most amiable lady who has lately engaged in the school line, but was compelled to decline it, my complaints requiring a change of climate, and that I should consult those medical friends who have been accustomed to prescribe for me. I much regret this circumstance, having no doubt but we might have suited each other extremely well, for she has proved herself a sincere friend in many instances and must ever possess my grateful esteem.

28th March.

I had the pleasure last evening, of being present at the marriage of Captain P. M——and my young friend Miss T——; the wedding was kept at Dr. Jackson's and of course they intended to have a little ball; but hardly any one could be prevailed on to dance so late in the season. I had given a solemn promise that nothing should induce me to run the risk, so to comply was out of the question.—At length Mrs. Jackson, senior, who is turned of sixty-five, opened the ball with a very good minuet, and afterwards footed it away for about two hours, as gaily as the youngest: her example took effect, and they made up a tolerable set. The dance was succeeded by a magnificent supper, to which nearly thirty persons sat down. After the customary toasts we retired, and I reached home before one. May they be happy is my sincere wish.

This is a terrible season for reaching the ships, none but stout vessels can venture down. Colonel Tottingham pays seventy pounds for a sloop to convey his family. I am in this respect fortunate. Sir R—— and Lady C—— are going to a place called Bearcole for the benefit of sea-bathing, and I shall accompany them to Ingellee; which is within a tide of the Valentine: my friends will then proceed by land to the bathing-place; and one of the sloops by Sir R——'s orders will convey me and my baggage to the Barrabola head where the ship is lying at anchor to complete her cargo.

5th April.

I have every thing now ready and only wait for the completion of Sir R——s preparations. I feel very impatient to get to sea, being persuaded that it will have a salutary effect on my health,—change of scene and company will also be of service. I have taken leave of every one, and for many shall preserve sentiments of the most grateful esteem.

ON BOARD THE VALENTINE,[43]
Barrabola Head, 14th April.

I left Calcutta, on Tuesday the ninth Instant with Sir R—— and Lady C—— the latter I am concerned to say is in a very weak state, but trust sea bathing will be beneficial. We had a boisterous trip of it down to Ingellee, and every one but myself was dreadfully sea-sick.

My kind friends quitted me on Saturday evening.—I felt quite forlorn at our separation. To be thrown among strangers after experiencing for near nine months, the attentive hospitality of such a family as I was torn from, almost overcame my fortitude,—but I soon lost every other sensation in that overwhelming one of sea-sickness, which lasted the whole way, nor could I go on board till the afternoon.—I shall keep this open till the Pilot goes, that you may have the satisfaction of hearing that we have passed the *first* dangers.

20th April.

Our commander is by no means the placid being we supposed.—I doubt he will prove a very tyrant—instead of paying attention, or shewing respect, he *exacts* both, and woe be to those who fail in either. We are still waiting for the remainder of our Cargo and Captain Lewis vents his rage in drinking "*confusion to the Board of Trade*" every day.

28th April.

We had a narrow escape last evening though I knew not of the danger till it was over. I was seized after tea with severe spasms in the stomach, and had the doctor with me; when suddenly the ship began to pitch and toss violently; and I heard Captain Lewis, call out in a *voice* of thunder "Stand by the sheet anchor, heave the lead." Presently all was quiet again, nor had I the least suspicion till next morning of our having been *adrift* on the Barrabola sand; and what might have been our fate Heaven knows, had not the sheet anchor brought us up; for it is a most dangerous place, surrounded by shoals and out of sight of land.

It is pleasant to see Captain Lewis so alert on perilous occasions; he appears to be an excellent seaman, but the roughest being surely that nature ever formed, in language and manners. The oaths he swears by, are most horrible and he prides himself in inventing new ones. How were Mrs. Wheler and I mistaken? I see he must be humoured like a child, for the least contradiction makes him almost frantic.

2nd May.

Now I must indeed say farewell—the Pilot is just quitting us, and has promised to put this on board the first vessel that sails for England; there is one under dispatch. God bless you. Within six months, I trust we shall all meet in health and safety.

I am,
Your's affectionately
E. F.

LETTER XXIII.

My Dear Sister,

A more uncomfortable passage than I have made to this place, can hardly be imagined. The port of my cabin being kept almost constantly shut, and the door opening into the steerage; I had neither light nor air but from a scuttle: thereby half the space was occupied by a great gun, which prevented me from going near the port when it *was* open.

Mrs. Tottingham at first took her meals in the Cuddy, but the gentlemen were in general too fond of the bottle to pay us the least attention; after tea, we were never asked to cut in at cards, though they played every evening. Captain Lewis swore so dreadfully, making use of such vulgar oaths and expressions; and became so very rude and boisterous, that Mrs. Tottingham withdrew intirely from table, and never left her cabin for the last thirteen weeks: but the Colonel took care to send her whatever was necessary; I had no one to perform the like kind office for me, and was therefore forced to venture up among them, or risk starvation below.

The table was at first most profusely covered; being our Captains favourite maxim " never to make two wants of one "; Every one foresaw what must be the consequence, but he would not listen to reason. Thus we went on till the beginning of August, when he declared that we had rounded the Cape of Good hope; offering to back his opinion by receiving twenty guineas, and return a guinea a day till we reached St. Helena: but no one accepted the bet; yet doubts seemed to hang on the minds of many. However on the 5th at noon, hearing that we were in Latitude 33. 32 S. I began to think with the Captain that, it was needless to *spare* our stock, since a few days would bring us a fresh supply—but alas! at 4 P. M. land was perceived on the *East* coast of Africa; so near, that before we tacked *flies* were seen on the shore—had this happened during the night, nothing could have saved us from shipwreck.—Can I sufficiently bless Providence for this second escape?

On examining the state of our water and provision, after the error was discovered, we were put on an allowance of a quart of water a day, for all purposes; and for nearly a month before we arrived here, we were forced to live on *salt* provisions; even the poor children and the sick, had no better fare.

While off the Cape, we encountered very stormy weather but happily sustained no injury, except the loss of a fore-top-mast which was easily replaced—Captain Lewis, one day, thought fit to refuse me a passage through his cabin, for which I had expressly stipulated. I retired, and in a few minutes he came down to apologize for his behaviour, and a most curious apology he made. He began by saying that he had been beaten at *piquet*, and that losing always made him cross, " besides, said he, to tell you the truth I do not like ladies, not, (with a great oath) that I have any particular objection to you, on the contrary I really think you are a quiet good sort of woman enough; but I cannot *abide* ladies, and I declare that, sometimes when you come up to me upon deck, and say, ' how do you do Captain Lewis ' it makes my back open and shirt (*sic*) like a knife " —so much for this gentleman's *respect* and politeness! I was forced to appear satisfied and he seemed very penitent for some days; till another cross fit came on.

Judge if I did not rejoice at the sight of this romantic Island; though its appearance from the sea is very un-promising,—inaccessible rocks, and stupendous crags frown-ing every side but one, nor is there any anchorage except at that point—The town is literally an ascending valley be-tween two hills, just wide enough to admit of one street. The houses are in the English style, with sashed windows, and small doors. Here are back-gardens, but no gardens; which makes the place intensely hot for want of a free circulation of air; but when you once ascend *Ladder Hill* the scene changes, and all seems enchantment. The most exquisite prospects you can conceive burst suddenly on the eye—fruitful vallies,—cultivated hills and diversified scenery of every description. The inhabitants are obliging and attentive, indeed, remarkably; so altogether I find it a most welcome resting place. After being kept on salt provisions for a month, one is not likely to be very fastidious; former abstinence giving more poignant relish to the ex-cellent food, which is set before us.

Lord North, and the Hastings, China ships, arrived soon after us, but we are all still detained for Convey—how vexatious.

18th October.

Yesterday Captain Lewis gave a grand entertainment on board the Valentine. I was obliged to preside for Mrs. Tottingham would not venture on the water till there was a necessity for it. We had a most brilliant party. I danced a good deal, but find no inconvenience from it. It is odd enough, that he should have fixed on your birth day. You may be sure I silently drank my own toast. Mrs. Comettee and the other ladies seemed highly gratified, and well they might, for no expence was spared to render it completely elegant.

20th October.

The *Chapman* is just arrived, in a most dreadful state, having lost near fifty of her Crew in her passage from Madras, from whence she sailed in Company with the Dartmouth, which was wrecked off the Carnicobar island the *very ship* I was, as I *then* thought, so *unfortunate* in *missing*: so that in this instance, as in many others, I may justly impute my safety to that Providence which

> " From hidden dangers, snares and death,
>   Has gently steered my way."

11th November.

Among the passengers in the *Dartmouth* were Mrs. Irwin and her infant son, a most interesting child, three years of age, who were wonderfully preserved through sufferings, enough to overwhelm the strongest constitution; and proceeded to St. Helena on the *Chapman* on board which were Mr. Casamajor and his mother, who secured accommodations on the *Lord North*, not choosing to venture farther on the *Chapman*.⁴⁴ Upon which I was applied to, to accompany Mrs. Irwin who could not well proceed without a female companion, and was not able to procure accommodations on the other ships—I instantly determined on accompanying her for the express purpose of endeavouring to soften the inconveniences under which she laboured, and to soothe her mind harrassed by the many hardships of her distressing voyage.

25th November.

This day we left St. Helena in company with the *Lord North, Valentine, and Hastings*. The Chapman unfortunately sails very ill and cannot keep up with the other ships. Captain Lewis told me at St. Helena in order to prevent my quitting the *Valentine*, that we should be left in the lurch the first fair opportunity; and so it happened long ere we reached England.

Our passage was tremendous, the Sea breaking over the ship and continually carrying some thing or other away; nor had we any naval stores to replace what was thus lost. Captain Walker and Mr. Gooch, the second officer, were daily employed with the people, repairing the sails and rigging, nor did they shrink from any labour. I never beheld such exertion: very frequently they were obliged to take the wheel, for scarcely a sufficient number could be found to keep watch.

On entering the channel the weather was so thick that no observation could be taken for five days. One night after remaining several hours in dreadful suspense respecting our situation, Captain Walker came down about half past ten o'clock, to tell us that we were off Scilly. What a declaration! off Scilly! on a stormy night in the beginning of February! This intelligence was not likely to tranquillize our feelings. Mrs. Irwin and myself passed a sleepless night, and in the morning, one of the sailors ascertained the place we were driven into to be St. Ive's Bay, a most dangerous place; but thanks to providence, we sustained no injury, except being forced round the Land's End, which was to us a serious misfortune, being utterly unable to beat back into the English channel, our men being worn out with illness and exertion, and our stores of every kind nearly exhausted.

No Pilot would venture to stay on board: The *Chapman* having no poop, looked so unlike an Indiaman, that she was taken for an American, and we poor forlorn creatures set down at once as prisoners. "Why don't you release those women," said they, "We will have nothing to do with you, we know better." We found afterwards that although the preliminaries of peace had been some time signed, no account of the important event had reached this

remote spot.   Captain Walker now proposed proceeding
to Milford Haven to refit, but the indraught, as it is called,
having brought us off Lundy, he changed his resolution
and took a pilot on board for King road, where we anchored
at 7 A. M. on the 7th February 1783.

THE END OF THE FIRST PART.

PART SECOND

CONTAINING AN ABSTRACT OF THE
AUTHOR'S THREE SUBSEQUENT
VOYAGES TO INDIA.

LETTER I.

To Mrs. L.——

BLACKHEATH, 12*th February*, 1815.

My Dear Madam,

 The interest which you are pleased to take in my welfare, and the kind inquiries you make respecting the voyages I have performed since my first memorable one, induce me to offer you a simple statement of facts relative to them; though to accomplish this even in the briefest manner, some circumstances must be revealed which I would rather consign to oblivion, and some wounds must be re-opened, which time has mollified, if not healed.—— The manuscript submitted to your perusal, closes with an account of my arrival in England, and thus ended my first eventful visit to India; a period which according to my own estimation, had comprized a whole life of suffering and anxiety, and dissolved for ever the strongest tie the human heart can form for itself; a period in which physical and moral evils had alike combined to inflict whatever can wound the heart to its inmost core, and destroy that confidence in our fellow creatures, without which the world seems indeed " a howling wilderness," peopled with terrific monsters, each prowling either by violence or fraud for his defenceless prey.

 Happily for me gentler beings had blended in my path their benign influences; my sorrows had been cheered and consoled by many. I was still young, and with buoyant spirits relieved in some degree from their late severe pressure, hailed my native land; yet a sigh of regret would mingle with my joyful anticipations, at quitting the society wherein, though assailed by tempestuous winds and mountainous seas, I had so frequently enjoyed, " The feast of reason and the flow of soul " amidst congenial minds.

For ever blest be the moment when I quitted the *Valentine*; from that circumstance arose a friendship which has constituted one of the sweetest enjoyments of my life, and which still remains unbroken, though my friend and I seldom meet; but her letters are invaluable. Few possess such epistolary talents: they have been my chief solace and consolation in distress; but to proceed: Mrs. Irwin, her little boy and myself went on to town, where a dreadful shock awaited me; my dear mother was no more; the tie to which a daughter most fondly clings was rent asunder; tho' I had still a father and two most affectionate sisters remaining, it was long ere I could justly appreciate their worth, or draw consolation from their society. For nearly a whole year I laboured under very severe indisposition, and incurred great expence for medical attendance, not less than £150. I was several times considered in imminent danger; Mrs. Irwin too was long, after her arrival, affected with the most distressing nervous debility. All this is not to be wondered at, for during the passage from St. Helena, both of us were in an infirm state, and our health had suffered much from the circumstances in which we were placed. It is true we experienced all possible relief from the kindness of those around us, whom we daily beheld subjected to privations and exertions the most trying, yet ever affording us comfort and attention. In each benevolent act Captain Walker was amply assisted by Mr. Gooch, and the Surgeon Mr. Crowfoot, a most worthy and scientific young man, to whose skill I was probably more indebted for the prolongation of a precarious existence, than I was aware of at the time. My health being in some measure restored, I tried various plans in pursuit of independence; but none seemed to promise success; my friends wished me to remain at home; but Calcutta appeared the most likely theatre of exertion; and you cannot wonder that my heart warmed towards a place, where I had met such friendship and generosity, and where so much general encouragement was given to the efforts of respectable individuals. I still bore in mind the offer which had been made to me in Bengal, and determined to pursue this plan; and having become acquainted with a Miss Hicks, a young woman of the strictest integrity, and who possessed many valuable qualifications, I engaged her to accompany me as an assistant. Captain Walker was about to proceed to Bombay, in command of the *Lord Camden*, and offered me a passage on very moderate terms, provided I took charge of four ladies, who wished to have a protectress during the voyage. Being desirous of seeing Bombay, I felt little reluctance to comply, especially as my friend Mr. Gooch held the same station in the *Camden* which he had, so meritoriously filled, in the *Chapman*. The passage to be sure, would be rather circuitous, but in a fine new ship, navigated by persons of whose nautical abilities I had such indubitable proofs, *that* appeared of little moment. The prospect of strengthening my connections in India, influenced me still further. Having therefore arranged my plans on a general ground, allowing for the deviations which in such a case as mine, might be allowed to arise from circumstances, I embarked on the *Lord Camden*, and sailed from the Downs for India, on the 17th March 1784.—Here let me pause for the present; I will soon resume my pen.

I am &c.

E. F.

LETTER II.

To Mrs. L.——

15th February, 1815.

My Dear Madam,

For some days we had rather boisterous weather, but this subsided as we approached the Canary Islands, where (to my great mortification) we did not stop.——On the third of April had a view of the peak of Teneriffe which is said to be 2,000 feet high, perpendicularly. It must have been formerly a considerable Volcano; so lately as the year 1704 there was an irruption from it which did immense damage. On the 10th we passed the Cape de-Verd Islands, but to my regret without touching at any; for curiosity was ever with me a predominant feeling. The Island of Fogo has a Volcano, which sometimes flames out in a terrible manner, and discharges pumice stones to a great distance. The weather at this time was intensely hot, but we had plenty of apples on board, which afforded great refreshment; and soon after they were finished, we spoke a Danish ship, whose captain made the ladies a handsome present of oranges and pine apples. It is not easy for you, my dear madam, to conceive the importance of such accommodations; but those who have been many weeks, perhaps months, shut up in a floating prison, without the power of procuring refreshments which even health demands, will be well aware of their value.——At length the trade winds visited us, " and bore healing on their wings; " we passed the Tropic of Capricorn very pleasantly, but soon afterwards a change took place: such are the vicissitudes of a sea life. I have not yet mentioned the names of the ladies who accompanied me, there were Mrs. Pemberton, and Misses Turner, Bellas, and Fisher, who with Miss Hicks and myself occupied two thirds of the roundhouse; and I note it as rather a singular circumstance, that we were only five times on deck during the passage, which was owing to a previous arrangement between the Captain and me, to guard against imprudent attachments, which are more easily formed than broken; and I am happy to say the plan succeeded to our wish——About this time, Captain Walker fell dangerously ill, but fortunately recovered before the 8th of June, when the birth day of Miss Ludlow, a Bristol lady, who subsequently became Mrs. Walker, was celebrated in high style: all the ship's company had a dinner of fresh provisions, and we sat down to a most sumptuous repast, vegetables and fruit having been provided in England, and salad raised purposely for the occasion.

We were now going at the rate of eight knots an hour, *off* the Cape, with a heavy swell; but the young folks, nevertheless, so earnestly solicited for a dance, that the Captain could not refuse; so all the furniture being removed out of the cuddy, I led off, by particular request; but had only gone down one couple, when a tremendous *lee lurch* put us all in confusion. I declined standing up again, but the rest during three or four hours, tumbled about in the prettiest manner possible, and when no longer able to dance, made themselves amends by singing and laughing; no serious accident happened to any one, and the evening concluded very agreeably.

On the 11th June we struck soundings at 7 A.M. off Cape L'Aguillas, this exactly confirmed Capt. Walker's observations, and was matter of greater rejoicing to me, than can be imagined by persons who were never brought into danger, by the ignorance or inattention of those intrusted with the command. The next day we shipped so many seas from the heavy land-swell, as to extinguish the fire; we were therefore constrained to put up with a cold dinner: however our good Captain, ever provident, produced a fine round of beef, preserved by Hoffmann, which well supplied the deficiency.

On the 24th June, we anchored in the Bay of Johanna, one of the African Isles to the northward of Madagascar. It is a fertile little spot. We here met with plenty of refreshments and very cheap. The oranges are remarkably fine: I took a good quantity of them: their beef is pretty good: Captain Walker purchased several bullocks for the ship's use and to supply our table. The inhabitants are very civil, but are said to be the greatest thieves in existence. We were much amused with the high titles assumed by them. The Prince of Wales honoured us with his company at breakfast, after which Mr. Lewin [45] one of our passengers, took him down to his cabin, where having a number of knick-knacks, he requested his royal highness to make choice of some article to keep in remembrance of him; when to Mr. L's astonishment he fixed on a large mahogany book-case, which occupied one side of the cabin; and on being told that could not be spared, went away in high displeasure, refusing to accept any thing else. The Duke of Buccleugh washed our linen. H.R.H. the Duke of York officiated as boatman, and a boy of fourteen, who sold us some fruit, introduced himself as Earl of Mansfield. They seem very proud of these titles—We all went on shore, and while those who were able to walk, rambled about to view the country, which they described as very delightful, I awaited their return in a thatched building erected for the accommodation of strangers. We were careful to return before sun-set, the night air being reckoned very pernicious to Europeans.—These people are almost constantly at war with those of the adjacent Isles. Being in great want of gunpowder, they prevailed on Captain Walker to give them the quantity that would have been expended in the customary salutes.

On the 2nd July we left Johanna, with a pleasant breeze, but were soon driven back and experienced great fatigue for many days, from a heavy rolling sea, but on the 20th, at day break, we saw Old-woman's Island, and at 11 A.M. cast anchor at Bombay. An alarming accident happened while saluting the Fort; the gunner's mate reloaded one of the guns without having properly cleansed it, in consequence of which he was blown off into the water. Never did I behold a more shocking sight. The poor creature's face was covered with blood, yet he swam like a fish till a boat reached him. Thank God he escaped with some slight hurts, and to my surprize was upon deck next day.

On the 21st we went on shore with Mr. Coggan the Naval store-keeper, who was Miss Turner's brother-in-law. We landed in the dock-yard, where the many fine ships building and repairing with the number of Europeans walking about, almost persuaded me, I was at home, till the dress and dark complexion of the workmen destroyed the pleasing illusion—Mrs. Coggan received me very kindly, and by her hospitable treatment, rendered my stay at Bombay as agreeable as possible. On Saturday the 24th we received a visit from the Governor (Mr. Boddam) which I find is to be considered as a great compliment. We went to church, on the 25th, and in the evening sat up to receive company as also the two following evenings, a tiresome ceremony to me who detest parade and was merely a traveller; but Mrs. Coggan assured me it would be an affront to the settlement if I submitted not to the established custom. The like usage formerly prevailed in Bengal, but is now abolished. On the 29th we went to pay our respects to the Governor at *Perell* his country seat, a delightful place and a charming ride to it. Indeed all the environs are beautiful; in this respect it has greatly the advantage of Calcutta; but the town itself is far inferior. They have a handsome church and a good assembly-room, where they dance all the year round.

We dined one day at Mr. Nesbit's, chief of the Marine, who gave us a repast in the true *old* Indian style. " The tables they groaned with the weight of the feast." We had every joint of a calf on the table at once; nearly half a Bengal sheep; several large dishes of fish; boiled and roasted turkies, a ham, a kid, tongue, fowls, and a long train of et ceteras. The heat was excessive, the hour two, and we were thirty in company, in a lower roomed house, so you may conceive what sensations such a prodigious dinner would produce. It is however a fact that they ate with great appetite and perseverance, to my astonishment, who could scarcely touch a morsel.

On the 1st August, the *Camden* being ordered to Madras without any prospect of proceeding from thence to Bengal, Captain Walker secured a passage for Miss Hicks and myself on the *Nottingham*, Captain Curtis, who offered us the best accommodations and refused to accept of any remuneration. He afterwards disposed of his ship, but under the express stipulation that we should retain our cabin. I dined on the 8th at Mr. D. Scott's with our fellow passengers Mr. and Mrs. Lewin; and a very agreeable day we passed, the whole of the cuddy passengers being invited, so that we sat down once more together, assuredly for the last time. On the 23d I dined with Miss Bellas at her uncle's gardens where I met with a most cordial reception, and was introduced to Captain Christie whom she married before I quitted the settlement; and alas! I must add survived her marriage only thirteen weeks. She died, as I afterwards heard, of a confirmed liver complaint. Her health was very bad during the whole passage; for on the least motion she constantly became sea-sick, and never overcame it: she was a most amiable young woman and generally beloved. I shall ever cherish her memory with affection. On the 25th Captain Curtis introduced the new Commander Captain Ross to me, and made as many apologies for quitting the ship, as if he had been accountable to me for his conduct. " But however " said he " go when you will, I will see you safe on board and clear of the Reef," which is a ridge of rocks at the entrance of Bombay harbour. This promise he performed on the 4th September, when having taken leave of our friends, he accompanied us on board the *Louisa*, for so was the *Nottingham* named in honour of the new owner's wife. He staid until seven in the evening, and then went on shore with the Pilot; first calling up all his late servants, whom he charged to pay me the same attention as if he were present. I shall ever esteem him. Our friendship continued unabated while I remained in India; he afterwards commanded the *Swallow Packet*, and mine was the first and the last house he entered on each voyage: since my return home I have seldom seen him, but that alters not my sentiments.—It was natural that I should quit Bombay with favourable impressions. I had been treated with much kindness and mixed with the first society on the Island: I refer you to other travellers for descriptions, observing only that provisions of all kinds are good, but rather dear, except fish, which is here in high perfection and very plentiful.

On the 15th September we anchored in Anjengo roads, to take in coir rope and cables for which this is the great mart. They are fabricated of the outer rind of the cocoanut, whose quality is such that the salt water nourishes it, and it possesses also an elasticity which enables it to contract or dilate itself, in proportion to the strain on it. This property is peculiarly useful in these seas, where squalls frequently come on with frightful violence and rapidity, and the preservation of an anchor is an object of importance. The surf runs very high here, and is at times extremely dangerous. Captain Ross brought off an invitation from Mr. Hutchinson the chief, to dine with him; but no one chose to venture on shore. I have not forgotten the fate of Mrs. Blomer, who was drowned some years ago with seven others in attempting to land on the beach.

Here is a pretty strong Fort on the sea side. Every one who went on shore spoke with rapture of the country. The vicinity of the great chain of mountains which separates the coast of Malabar from that of Coromandel, and which are said to be the highest in the world, (the Alps and Andes excepted) gives an awful termination to the prospect. The water is here so indifferent that few Europeans attempt to drink it. Formerly Anjengo was famous throughout India for its manufactures of long-cloth and stockings, but these have fallen to decay. We left this dangerous place on the 22nd; the wind several times blew so strong, we had great apprehensions of being driven on shore; and a very narrow escape we certainly had; for on examining the anchor, only one fluke was found remaining; the other must have been so nearly broke by the strain on it, that it would not bear heaving up. Our passage was remarkably tedious, though we had a pleasant man in command, who kept an exceeding good table, but not expecting to be more than five or six weeks at sea, instead of *twelve*, our stock of fresh provisions was quite exhausted long ere we reached Calcutta, and only distilled water to drink. On the 27th November we arrived, and to my great surprise after all that had been said against the probability of such an event taking place, found the *Camden* had been some time in the river. Mr. Baldwin the chief officer died soon after, and my friend Mr. Gooch succeeded him. In this situation he remained for several voyages, with Captain Dance till he obtained the command of the *Lushington*, and I had frequently the pleasure of seeing him during my residence in Bengal. Being now about to enter on a new scene, I will take leave for the present and remain,

Your's &c.
E. F.

LETTER III.

To Mrs. L.——

My dear Madam,

At Calcutta I met with great kindness from many whom I had formerly known, and who now appeared desirous of forwarding any plan, I might adopt. At length with the approbation of Captain Walker, and several other friends, I determined on placing Miss Hicks in business as a milliner. It was agreed that my name should not appear, although I retained in my own hands the entire management of the concern, allowing Miss H. one third of the profits. Mr. Berry purser of the *Camden* had the goodness to open a set of books, and to give me every necessary instruction how to keep them in proper order, which afterwards proved very advantageous in the prosecution of my concerns. You are aware how many difficulties both from within and without must have opposed themselves to this design, and how much even the same feeling operated in contrary directions; at least, if the wish for independence may be termed pride, to which it is certainly allied. Soon after, a proposal was made me to engage in a seminary for young ladies, on so liberal a plan, that I have since frequently, regretted not having complied with the solicitations of my friends; but I had in fact gone rather too far to recede, having made several large purchases, which could not be disposed of suddenly but at considerable loss. Within four months after our arrival, Miss

Hicks married Mr. Lacey; [46] and the following Christmas lay in of a fine boy, but unfortunately lost him at the end of six weeks; after which her health declined so fast, as to render it absolutely necessary that she should proceed to Europe. I took that opportunity of sending home for education, a natural child of my husband's, whose birth had caused me bitter affliction; yet I could not abandon him, though he was deserted by his natural protector. They accordingly embarked on the 5th of September 1786, on the *Severn Packet* Captain Kidd, with every prospect of a favourable passage; but on the 9th, owing to the rapidity of the current, the vessel struck on a sand, called the Broken Ground, just below Ingellee, and every European on board unhappily perished, except the second officer in whose arms the poor little boy expired; but Mrs. Lacey supported herself in the fore chains with exemplary fortitude, till a tremendous sea broke over them, and he saw her no more, but by great exertion reached the shore on a broken spar. I felt her loss severely, for she possessed a mind and spirit that would have graced any station.

After this melancholy event I was compelled to conduct business in my own name, but on a more extensive scale, and succeeded tolerably well, till the unlucky year 1788, when such immense investments were brought out, that nearly all concerned in that branch of commerce, were involved in one common ruin. Yielding to the storm, for I had large consignments which I was compelled to receive, my brother having become security for them at home, I solicited and obtained the indulgence of my creditors for eighteen months under four trustees, Messrs. Fairlie, Colvin, Child, and Moscrop, whose names were sufficient to sanction any Concern; and such was the confidence reposed in my integrity, that every thing remained in my own hands as formerly. Never, I am proud to say, was that confidence abused; pardon the seeming vanity of this assertion; in justice to my own character, I must say thus much, and can boldly appeal to those who are best acquainted with the whole transaction for the truth of my statement. Having received several consignments from my kind friends at home, which sold to great advantage, and various other means suggesting themselves, wherein I was benevolently assisted by many who saw and compassionated my arduous struggles after independence, I succeeded in settling either in money or goods, every claim on me, and again became possessed of a little property; when in the beginning of 1794, anxiety to see my dear friends, led me to resolve on returning once more to Europe. I must here mention what operated as a strong encouragement to prosecute the plan immediately. In May 1791 Mr. Benjamin Lacey brother of my lamented friend's husband came to Bengal, bringing out a small investment for me. I received him into my family, and altho' only nineteen years of age, he evinced such abilities, that I soon obtained a situation for him, where he conducted himself so much to the satisfaction of his employers, as to be intrusted with confidential commissions to Madras and elsewhere, which he executed with judgment and integrity. This young man happening to be in Calcutta, I embraced the opportunity of leaving to him the management of my concerns. As a proof that my confidence was not misplaced, allow me here to notice, that altho' my stock and bills were delivered over to him without inventory, or engagement on his part when I left India, he in the course of *eleven* days after, transmitted regular accounts of the whole, and where placed, making himself answerable for the proceeds in the strongest manner; so that had we both died, my friends would have found no difficulty in claiming my effects. Having by his assistance laid in a small investment, I embarked on the 25th March on board the American ship *Henry*, Captain Jacob Crownin-shield, bound for Ostend; and on the 29th the pilot quitted

us.   I found the *Henry* a snug little vessel, Capt. C. a well
behaved man, and his officers, though not of polished
manners, yet in their way disposed to offer me every
attention that could render the passage agreeable.   I
suffered at times from the heat, but on the whole enjoyed
better health than during my former voyage.   Having only
one passenger on board besides myself, but little occurred
to relieve the monotony of a sea life: I frequently played
chess, and was almost constantly beaten.   Cards and backgammon had their turn, but I grew tired of all; till at
length, on the 2nd July we anchored off St. Helena.

I went on shore in the afternoon and learnt with some
vexation that a large fleet sailed only the day before.   I
wished to have written, specially as we were not bound
direct to England.   Many changes had happened in this
curious little Island, during my twelve years absence.
Few recollected me; but Captain Wall of the *Buccleugh*
formerly chief officer of the *Valentine*, behaved with the
greatest attention,—I shall ever acknowledge his kindness.
Fresh provisions were very scarce, a drought had prevailed
until this season for four years, and it would require three
good seasons to repair the damage sustained, by their stock
perishing for want of water—A circumstance happened
during our stay, the like of which was not remembered by
the oldest inhabitant, though from the appearance of the
place, one would conclude such events were common: a
large fragment of rock, detached by the moisture, fell from
the side of Ladder Hill, on a small out-house at the upper
end of the valley; in which two men were sleeping in
separate beds.   The stone broke thro' the top and lodged
between them, the master of the house was suffocated, it is
supposed, by the rubbish, as no bruises were found on his
body; the other man forced his way through, and gave the
alarm, but not time enough to save his companion.   This
accident has caused many to tremble for their safety, since

all the way up the valley, houses are built under similar
projections, and will some time or other probably experience
the same fate. Among the Alps such things are common.
An unpleasant affair also occurred to me. I had, when
last here, given a girl who had attended me from Calcutta,
and behaved very ill, to Mrs. Mason, with whom I boarded,
under a promise that she should not be sold, consequently
no slave paper passed. Mr. Mason, however, in defiance
of this prohibition, disposed of her for £10. This act
militating against the established regulations, advantage
was taken of my return to the Island, to call upon me as
the original offender, not only for that sum, but a demand
was made of £60 more, to pay the woman's passage back to
Bengal with her two children! ! ! After every effort, I
could only obtain a mitigation of £10, being forced to draw
on my brother Preston at sixty days sight in favour of the
Court of Directors, for £60, a sum that I could ill afford to
lose, but the strong hand of power left me no alternative.[47]
On the 6th July we quitted St. Helena, and on the 11th
anchored off Ascension. Our Captain and the gentlemen
went on shore to look at the Island. The following
remarks I extract from his journal. " The soil near the
sea, appears dry and barren in the extreme, like cinders
from a fire; indeed the whole Island bears evident marks
of the former existence of volcanoes, several craters still
appearing on the hills; perhaps it owes its origin to some
great convulsion of nature, as I am persuaded does St.
Helena: altho' the sea coast presents a dreary view, yet
on walking farther the prospect becomes enchanting; a
most delightful verdure covers the *smaller* hills, and the
vallies; and no doubt they afford plenty of water, tho'
not being very well, I was too much fatigued to examine.
The 2nd officer saw five or six goats, but could not get
near enough to fire at them."

Numbers of man-of-war birds and eggs were taken,

which proved to be good eating; they likewise caught the finest turtle I ever saw, weighing near 400lbs., but by an act of unpardonable negligence in people so situated, it was suffered to walk overboard in the night. We had however the good luck to catch a fine albercuore which weighed near 100lbs., its flesh when roasted resembled veal; we were fortunate in having an excellent cook on board, who really made the most of our scanty provisions. On the 3rd of August, three large ships hove in sight, one of which bore down towards us and fired several guns to bring us to. They sent a boat on board with orders for our Captain to attend the commander; he came back, to our great joy, in about half an hour, having been treated with much civility by the French Captain. It was now we heard the distressing news of Ostend being in the hands of the French; indeed they boasted of having gained the advantage every where, except in the West Indies.—These were three frigates mounting from 28 to 32 guns, they had been 20 days, from Brest and had taken 22 prizes. We had been assured by Captain Wall, that the French dared not shew their *noses* in the channel, but I with sorrow now witnessed the contrary, not on my own account, being safe enough on board an American; but Captain C. informed me, there were more than 200 English prisoners on board those ships.—He now acquainted me with his determination to proceed to America, and very politely offered me a passage, that I might witness the disposal of my property, which I of course declined, not feeling the least desire to prolong my voyage. So having arranged my affairs in the best manner possible under existing circumstances, I took a final leave of the *Henry* on the 4th September, and landed with my baggage at Cowes in the Isle of Wight.—From this place I soon reached London; pleased as I went, to behold scenes from which I had been so many years banished, and anticipating the delight with which my dear father would receive his long absent child. Alas! I was doomed to behold him no more. He expired only four months before my arrival—The remainder of my family I had the happiness of finding in perfect health—The property sent to America came to a tolerable market, but Captain Crowninshield instead of making the returns in cash, sent a ship called the *Minerva*, with his younger brother Richard Crowninshield in command of her, which ship it was proposed that I should take out to India under certain conditions. She was a fine new vessel of about 300 tons burthen; I had her coppered, and proposed her first making a voyage to America, and on her return sailing for Bengal about Christmas: But when completely fitted for sea, with a *picked* cargo on board for Boston, she took fire by the bursting of a bottle of aquafortis, which had been negligently stowed among other goods, and though immediately scuttled and every precaution taken, sustained material damage. This involved me in a series of misfortunes. Mr. P. Wynne who had shipped to the amount of £428 on the *Minerva*, by mere accident discovered that, contrary to the general opinion, the Captain was responsible for all goods committed to his charge under regular bills of lading; and accordingly commenced an action against him, in which he was successful, the whole debt and costs near £600 falling on the Captain, and from his inability, on me: this decision caused a change in the tenor of bills of lading, which now contain clauses against fire and several other casualties, whereas before "the dangers of the seas" were alone excepted. Thus did my loss operate to the advantage of others. To prevent the total wreck of my little property, I was compelled to proceed immediately on the original plan, as affording the only chance of attaining independence, and ultimately securing a home in my native country.

Having resolved never again to travel alone, I engaged a Miss Tripler as a companion, for two years, at £30 per annum; but had soon cause to regret the agreement. A proposal being made by my dearest friend Mrs. Irwin to take out a young lady, who had been educated in England, and was going to rejoin her friends in Bengal, I felt no disposition to refuse, having frequently seen Miss Rogers and knowing her to be a most amiable little girl; besides as I had a piano-forte, and a pair of globes with me, and a good collection of books, I was pleased with the idea of contributing to *her* improvement, and amusing myself at the same time—The ship being obliged to touch at Guernsey, I determined to join her there; so, on the 17th July she sailed for that place. Miss Tripler and my Bengal servant proceeding on her, as the most saving plan. Here let me pause, reserving the account of my third voyage for another letter.

I remain truly your's
E. F.

LETTER IV.

To Mrs. L.——

BLACKHEATH, 24*th February*, 1815.

My Dear Madam,

On Sunday the 2nd August 1795 at 5 A.M. Miss Rogers and myself, accompanied by Captain Richard Crowninshield quitted London for Southampton, from whence the packets sail for Guernsey. I did not leave my sister and nieces without deep regret; they were *always* very dear to me, but now, having lost my parents, the tie was drawn still closer; abstracted from this consideration, I rather rejoiced at quitting England, as the whole time of my stay had been imbittered by a succession of losses and disappointments, arising partly from my individual misfortune respecting the ship, and partly from the general state of commerce at this inauspicious period. Alas! in the number of wretched Emigrants whom I saw crowding the port of Southampton, I felt that I had but too many fellow-sufferers, and it was easy to read in many a sorrowful countenance that, " the times were out of joint."

On arriving there, we were advised to go on by land to Lymington, and embark from thence; this gave me an opportunity of passing a few hours at Newtown Park, a short mile from *Lymington*, the residence of Mrs. Irwin's sister Mrs. P—n. The house and grounds are strikingly beautiful, and an Observatory at the top of the former, commands an extensive view over the Isle of Wight, and great part of the channel; and Mrs. P.—n assured me, that not long before, she saw from thence near four hundred vessels sail together. The wind becoming fair, we embarked on the 5th August, and next evening safely reached the *Minerva* at Guernsey. We found all on board greatly fatigued, the ship having arrived only the night before, after a most harrassing passage of eighteen days. What an escape we had! On the 8th we went on shore; passed through the market, which appears to be well supplied, particularly with fruit, vegetables, poultry, and butter; we took a quantity of the latter, which lasted perfectly good all the way out. I was pleased with the market people, they were so remarkably clean and civil. The women wore bonnets with enormous stiffened crowns, underneath which, they had becoming laced mobs. Provisions are in general good and cheap; the fish excellent; such delicious soles I never tasted any where. We went to church and heard prayers both in French and English; a dialect of the former prevails here, but it is a vile jargon, I could scarcely understand one word in ten. This must be a very healthy place; I saw here a lady who, at the age of ninety-four, had full possession of her faculties, and I heard there were several others on the island nearly of the same age. Mr. Tupper, a gentleman to whom I had a letter, was in his 76th year; he and his whole family paid Miss Rogers and myself the greatest attention. I was surprised to see the magnificent style in which their house was fitted up, the drawing room stove was of silver, the curtains rich silk, with gilt cornices; the chimney piece cost eighty pounds, and every other article corresponding; but even these were trifling, when compared with the many capital paintings and valuable prints which adorned every room in the house. I afterwards found that the prevailing taste with the wealthy here, is for expensive houses; for the roads are so bad and steep, that single horse chaises are the only carriages in use. On the 17th August, Mr. J. Tupper came by appointment to shew us the Island, of which we made almost the tour. The lands are highly cultivated, but such roads I never saw; they are barely wide enough to admit a chaise; fortunately we met only one, which backed for us to pass. I admire the exact manner in which the hedges are kept, they add great beauty to the prospect. I have seldom seen more picturesque views; the land and sea vallies are particularly striking. Their parties, though elegant, are by no means expensive; for liquors are duty free, and the best wines do not cost more than 16s. per dozen, except claret, which is at from 25 to 28s. The hospitality with which we were all treated by this worthy family, excited the most grateful emotions; and I bade them adieu with sincere regret.

I am yours truly,
E. F.

LETTER V.

My dear Madam,

We were a pretty large party on board; Mr.
Campbell, fresh from the Highlands of Scotland, on whom
the officers were continually playing their jokes; Mr.
Smith, a youth going to the Madeiras, and Mr. Regail,
who was one of the most interesting young men I ever
met with: his manners were elegant, his mind highly
polished, and his disposition placid and benevolent; but
he appeared bending beneath a deep dejection; he never
joined in conversation, if it were gay; he ate no more than
barely sufficed nature, and tho' from politeness and native
suavity, he never refused to join our evening parties at cards,
yet his depression was visible even in the moments of
amusement. He had been brought up in Russia, and had,
for his age (which could not be more than 24) seen much
of the world, and evidently mixed in the first society, and
I apprehend some singular blight had happened in his
fortunes.

On the 7th September we landed at Funchall, the
Capital of Madeira. I was exceedingly delighted with our
approach to the Island: the town is built on rising ground,
and as you draw near to it, appears imposing and magnificent, having several churches and convents. Behind the
town the ground rises abruptly into steep hills, covered with
vineyards, and ornamented with pleasure houses, at once
exhibiting the appearance of prosperity and cultivation, and

the charms of picturesque and romantic scenery.—A Mr. L.— to whom I had letters, went with us to a Hotel; for unfortunately his lady being in England, he could not entertain us at his own house. Living in this manner was very expensive and disagreeable also, we paid 5s. each for dinner, exclusive of wine; and neither the waiter, nor any other servant, understood a word of English, or any other language we could speak. It was only with the landlady we could have any communication. We found Funchall much less beautiful than its first appearance promised; the streets were ill paved, narrow, dirty and solitary; but the great church is a handsome building, and the hospital a very excellent one, before which is a fine fountain, which is always a refreshing sight in a country like this. The American Consul visited us the next morning, and invited us to his country house, for which we sat out at 5 o'clock. Miss R—s and I were in silk net hammocks, slung upon poles, and each carried by two men, who went at a great rate, considering the road lay up a steep hill; this is the only mode of conveyance, except riding on horse back, as no wheel carriages can be used in a country so hilly—They employ a kind of dray or sledge drawn by oxen to transport goods.

We found a large party assembled; the lady of the house, a pleasant Irish gentlewoman, had all the frankness and hospitality of her country, and with her husband, a most amiable and companionable man, made us quickly forget we were strangers. Even the Portuguese ladies, seemed familiar with us, tho' unluckily we could not converse with them. We had a ball at night, but the weather being too warm for dancing, we exchanged it for whist. I cannot help observing here, how frequently people who travel, will find an advantage in knowing some thing of this game, as they may sit down with persons of different nations and languages and enjoy with them an amusement, that for the time, admits of an interchange of ideas and facilitates good-will, even where conversation is denied. We sat down above thirty to an elegant supper; the grapes I found delicious here, but the season for other fruits was over. The vineyards are tended with unusual care; the grapes of which wine is made, are not suffered to ripen in the sun, which they told me is the reason of the superior flavour in Madeira wine. The Consul's house was most delightfully situated; it overlooked the whole town of Funchall, the surrounding country, and the wide spreading ocean; it had a beautiful garden, which produced abundance of peaches, apricots, quinces, apples, pears, walnuts, bananas, guavas, and pine-apples, and behind rose a fine grove of pine trees. I quitted this paradise with regret, and found my ride down-hill very fatiguing and disagreeable.

We staid here till the 21st, and by means of our first friend, spent several pleasant days, and gay evenings, but the weather was so intolerably hot, and the travelling so disagreeable, that if I had not been detained by business, I would much rather have passed my time on board. One day we went with the American Consul to visit a Convent of Ursulines; we found the Chapel door open, but were not suffered to pass the threshold: the nuns were very chatty, and like most ignorant persons, exceedingly curious, asking a hundred ridiculous questions. How very differently do human beings pass the time allotted them in this probationary existence! Surely, to consume it in supine indolence or " vain repetitions " can never render us more acceptable to Him, who is the fountain of light and knowledge. We ate some preserved peaches with them, which the Consul paid for, and then took our leave; but were forced to submit to a salute from the sisters, which we would gladly have dispensed with, for they all took an enormous quantity of snuff. These are the only nuns I ever saw who do not conceal their hair. On leaving these pious ladies, we went to Golgotha, or the chapel of skulls, (as it is called) being entirely lined with skulls and other human bones. What an idea!

We drank tea the same day, with Signor Esmerado, whose large house and extensive grounds once belonged to the Jesuits. This is one of the richest families in the Island; the display of plate surprised me; the tea tray was the largest I ever saw, and of massive silver; wine and sweetmeats, were served in the same costly style. After tea there were several minuets danced; they with difficulty suffered us to depart, and were the means of introducing us to another pleasant evening party, where the lady of the house played remarkably well on the piano-forte, and sung in a style of superior excellence.

One day we went on horse-back, to visit the church of Nossa Senhora de la Monte, (our Lady of the Mount) about three miles from Funchall, upon a very high ground which must have cost a large sum in building. The ascent to it, is at least by a hundred steps. The church is not large, but richly ornamented: there is a wonder-working image of the virgin, in a chrystal shrine, very small, not more than two feet high, it looks exactly like a doll; but her little ladyship, however insignificant her appearance, had more votaries than any other saint on the Island. Here we saw some paintings, which considered as the work of a self-taught Genius, (and I was assured this was a fact) had extraordinary merit. In this little excursion, I was surprised to see the diversity of climate exhibited in a short distance; the vintage was over, below; while the grapes around us were like bullets, and I am told they never completely ripen; we observed the same effect in Mr. Murray's plantation, half a mile lower. This gentleman, who was the English Consul, had laid out above £20,000 in improving a spot, which after all, will never bring any thing to maturity; yet it is a most charming place; there are three ranges of gardens, one

above another, the lower are very large and well laid out, on
a level, artificially formed, in the midst of which stands a
good house, but not sufficiently elegant to correspond with
such extensive grounds.   In these are several reservoirs,
containing gold and silver fish, which are supplied with
water by small cascades, as as to be kept constantly full:
Nor are Mr. Murray's improvements confined to his own
estate; the road up to the mount and the wall which
secures it, with many fountains, conduits, and reservoirs,
were made by him.   He has also opened many cross-paths,
winding round the hill in the prettiest manner imaginable,
with stone seats, and alcoves, to rest on from time to time;
and has planted the hollows with chestnut trees, entirely at
his own expence.   Poor man! he had been obliged by ill
health to abandon his little paradise, and was at this time
in Lisbon.   We afterwards called upon the British Vice-
Consul Mr. C——k, at his country seat, which was remarkable for its extensive prospect; we thought him and
Mrs. C. very good kind of people, but were surprized to
find that altho' the latter was English, she had resided
abroad from infancy, and knew scarcely a hundred words
of her native language.

Altho' we were certainly treated with much kindness
and hospitality at this place, yet were we assured, that the
inhabitants had little enjoyment of society with each other;
that being all engaged in one line of merchandize, the
pursuits of interest, were found to jar with those of good-
fellowship; and that on the whole, Madeira was an unpleasant residence, except to the sick, and the way-faring.

I am yours truly
E. F.

LETTER VI.

To Mrs. L——.

MY DEAR MADAM,

We were much tossed by the equinoctial gales on quitting Madeira, as might be expected; but on the 23rd September we obtained a sight of the peak of Teneriffe: all that day we kept standing in for the land, but to little purpose, as the mountains are too high to admit of approach, except in a calm. On the 26th we cast anchor in the road of Oratavia: the visit-boat came out, and as soon as our bill of health had been examined, the Captain was permitted to go on shore. I sent by him a letter which, Mr. P—— the American Consul at Madeira, had given me, and received in reply a most cordial invitation from Mr. and Mrs. Barry for Miss Rogers and myself, to take up our abode with them during our stay with which we thankfully complied in the evening. The appearance of this country, pleased me much better than Madeira, as it is more culti-vated and better inhabited: the city of Oratavia constitutes a fine feature in the beautiful scene. We were received most kindly by the worthy couple who invited us, and at whose house we met with the best society in the Island. I greatly prefer the Spanish ladies to the Portuguese, finding them more easy in their manners, and much better educated. Many spoke French and Italian with facility, and several had been so connected with the English, as to

have attained enough of the language, to be tolerably
intelligible in it: their persons were pleasing, and some
would have been really handsome, but for the presence of
Mrs. Barry, who altho' in her thirty-fourth year, I thought
the most beautiful woman I ever beheld. She was in
England just before Sir Joshua Reynold's death, and he
declared repeatedly, that would his health permit him ever
to take another picture, it should be Mrs. Barry's. Her
height was commanding, with just enough of the *enbonpoint*
to be agreeable. Dimples have been called " the first of
the graces." I never saw a countenance display more of
them; her smile was perfectly fascinating.

I was disappointed in my intention of ascending the
Peak of Teneriffe, the season being too far advanced; and
I was assured by many, that I was quite unequal at any
time to have endured the fatigue. After travelling 15 miles
over loose stones and rugged ascents, you find yourself still
at the foot of the Peak; here it is necessary to remain till
two in the morning, when the task of clambering begins,
over pumice stone and ashoo, and should you reach the
top by sunrise, you may esteem yourself very fortunate:
four hours are generally allowed for the ascent, and after
all, should the Peak be enveloped in clouds, which is
frequently the case, you have your labour for your pains;
but on a clear day the view is truly sublime; you can
distinctly see the seven Canary Islands; some assert that
both the Continent of Africa and the Island of Madeira
have been seen from hence; but I cannot suppose the
human vision capable of extending so far, tho' I do not
doubt that both places are comprehended within the
immense horizon such a prodigious height may command.
Having heard a very good account of Santa Cruz, which is
between 20 and 30 miles across the Island, we determined
to visit it, little aware of the roads we must encounter.
Ladies here travel on Asses, on which are placed a sort of

armed chair, with cushions and a foot-stool; this plan
appeared to be easy, but we soon found that the roads at
Madeira, were bowling greens compared to these; how the
poor animals that bore us, contrived to keep their legs,
clambering over the rocks that from time to time had
fallen in the path, I know not; the shocks they gave me I
shall never forget.   Mr. Barry had provided a cold turkey,
wine &c. for a repast, and when ready for it, we went into
a peasant's cottage, and dined comfortably, endeavouring
to laugh away our fears and fatigues; the remains of our
meal afforded a feast to the peasants, who live in a most
wretched style, seldom tasting either meat, eggs, or milk:
the mother of the mistress of the cottage was near eighty,
and to see, with what eagerness the poor old creature
watched every morsel we put into our mouths, was really
affecting.   Notwithstanding their coarse fare, the common
people here, are a stout, hardy race; fair complexioned,
well featured, and remarkably lively, as we found by our
attendants, for as each animal has a man to guide it, we
were almost stunned by their incessant chatter.   Soon after
dinner, we renewed our journey; my animal fell down, but
I was not hurt, and for the next five miles, our road was
easy, and lay over a delightful plain which brought us to
the ancient city of Laguna, the Capital of the Island, which
is tolerably large, well inhabited, and has two good churches,
with several convents; from thence the road to Santa Cruz
lay entirely on the descent, over large stones and fragments
of rock.   The jumbling was horrible, and *pour surcroit de
malheur*, so strong a wind blew from the sea, that my whole
strength was scarce sufficient to hold my umbrella; yet I
did not dare give it up, the rays of the sun were so powerful, and the reflection from the stones intolerable.   I was
at one time so exhausted, that I declared I must give up the
journey, but the creature I rode, carried me on in spite of
me, and stopped not until we arrived at the house of Mr.

R——y in Santa Cruz, who gave us all a hearty welcome. This gentleman lived in a most delightful situation fronting the Mole, where notwithstanding our fatigue, we walked in the evening, when our good host got tipsy for joy, and with great difficulty allowed *us* to retire.   Alas! weary as we were, the musquitoes would scarcely permit us to sleep; my companion suffered terribly from them.

Santa Cruz is indeed a fine place, and the country around, well deserves the pen of Mrs. Ratcliffe to celebrate its cloud-capt mountains, vallies teeming with abundance, that in the language of Holy Writ, seemed to " Laugh and sing " beneath the eye of their majestic mountains; and here to render every *coup d'oeil* complete, the vast Atlantic occupies the front, and offers its immense world of waters to our contemplation.

The most curious, perhaps I ought to say the most *interesting* circumstance that happened to me in this expedition, was the violent passion our kind entertainer conceived for me, and which was certainly opened in a manner perfectly new.   " My *dare* soul, what shall I do to *plase* you?   Is it fifty pipes of wine you would like? but why will I talk of wine? you shall have my house, my garden, all I have in the world! at nine o'clock to-morrow I will resign every thing up to you, and by J——s if you'll consent to marry me, I'll be drunk every day of my life just for joy."   Irresistible as the last argument was, my heart of adamant withstood it.   Poor R——y! never did a kinder heart, a more generous spirit exist, and but for a fault which indeed proceeded really from the warmth of his heart, he would have been a most agreeable companion; he was beloved by every one.   Poor man! let me here close his history, by recording that he was since killed by a shot in the streets of Santa Cruz, at the time of Lord Nelson's attack against it.   We returned soon after this declaration, and found the road present objects of new beauty, because we were a little more at ease in our con-veyance, from habit.—We found a new guest with Mrs. Barry, a Mr. Edwards, who was just arrived from Turkey and attended by a native of that country; he was completely a citizen of the world, held a commission in the service of the Grand Signior, had been every where, and seen every thing; he was elegant, accomplished, and every way agree-able. Our fellow voyager Mr. Campbell, during all the time we were at Teneriffe, continued the butt of the Captain's jokes, in which others were too ready to join him; on our return, they persuaded him that his legs were swelled, which was ever the precursor of mortal disease in the Island, and the poor fellow submitted to be swathed in flannel, and dosed with every nauseous mess they gave him, with the utmost patience, until Mr. Barry's good nature released the victim, who was to be sure the most ignorant creature in the ways of the world, I ever met with.

I cannot omit to mention, that when we left Santa Cruz, one of Mr. B.'s servants walked over from Oratavia that morning, and returned with us apparently without fatigue, as he laughed and talked all the way home, tho' the real distance was fifty miles, and the badness of the roads of course rendered the exertion much greater, but I was assured this was not remarkable.

On the 6th October after breakfast, we took leave of our kind hosts: and here instead of putting on a semblance of concern, I was obliged to stifle my actual emotions, lest they should appear affected. I never recollect being equally moved at a separation, after so short an acquaint-ance. But Mrs. Barry is so truly amiable, and we were treated with such generous hospitality by both parties, that it seemed more like a parting between near relations, than casual acquaintances. Since then Oceans have rolled be-tween us, and time and sorrow have combined to efface the traces of recollection in my mind of a variety of circumstances; yet every thing I then saw and enjoyed, is still fresh in my memory.   Adieu, my dear madam, for a while: believe me

Yours truly
E. F.

LETTER VII.

To Mrs. L.——.

My dear Madam,

On the 7th October 1795, we set sail from Oratavia with a fair wind, and as it continued, I was sorry we were obliged to stop at St. Iago, where we anchored, on the 13th, in Port Praya Bay. This Bay makes a noble appearance; the surrounding hills rising like an amphitheatre from the sea. The next morning we went on shore about eight o'clock, but were excessively incommoded by the sun, which in these climates rises very rapidly when once above the horizon. Signor Basto the Commandant of the Island, received us very politely, and most of the principal inhabitants came out to pay their respects to, and gaze at, the strangers; among the rest a tall Negro priest, whose shaven crown had a strange appearance. Signor B. led us to a summer house which he had built for the sake of *coolness*, and where there was indeed wind; but the air from a brick-kiln would have been equally pleasant and refreshing; while the glare was insupportable, as the place was open on all sides; fortunately I had brought a pack of cards, so to whist we sat, and his Excellency the Governor joined us, and did us the honour to play several rubbers; and as he spoke neither English nor French, I know not how we could have amused each other better, as I have observed before. An elegant dinner was provided for us, at which I was obliged to preside. In the evening we walked out to see the country, which is well cultivated and highly picturesque; but the inhabitants make a wretched appearance, generally living in huts, even when they are rich. The sugar-cane raised here is remarkably strong; they have also very good cotton, which they manufacture into a pretty kind of cloth; but it is very dear, and exceedingly narrow, being only about a quarter wide. After tea we returned on board, tho' Signor Basto offered to accommodate us with a house to ourselves; but as it is considered dangerous to sleep on shore, we declined his offer, and bade him adieu with many thanks for his civilities. In the course of the day we learned, that this place is so unhealthy, that out of twenty who land here, fifteen generally die within six months. What a pity! every production of warm countries thrives here in abundance, but Man, who cultivates them, sickens and dies.

Our Captain here laid in a stock for a long voyage, and we set sail with a pleasant gale; the day following we caught a fine dolphin; I never saw any thing so beautiful as the colours it displayed when dying. On the 29th October we crossed the Line, and again poor Mr. Campbell was the butt of the party; he had been taught to expect a great shock on passing it, and really stepped forward to look at it, but the boatswain, who was his countryman, advised him to keep aloof; he however declared very seriously that, " he felt a very great shock, he must say, at the time." Nothing further occurred worthy of notice till our arrival at Madras, which took place on the 25th January 1796. I found this town much improved since my former visit, and was particularly pleased with the Exchange, which is a noble building, ornamented with whole length pictures of Lord Cornwallis, Sir Eyre Coote, and General Meadows. The Theatre and Pantheon, where the assemblies are held, are three miles from Madras. At this place we parted with poor Mr. Campbell. I shall never forget the agony of tears

I one day found him in. " What is the matter " said I.
" Miss Rogers is going away and I am *here*," answered he;
the words were very comprehensive; many young people
will be aware that they express love and misery in the
extreme. Poor Mr. C— must mourn in vain, for alas!
" his love met no return."

On the 6th February we again set sail, and were fortunately but little annoyed by the surf. On the 22nd we
reached Fulta, where the pilot being over-anxious to get
forward, made sail at night, when the soundings suddenly
shallowing he found it necessary to cast anchor, tho' not
quite early enough, for in swinging round the ship struck.
At first she lay easy, having made a bed in the sand, but
when the tide came in, she heeled terribly, and it was the
opinion of most on board, that she would never be got off.
The chief officer advised us to secure whatever valuables we
had, about our own persons, for fear of the worst; (which
precaution I had already taken) and used all possible means
for the preservation of the vessel himself. Happily the
rising tide floated her off.—You cannot judge of the acuteness of my feelings on this occasion; to see all my hopes
and cares frustrated; and the quick transition from sorrow
and disappointment on seeing the ship afloat again, without
having sustained the least injury, can only be imagined, by
those who have experienced such changes.

On Wednesday the 24th February we reached Calcutta
in safety, where we remained several months. Here we
found a resting place after a long voyage, diversified by
many pleasant and perilous occurrences, and here therefore
I shall make a pause in the narrative.

> I remain,
> My dear Madam,
> Yours truly,
> E. F.

LETTER VIII.

To Mrs. L——.

BLACKHEATH, *3rd March*, 1815.

My dear Madam,

On Wednesday the 24th February 1796 (as I mentioned in the conclusion of my last letter) my feet once more pressed the ground of Calcutta. Miss Rogers, Miss Tripler, and myself, went directly to a large house which Mr. Benjamin Lacey had taken for us by my desire. We procured a freight for the *Minerva* and sent her off, within a month after her arrival. The ship had been detained so long on her passage from various causes, that our goods came to a very bad market; we were compelled therefore to sell part by retail, and dispose of the remainder by auction. A small copper bottomed ship called the *Rosalia*, a very fast sailer, was purchased, and the command given to Capt. Robinson, an American, who came out with us, and on the 26th of August following, I embarked on her, with Mr. Benjamin Lacey and Miss Tripler, for the United States, after bidding a painful adieu to my dear young friend and companion Miss Rogers, whose place Miss Tripler had neither inclination nor ability to supply; but having fettered myself by an engagement, I was forced to submit; besides I could not well have proceeded alone.—We set sail with a fair wind, but a very strong current running astern. On the night of the 29th the water broke with such violence against the ship, that I called for dead-lights, but was assured by the Captain that there was not the *least* occasion for them; loth to be thought cowardly or an ignorant sailor, I instantly gave up the point, but had great reason to lament my acquiescence: in less than a quarter of an hour, a most tremendous sea broke in at the starboard side of the cabin, and half filled it with water, which soaked a bale of valuable muslins, with me their unfortunate owner. On this the pilot bawled out, that if the dead-lights were not put up instantly, he would cut cable and get under weigh; so at length they were fixed.—In the morning we had the additional mortification to find, that the ship had sprung a leak, and what was worse than all, that she appeared generally too weak to support the voyage; but as it would have been wrong to give her up without a trial, we proceeded with the tide to Ingillee, in the faint hope of the leak closing.— On the 30th we reached the lower buoy of the Barabulla. Our leak still continuing to increase, on the 1st September we were obliged to put back for Calcutta. In the evening of the 4th, we anchored off Cooly Bazar, and the next day went on shore at Calcutta, where the *Rosalia* was examined, and pronounced totally unfit for the voyage.

On the 11th September I went on board the *Swallow Packet* with Captain Simson, who was a Guinea pig (as it is called) on board the *Camden* when I came out in 1784. He has been a very fortunate young man, so early in life to obtain a command. We had a very elegant repast or Tiffin, and I must say, Captain S. seemed heartily glad to receive his old shipmate. Mr. L— and Miss T— having accompanied me, the former was suddenly taken ill with an ague and fever: this added to the fatigue, loss, and disappointment, I had so lately endured, was very near too much for me. I brought him back, procured the best advice for him, and in a few days he was relieved; but before he was able to crawl out, I was in the same situation with a similar intermittent, but escaped the cold fit: I was exceedingly reduced but restored by the free use of bark, and other prescriptions from Dr. Hare, who never failed to relieve me.[48]

On the 22nd October Mr. Lacey engaged for our freight and passage, on board the *Hero*, Captain Jackson, bound to New York, to sail between the first and the tenth of December. As soon as my strength returned, I bustled about my business, endeavoured to repair my losses, visited my friends, and bade them farewell, and every necessary preparation being completed, on the 18th of December we went on board at Garden Reach, and reached Culpee the 22nd, after a tedious passage, kedging all the way. Here we went on shore, and laid in provisions. On Christmas day we anchored off Kedgeree. On New Year's day we got under weigh; but unfortunately the wind failed us; and at six in the evening, the Pilot received instructions not to take us out till further orders. This was a sad beginning of the New Year; the embargo lasted 18 days, after which we proceeded, though very slowly, and on the 30th arrived at Vizagapatam, where we ran some risk from the *Hero* being mistaken for a French Frigate. On the Captain's going on shore, I sent a letter from my good friend Mrs. Child, to Captain Hodson, who returned me a pressing invitation, and the next day I found him on the beach with four palanquins for me and my friends. We proceeded to Waltair, where Mrs. Hodson, Mrs. Child's sister, gave us a most cordial reception, and insisted on our staying till the ship was ready to sail. The next morning I breakfasted with Captain Pitman, one of the most elegant young men I ever saw. He obligingly drove me in his Curricle round Waltair, and shewed me Sardinia Bay, and several other spots remarkable for their beauty.

His own house was charmingly situated on a hill, half way between Vizagapatam and Waltair. Land here is considered of so little value, that every person who built, took in as much as he could employ.

To one whose eye has been fatigued with viewing the flat country of Bengal, this place appears delightful, but yet diversified prospects do not repay the want of fertile plains. Here I bought some beautiful sandal-wood and ivory boxes, for which this place is famous.   Captain and Mrs. Hodson behaved to us with unbounded kindness.   In the evening we quitted Vizagapatam.   The town makes an agreeable appearance from the sea, not unlike St. James Valley in St. Helena.   All who can afford it, live at Waltair, which however does not contain above ten houses.

On Friday the 24th February I once more landed on Madras Beach, and the day following saw many of my friends; among others Captain Gooch, who looked remarkably well: there is nothing more pleasant than to meet unexpectedly an old friend, after a long absence and in a foreign country.   He dined with us, and every one was charmed with his behaviour, so different from many who on getting into commands, fancy that insolence establishes superiority.

On the 27th we dined at St. Thomé, with Mr. Stevens, Mr. B. Lacey's agent; in the evening we sat down to vingt-un, at a rupee a fish, which Mr. S. assured us was very low. I lost only two dozen.   We rose from the card table at half past eleven, and for the honour of Madras hospitality, were suffered to get into our palanquins at that time of night, without the offer of a glass of wine to support us during a four miles' jumble, or a shawl to keep us from the damp air.

On the 2nd of March Captain Gooch paid us a farewell visit: I was a good deal affected at parting; how many thousand miles had each to traverse before we met again! At 5 P. M. we left Madras; there was scarce any surf, but the sea ran high.   I found every thing very dear here, consequently made few purchases.

On the 4th of March we got under weigh at day break,

and set sail for a new country, towards which I now looked with eager expectation. On the 15th I had the misfortune to fall into the after-hold, which opens into the great cabin; the steward having carelessly left the scuttle open, while he went for a candle. I was taken up senseless, having received a severe blow on the head and many bruises, but thank heaven, no material injury. There was a large open case of empty bottles under the opening, and had I fallen the other way, I must have gone directly on it; judge what the consequences must have been.

About the 20th we began to be troubled with calms and southerly winds, when our Captain politely accused Miss Tripler and me of being two Jonahs, saying he never knew a good voyage made, where a Woman or a Parson was on board. I had a very agreeable revenge, for that very afternoon a breeze sprung up, which proved to be the trade wind, and for some time we enjoyed a fine run; but the ship was the most uneasy I ever sailed in, rolling and pitching on every occasion. On the 23rd of April a violent gale came on, and for several days we had very unpleasant weather. I was in great fear of the passage round the Cape, and we were all in trouble, as provisions ran very short: all our wine and spirits were expended, and we had neither butter, cheese, nor coffee remaining. On the 18th of May we arrived off False Bay, and on the 20th at noon, Mr. D. Trail the Harbour-Master came on board, and we cast anchor soon after. Mr. Lacey wrote to Lord Macartney for leave to proceed to Cape Town, as without his permission no passengers are suffered to land. We received a visit from Mr. Gooch First Lieutenant of the *Jupiter*, an elder brother of Captain Gooch, of whose arrival at Madras we brought the first news. I called by invitation on Captain Linzee to look at the *Dort* late Admiral De Lucas' ship. Captain L. has been three years a Post Captain, tho' not yet four and twenty. When in command of the *Nemesis*, he cut out two French vessels from some Mahomedan Port in the Mediterranean, and was afterwards taken himself. He but just saved his distance now, for hearing at Cape Town on his arrival ten days ago, that the *Dort* was under sailing orders, he sat off on horse-back, and arrived but twelve hours before she was to have sailed. Mr. Gooch brought Mrs. Losack the wife of the Captain of the *Jupiter*, to visit me, and they took us with them on board that ship, where we drank tea and supped.

On Monday the 22d we went on shore at noon, and were received by Major Grimstone the Commanding Officer, who politely apologized for detaining us so long. At one, six of us mounted a waggon with eight horses, which to my great surprize were driven by one man in hand, at the rate of six miles an hour, over loose stones, or whatever else came in the way; so that we were almost jumbled to death. We passed three beaches, and to avoid quick-sands, they drove through the surf; the roaring of which, the horses splashing as they gallopped along, added to the crack of the driver's long whip, formed altogether a charming concert. As the driver cannot wield these enormous instruments with one hand, another man sits by to hold the reins, while by lengthening or shortening his arm he dexterously contrives to make every horse in turn feel the weight of the lash. At length we reached Cape Town in safety, but were terribly tired and bruised. Between the beaches, the road (such as it is) passes along stupendous mountains, from whose craggy tops, masses of stone are continually falling, some of them large enough to crush a church; many have rolled into the sea, where they form a barrier against the surf, and may defy its force for ages.

We heard that the former Governor, General Craig, sailed from hence on Tuesday preceding; he was once forced to put back, but the second attempt succeeded.

There were no less than six vessels here. The flag was

struck on the 15th, and would not be hoisted again until the
15th August, during which interval the Dutch suffered no
ships to remain in Table Bay. Our people are not so
cautious; perhaps, experience may render them so. I like
the appearance of the place; for altho' the houses are
generally low, they occupy much ground; being built of
stone, or covered with plaster, and containing five or six
rooms on a floor, they look well; and though with only one
upper story, yet the ceilings being lofty, they do not seem
deficient in height. The church is handsome; the service
is performed in Dutch and English; there are no pews but
benches and chairs, which I greatly prefer, as it gives the
idea of social worship more, and is consistent with that
equality, which in the more immediate presence of God,
becomes his creatures, as being equally dependant on Him.
It is true this was partly lost here, because the Governor and
his family use benches, covered with crimson velvet. We
sat off after service for Simon's Town and reached the ship
at 4 P. M. On Monday Mr. Gooch took us in the morning
to see the *Tremendous*, Admiral Pringle's ship. Here we
saw furnaces for heating balls.

On Wednesday the 31st we dined on board the *Dort*,
where we met Captain and Mrs. Losack, Lord Augustus
Fitzroy, Captain Holles of the *Chichester*, and Captain
Osborne of the *Trusty*; we went and returned in Captain
L—'s barge. Next day we dined on board *L'Imperieuse*
with Lord Augustus Fitzroy. In addition to our yesterday's party were Captain Stevens of the *Rattle-Snake*,
Captain Granger of the *Good Hope*, Captain Alexander of the
Sphinx, Mr. Pownall Naval Officer and his wife, and Mr.
Trail. His Lordship gave us a most magnificent dinner,
and to my great joy, was too much the man of fashion, to
urge the gentlemen to hard drinking, as had been the case
on board the *Dort*. He has an excellent band. When we
retired Mrs. Losack and Mrs. Pownall entered into con-

versation, about the Cape, which they both agreed was the vilest place imaginable; Mrs. L— is a fine dashing lady. Since her marriage, the *Jupiter* has been on a cruize. I asked her if they were ever fired upon. " Oh yes, from a battery and returned the fire." " Did you go below? " " Not I indeed." " Then I suppose you must have been greatly alarmed for fear of being shot? " " Why to tell you the truth I was so much engaged in observing how they loaded the guns and manœuvred the ship, that I *never* once thought of danger." There is a courageous lady for you!

We played at whist in the evening and retired at eleven. Captain Alexander took us on board in his Barge. On the 4th of June the Admiral, at one, fired two guns, then all the Men of War in the Harbour followed with twenty one each: the effect produced by the reverberation from so many stupendous rocks was most noble! Mr. Gooch and the Doctor came on board to take leave, and on going away, the boats crew gave us three cheers, which our people returned. On the whole, our time passed here pleasantly; the politeness of my Countrymen, contrasted with the manners of our American officers served to soothe the irritation of our minds, and teach us to endure that for a season, with patience, which we had often found to be a trial of our spirits and temper, in the hopes of meeting by and by with Gentlemen.

On the 5th of June the wind was as foul as it could blow, and split our only main sail. It is a great misfortune to sail in a vessel ill provided with stores and necessaries: we had an opportunity of observing this day, what a good ship can perform; *L'Imperieuse* Frigate being ordered on a cruize, got under weigh at noon, passed us at 3 P. M. and was safely out before night. Lord Augustus was polite enough to hoist his colours while going by, and struck them immediately afterwards. Our Captain was too much of a Yankee however to return the compliment. I forgot to mention, that yesterday four large ships came in; they proved to be the *Rose*, the *Hillsborough*, and the *Thurlow* East India-men, under convoy of H. M. 74 Gun ship the *Raisonable*.

On the 8th of June we were still in sight of Simon's Town, though we were out two days. On the 11th of July we crossed the equinoctial Line, and I felt satisfied in thinking, that I was once more in my own hemisphere. There are cases in which it is wisdom to please ourselves with trifles; at this time my spirits were very low, and sunk with what I might now term a presentiment, as I approached another people and another world, which was eventually the grave of that property, for which I had toiled so long. On the 28th of August a pilot came on board from Philadelphia, and from him we had the mournful account, that a sickness raged in the city, almost as fatal as that which ravaged it a few years before, and that a general distress prevailed in America: frequent Bankruptcies, Trade at a stand, and an open war with France daily expected, as they took every thing from America which fell in their way—As we did not like to proceed to Philadelphia after hearing this account, we tacked and stood to the northward, but we had a succession of vexatious hindrances, having narrowly escaped shipwreck in Egg Harbour, and did not reach New York till the 3rd of September, when we landed at 6 in the evening, and went immediately to a house recommended by my friend Captain Crowninshield, most happy to part with the strange beings with whom we had been so long and painfully immured.

Now having arrived in the land of Columbia, I will bid you adieu for a while.

I am, My dear Madam,
Yours truly,

E. F.

Advertisement.

The work had been printed thus far when the death of the author took place. The subsequent parts of her journal, not appearing to contain any events of a nature sufficiently interesting to claim publication, no additional extracts have been deemed necessary by the administrator, who from a view of benefiting the estate has been induced to undertake the present publication.

TERMINAL NOTES

By E. M. FORSTER

[1] P. 37. THE QUEEN: Marie Antoinette, aged 23.

[2] P. 41. DUC DE CHARTRES: afterwards Duke of Orleans (Philippe Egalité).

[3] P. 56. THE KING OF SARDINIA: Vittorio Amadeo III.

[4] P. 63. THE BARETTO BROTHERS: probably Joseph and Luis. A big Indo-Portuguese firm, engaged in the Eastern trade. Joseph built churches in Calcutta. W. Hickey found Luis " endowed by nature with extraordinary talents and elegant address, though under the unfavourable circumstance of an extremely dark skin, indeed, nearly black." See also Campos, *History of the Portuguese in Bengal*.

[5] P. 69 *seq.* ALEXANDRIA. Topography. Two harbours, divided by the promontory of Ras-el-Tin, on whose western spur stood the lighthouse. (The Pharos of the ancients occupied the eastern spur and has long since vanished.) The native town lay across the neck of the promontory. The present city had not been begun. Mrs Fay's account is interesting. She visits (i.) " Pompey's Pillar," which has nothing to do with Pompey; probably erected to Diocletian, A.D. 297; height 84 feet: proportions—execrable. (ii.) Mosque built in the seventh century over the site of the Church of St. Athanasius, at the junction of the present Rue Rosette with the Rue Sidi el Metwalli. It was a large building, of the court-yard type; the wedge-shaped Attarine Mosque now occupies part of its site. (iii.) " Cleopatra's Palace "—probably a fraud, and in any case not visible in these days. (iv.) " Cleopatra's Needles " had nothing to do with her either, though they were brought to adorn a temple she had begun. Originally set up by Thothmes III. (1500 B.C.) before the Temple of the Rising Sun at Heliopolis, they were brought to Alexandria in 13 B.C. and set up in the forecourt of the Temple to Augustus. They remained *in situ* till the nineteenth century when one of them went to the Thames Embankment, the other to the United States.

For the appearance of Alexandria as she saw it, cf. the illustrations in Volney, *Voyage en Syrie et en Egypte*, 1783–85; Volney's pencil exaggerates, but so does her pen.

Society. The Fays did not see anything of the English community while at Alexandria, but, though small, it already existed. A Dane, who landed twenty years earlier, says:

The English keep themselves quiet and conduct themselves without making much noise. If any nice affair is to be undertaken they withdraw themselves from it and leave to the French the honour of removing all difficulties. When any benefits result from it they have their share, and if affairs turn out ill they secure themselves in the best manner they can.

[6] P. 70. MR. BRANDY. The news the Consul brought was bad: the previous Suez caravan had been plundered. Mrs. Fay dare not put this in her letter for fear of the Turkish censor (p. 90).

[7] P. 76. ROSETTA: 40 miles from Alexandria, and 10 from the Rosetta mouth of the Nile. It was then a prosperous city. Edward Wortley Montagu (Lady Mary's son) had, until recently, lived there in semi-Oriental state (Nichols, *Literary Anecdotes*, iv. 640). The place is still delightful, though the sands are choking it; in the nineteenth century when Alexandria expanded, it decayed.

[8] P. 77. THE PYRAMIDS. These are of course the three Gizeh pyramids, visible long before boat or train reaches Cairo. The Great Pyramid is 451 feet high. What does "steps three feet distant of" mean? Probably " of " should be " on."

[9] P. 78. GEORGE BALDWIN was the East India Company's agent at Cairo. He reported at length to Calcutta on the hardship endured by the English in Egypt, and particularly on the catastrophe of the Suez caravan, which Mrs. Fay is about to describe. (India Office Records: Original Consultations of the Supreme Council for December 23, 1779.) Baldwin says that if his advice had been followed all would have been well; with which, however, the Supreme Council did not concur.

[10] P. 78. MRS. FAY'S DRESS. See frontispiece, also note, p. 24. If, as is probable, the picture was done in India, she must have brought her costume safely through the various misfortunes of the journey.

[11] P. 81. CUTTING OF THE CANAL. This was the Khalig Canal (now filled up). The ceremony dated back to Ancient Egypt, and had at one time involved human sacrifice. The dyke was broken when the river, as measured by the Nilometer on the Island of Rodeh opposite, had risen to 16 cubits. Lane, *Modern Egyptians*, ch. xxvi., has a detailed account.

[12] P. 83. MR. FAY'S LETTER: the only example of his epistolary style, and the only indication that his wife had been a Miss C. If C should happen to be a misprint for P, then her maiden name would be Preston (p. 242).

[13] P. 86 *seq.* THE *NATALIA* AND THE PLUNDERED CARAVAN. A note is now due on this mysterious and agitating subject. Mrs. Fay had to bottle herself up so long as she was on Egyptian soil; once on the *Natalia*, she

explodes. Her account is fairly accurate; let us check it by the long complaint which John O'Donnell, who was part owner of the merchandise, addressed to the Supreme Council at Calcutta (India Office Records: Consultations of the Government, June 12, 1780).

O'Donnell first went to India in 1771 as an E.I.C. Cadet; then he became Deputy Paymaster to the Nawab of Oudh. The Fays met him in Egypt, and, later, on their voyage round India. According to his account, the *Natalia* was a Danish boat, but her captain was Dutch, not Danish, and named Van der Velden, not Vanderfield. Chenu (of whom we shall hear much in a moment) was second mate. The two French Chevaliers were Pierre Mathieu Renault de St. Germaine, a godson of Dupleix (Mrs. Fay's " Monsieur Chevalier "), and his brother Renault de Chilly. The *Natalia* reached Suez on May 24, 1770. The catastrophe proceeds much as Mrs. Fay relates. The caravan is plundered as it crosses the desert, and the party splits—some continuing to Cairo, others returning to Suez. Only Renault de St. Germaine reached Cairo, to spread terror among the Europeans there; his brother de Chilly, Messrs. Barrington, Jenkins, Van der Velden, some servants, and an Armenian linguist all perished. Those who returned to Suez fared better; they included O'Donnell himself, Chenu, the cook, and a Captain Waugh. Nevertheless, says O'Donnell, " under the intense influence of the Sun which equally affected us by its vertical Rays from the Heavens as by its reflected Heat from the burning Sands, we also suffered from Thirst which was beyond Idea painful and troublesome. . . . We were reprobated by the People as if we had been the most abandoned Delinquents. . . . Our servant boys (sons of Christians) were against their Inclinations notwithstanding their Fears and Deprecations circumcised and underwent the Ceremonies of being made Mussalman." He did not suffer in silence; his threats to the Egyptian Government endangered the Europeans in Cairo, and nearly led to the seizing of the property of Mr. Moore.

The *Natalia*, lying all the time off Suez, had been gutted; now, with Chenu as captain, and the Fays and other passengers on board, she proceeds to her final doom at Calicut.

[14] P. 90. THE GOVERNMENT OF EGYPT: a well-informed account of the confusion. The dual system of a Pasha sent from Constantinople and of 24 local Beys or Mamelouks had broken down ten years previously. The country remained in anarchy until 1790, when a Turkish army subdued it.

[15] P. 102. CHEVALIER DE ST. LUBIN. His mission was not to Hyder Ali but to the Marathas at Poona, where he did great damage to English interests. Mrs. Fay cares nothing for her beloved country as long as she can get her letters delivered safely.

[16] P. 105. TULLOH: probably the eminent Calcutta auctioneer of this name. Zoffany the painter is said to have quarrelled with him a few years

later, and to have introduced him as Judas Iscariot into a picture of the Last Supper—having induced him to sit on the understanding that he was representing St. John. The picture is still in St. John's Church, Calcutta. Mr. Tulloh (if he it be) appears as a robust and handsome man. But Zoffany quarrelled with so many people that there is a doubt which he selected for Judas; some say it was a Mr. Paull.

Tulloh & Co. sold Mrs. Fay's effects after her death.

[17] P. 107. JOHN HARE. How she loathes this chattering mannikin! Wm. Hickey (i. 274) did not find him so bad: " A genteel-looking young man of very slight form and apparently in bad health "; they met in London in 1772. Hare built up a good practice at Calcutta; he and Fay were both employed to defend J. A. Hicky, the editor of the *Bengal Gazette* (p. 183); he became sheriff of the city in 1782. His end was tragic. He was returning home overland (1784) with letters of introduction from Sir Elijah Impey to Lord Thurlow, and he had some diamonds with him which he allowed his attendants to see; they murdered him and threw the body into the Euphrates. Thus the ostentation and expansiveness that Mrs. Fay censures proved his death. She certainly sums up his faults well; and his letter to Sirdar Khan (quoted on p. 277) fully bears out her charge of pomposity. But he was probably nicer than she says. We must never forget that she herself was a most trying woman, particularly on a boat, and that Mr. Hare would not have found her table manners funny, or appreciated her contempt for the violin.

[18] P. 110 *seq.* IMPRISONMENT AT CALICUT. This important episode calls for detailed comment.

Names of the prisoners: Mr. and Mrs. Fay, Mr. and Mrs. Tulloh, Mr. Hare and his servant Lewis, Mr. Taylor, Mr. Manesty, Mr. Fuller, and one other, possibly John the Gunner. The Fays were imprisoned from November 5, 1779, to February 17, 1780; the others got free on December 16.

Place: the English Factory (Residency) at Calicut; then the Fort, then back to the Factory.

Calicut was an old Hindu city. The name, Colicoda, means " cock crowing "; a cock was supposed to have crowed on the fort, and the city to extend so far as the sound could carry. Hyder Ali acquired it peaceably from the Hindu ruler (Zamorin) in 1766, but had to reconquer it in 1773. His brother-in-law, Sirdar (Sudder) Khan was now governor. When the *Natalia* arrived war with the English was contemplated, and the English factor had already fled. The *Natalia* was a Danish boat—hence the appeal to the Danish factor Passavant—and her captain was French; but Sirdar Khan rightly surmised that the chief financial interests in her were English. The Fays roused his suspicions first by refusing to place themselves under Danish protection. He began by imprisoning them, and added the other passengers in a few days. The imprisonment was monstrous. Nevertheless, Hyder Ali had good reason to suspect English intrigues against him that autumn. He was driven out of Calicut in 1782. His son Tipu Sultan got it back in 1789. It is now British. The population is largely Moplah—fanatic and turbulent to-day as in Mrs. Fay's time.

We possess—most fortunately!—the portentous memoir that Mr. Hare drew up and presented to Sirdar Khan on November 18, just after he had been robbed of his luggage. (Quoted in *Bengal Past and Present*, vol. xii. 257 *seq*. He sent it in duplicate to Madras, and it has thus been preserved in the E.I.C. archives.) It entirely confirms Mrs. Fay's account—also her estimate of Mr. Hare's character and oratory. How sublime is its exordium!

Your Memorialist begs leave in the first place to remind your Excellency that the Humanity and Policy of enlightened ages have suggested Certain Rules of universal Conduct under the denomination of the Laws of Nations. . . .

That the progress of civilisation has tempered and refined these Laws, so that a minute attention to them forms in some measure the perfection of National Character. . . .

In a season of public peace and alliance between the powers of the Nabob and Great Britain, nine English subjects have been seized by an armed force and their persons confined without the necessaries of life, separated from their property, the whole of it has been violently plundered and such parts of it as remained are damaged and rendered useless by the salt water.

Their imprisonment being in the first instance against and contrary to the Laws of Nations is aggravated by circumstances of peculiar and wanton cruelty. The indecent noise and insolence of the numerous force which constitute their Guard, molest equally their peace by Day and their rest by Night, their situation is moreover destitute of every domestic convenience and consolation, and the whole of their money has been taken from their chests and publickly confiscated (Rs.6000 in all).

Sirdar Khan was unmoved. On January 1, 1780, a letter from Mr. Passavant, the Danish factor, was received by Mr. Church, the English factor, at Tellicherry (*Bengal Past and Present*, iii. 168), and no doubt it was partly owing to this letter that Mr. Church sent his ill-omened assistance to the Fays.

Meanwhile the missionary Schwartz was at Seringapatam, trying to patch things up between Hyder Ali and the Madras Government, but he did not know of the Calicut outrage. A second mission was now despatched under George Gray with a letter from the Governor of Madras to Hyder Ali, requesting the release of " Mr. Hare and ten other Europeans " (Feb. 1780). Gray reports on his arrival that they had all been released by February 17 —the very date Mrs. Fay's narrative implies. Gray's own reception was cold, and in the following June the war started. The Fays only just escaped.

If they had been sent up country as Captain Ayres advised (p. 124), how would they have fared? The answer is to be found in two most interesting

little memoirs, *The Imprisonment of James Scurry*, published in 1824, and
The Imprisonment of James Bristow, published 1794. Scurry and Bristow
were two young sailors, captured by the French admiral during his naval
operations and handed over by him to Hyder Ali. They remained in the
interior several years, drilling recruits. They were circumcised and went
semi-native and Bristow was assigned a wife, from whom he parted with
great regret when peace was declared. Similar experiences would doubtless
have overtaken Mr. Fay.

[19] P. 124. She got the information about this plot from West in Calcutta
(p. 187).

[20] P. 134. THE NAYHIRS—*i.e.* Nairs—are a Hindu community who
interest anthropologists. They practise matriarchy and to a certain extent
polyandry also. Mrs. Fay is wrong in supposing they were attacking the
English. On the contrary the English had instigated them to rebel against
Hyder Ali, and their operations near Tellicherry were probably to this end.
The rebellion was soon crushed.

Mahe was another cause of dissension between Hyder Ali and the English
(p. 17).

[21] P. 135. KANHOJI ANGRIA was a Mahratta freebooter of the earlier
eighteenth century who infested the western coast; sometimes he is called
an admiral. For his encounters with the English in Bombay, see Clement
Downing, *History of the Indian Wars*, recently edited by W. Foster.

[22] P. 137. CALICUT: see note on p. 276.

[23] P. 164. MR. POPHAM and his projects made much dust in Madras
at this time. When William Hickey landed in 1783, he was erecting sixty
houses at once, having purchased as building material the stranded hull of an
East Indiaman. He came to grief, so did every one who trusted him. "A
hard marriage settlement, some extravagance, and Mr. Stephen Popham
have forced me to quit my country perhaps for ever," complains a Mr.
William Cane; and a Mrs. Augusta Barclay censures "his *peculiarities*, I must
not presume to use a stronger word," and is glad to feel that she sees as little
of him as possible. (Hickey, vol. iii. *passim*.)

[24] P. 166. ST. THOMAS MOUNT. There are two "Mounts" near
Madras connected with St. Thomas. A legend brings him to India to found
Nestorian Christianity on the "Little Mount" by the banks of the Adyar.
There he was pierced by the lance of a Brahmin, and ran six miles in a wounded
condition to the "Great Mount," where he died (A.D. 68). It is the Great
Mount to which Mrs. Fay refers. The church on the summit was built by
the Portuguese in 1547, when Nestorianism was dying out; it contains early
inscriptions, also a picture of the Virgin Mary by St. Luke, which St. Thomas

brought with him from Palestine. He is buried in a third locality, Saint Thome, close to Madras, on the shore.

[25] P. 174. THE CHAMBERS were Mrs. Fay's chief protectors at Calcutta. Sir Robert (1737–1803) had gained distinction in England; Vinerian Professor of Law at Oxford; friend to Dr. Johnson, whom he made laugh immoderately for reasons not obvious to Boswell (Boswell, iii. 304). He came East in 1774, as judge in the Supreme Court. Here he did not increase his reputation, being weak in the Nuncomar trial, and generally undignified and frivolous. William Hickey addressed him as a " contemptible animal " (iii. 255), on which " a look of surprize pervaded the whole Court," but the animal took no action. J. A. Hicky satirised him as Sir Viner Pliant in the *Bengal Gazette*. Chambers became Chief Justice after Impey's resignation, and returned to England in 1799.

His wife, Fanny, was the daughter of the sculptor Joseph Wilton. She was renowned for her beauty, smartness, and goodness. At the age of sixteen she " stood for Hebe at the Royal Academy," and in later life composed a volume of family prayers.

Old Mrs. Chambers was also of the party. Also several children, one of whom perished on the *Grosvenor*. Their Calcutta house was probably in Old Post Office Street; they acquired a good deal of property, and had some country estates; they have a vault in the South Park Cemetery. Mrs. Fay does not mention them in her subsequent visits; possibly they had seen sufficient of her.

[26] P. 175. MRS. HASTINGS: Anne Maria Apollonia Chapuset (Marian), Hastings' second wife. They fell in love coming out on the boat. She was still married to a Baron Imhoff, whom she did not care for and who did not care for her. A divorce was arranged after the trio reached India, and she and Hastings were married in 1777, and lived together for many happy years. " An unsavoury episode," complain the historians. A contemporary writes: " She has a good person and has been very pretty, is sensible, lively, and wants only to be greater mistress of the English language to prove she has a great share of wit." When Mrs. Fay called on her, she was about 43. Zoffany has painted her. " Belvidere House " raises a small difficulty, for Hastings had sold the bungalow bearing that name a few months before Mrs. Fay's visit; the present residence of the Governor of Bengal is on its site.

[27] P. 176. NORTH NAYLOR, the Company's attorney, had given Hastings advice which the Supreme Court held to be illegal and, after a complicated quarrel, he was committed to prison for contempt of court. He developed dysentery in the Calcutta Jail, and, though he was released, died soon after.

[28] P. 181. Food. From various passages it is clear that our heroine was of the hungry type. People who write long letters often are. That very June " the Surgeon of an Indiaman fell dead after eating a hearty dinner of beef, thermometre being 98° " (Busteed, *Old Calcutta*); but the warning did not deter her. She ate and ate till the end—asparagus, pork, tunny, turtle, preserved peaches, ghi.

[29] P. 183. The *Calcutta Gazette*, a respectable Government paper, did not appear until 1784, so Mrs. Fay must mean the *Bengal Gazette*. A disreputable weekly, and interesting as the first paper to be published in India. J. A. Hicky, editor. First published, February 1780. Here is a specimen of its news :

A few days ago a dispute arose between two young gentlemen not many miles from Serampore about a lady of a sooty complexion. The friends of both were of some apprehension that a duel would have been the consequences, but it happily ended in a reciprocal bastinado.

Here is a poem from it :

> O lovely Sue
> How sweet art thou,
>   Than sugar thou art sweeter;
> Thou dost as far
> Excell sugar
>   As sugar does saltpetre.

A footnote explains that " thou " must be pronounced as in Scotland. The paper was suppressed in 1782 because of its attacks on Hastings and general tiresomeness and vulgarity (Busteed, *Echoes of Old Calcutta*, 182-222). J. A. Hicky was unsuccessfully defended by Anthony Fay.

[30] P. 185. Duel between Francis and Hastings. In the words of a contemporary Mohammedan historian: " At the end of Redjeh or the beginning of Theban both parties, according to the established custom of the nation, went out by themselves and fought with pistols. The Governor being befriended by destiny came off harmless, but Mr. Francis was wounded. As he was predestined to live a great deal more, the pistol ball, although it entered at his right side, did neither break the bone nor even rend the curtain; it stopped between bone and flesh and in a few days he was cured."

They had quarrelled over an alleged promise of Francis' not to interfere with the military operations that Hastings was conducting. Had he, or had he not, given such a promise? The provocative minute was really Hastings', not Francis'. It is full of deliberate insults, such as " I judge of his public conduct by my experience of his private, which I have found to be void of truth and honour." A challenge arrived in due course. Francis, who had courage, entered in his journal for August 16: " Employed in settling my affairs, burning papers, etc., in case of the worst—dull work." They met under the " Trees of Destruction " near the Alipore Bridge. Much gentlemanly business—enquiries and so on—ensued; and just as much hatred and suspicion remained. They achieved a certain amount of pleasure for an old village woman who happened to be passing and thought the encounter between the mad sahibs great fun (Busteed, *Echoes from Old Calcutta*, ch. 6). And Hastings was so far successful that Francis did not interfere further on the Council, but shortly after left for England.

[31] P. 186. COLONEL BAILLIE: defeated by Hyder Ali near Madras (Sept. 1780), and carried away as prisoner to Seringapatam, where he died in misery two years later. His misfortunes recall her own imprisonment to her.

Her hopes of Sir Eyre Coote were justified. He checked Hyder Ali at Porto Novo, and ended the invasion of the Carnatic (1781). His previous Indian career had been distinguished: fought at Plassey. He died at Madras, and on her next visit she sees a picture of him in the Exchange there (p. 261).

[32] P. 188. ROWLAND JACKSON: a doctor of ability, who had lost his estates in Ireland owing to a lawsuit, and was obliged to take service in India. He wished to be appointed " Physician " to the Calcutta Hospitals, which Hastings opposed, on the ground that the other practitioners were only " surgeons," and that the distinction was unfair. He died in 1784. His son's name was Edward; the name of the young lady whom Edward married was Phœbe Tuting; the other young lady's name was Maria Chantry (Firminger).

[33] P. 190. JOHN HYDE: one of the judges in the Supreme Court. A fantastic and hospitable person. The " public breakfast " is described in detail by Wm. Hickey. Hyde's house was close to the Court (site of present town hall), so the Bar procession had not far to go. He was himself a hearty feeder: satirised by J. A. Hicky as " Turkey Cram." His notebooks at Calcutta contain (says Firminger) several references to Anthony Fay, but I have not had the opportunity of examining them. He died at Calcutta, 1796.

[34] P. 192. THE HARMONICON — dancing house, concert hall, and tavern—stood in the Lal Bazaar, opposite the Jail.

[35] P. 193. LADY COOTE, wife to the Commander-in-Chief. Her father had been Governor of St. Helena.

[36] P. 194. THE PLAY HOUSE, " erected in 1775, stood close to the northwest corner of the present Lyon's range " (Firminger). It consisted of pit and boxes; Mrs. Fay, for her gold mohur, would have sat in a box. This particular performance of Otway's *Venice Preserved* made a stir. The *Bengal Gazette* of February 11, 1781, says of it: " Captain Call played Jaffier admirably well, and may be styled the Garrick of the East. Mr. Norford played Belvidera with such an amorous glow of features and utterance —and was so characteristic in the description of madness—as to procure him (as usual) universal applause."

[37] P. 198. HENRY WATSON: chief engineer at Calcutta, also ship-builder and speculator in marine stores. He had lately quarrelled with the Government over his dock-scheme, and had acted as second to Philip Francis in the Warren Hastings duel (p. 185). His retention of Mr. Fay might well alarm Eliza; it showed that her husband had gone over to the opposition, and turned against Impey and Chambers, his former patrons. Did he now send Mr. Fay back to England, to prepare the impeachment against Impey? And did Mr. Fay make a muddle of this, as of everything else he touched? Probably. Watson had a superb house on Garden Reach. He loved Calcutta, and did not leave it until he was dying (1785). He bequeathed his fortune of £300,000 to his natural daughter; his widow only inherited the dock projects, but she did well out of it in the long run.

Mrs. Fay's account of her husband is confirmed by an illuminating and scathing passage in the Impey MSS. (B.M. 16260). Writing from Patna, under the date of August 31, 1781, Sir Elijah Impey speaks of Colonel Watson's hostility and then continues:

This very man is at this time pushing his animosity against me in another way. There is a very low man here of the name of Fay, who had been called to the Bar in England, and, therefore, I thought it proper he should be admitted an advocate here. This man at Watson's instigation as I believe has drawn the paper a copy of which I herewith transmit.

He entertains him, as I am informed, in his house, and means to send him to England with the paper. Fay sent it to me in an hand imitating printing. . . . He did not say who was the prosecutor employing him.

[38] P. 201. CHINSURAH, a Dutch settlement on the Hoogli, was seized by the English as soon as news of hostilities with Holland reached them —i.e. in July 1781. It was finally ceded to us by treaty in 1824.

[39] P. 201. MRS. WHELER. Charlotte, second wife of Edward Wheler, member of Council; important people. Mrs. Fay's misfortunes seem to have raised her into society from which she subsequently sank.

[40] P. 202. CHURCH AT CALCUTTA. There was none for the moment; St. John's was not begun until 1783. When Mrs. Fay returned to Calcutta and set up a millinery establishment, her shop abutted on to its graveyard. The sacred edifice, whose absence she had deplored, then became a nuisance, for the Vestry erected a wall which deprived her shop of light and air. She wrote complaining. Her letter must be quoted in full, since it is the only additional letter extant; and it is not without native acidity.

To the Rev. Mr. Blanshard, the Rev. Mr. Owen, Mr. Cockerell, Mr. Thornhill, Mr. Sealey, Mr. Johnson, members of the Church Vestry.

13th April, 1789.

GENTLEMEN—Pardon the freedom I use in making an application, which I flatter myself, however, will be attended with success having nothing for its object that can in the smallest degree injure the property of the Church.

Permit me then to acquaint you that, about five years since, I became an inhabitant, and, sometime after purchaser of the house I now reside in, formerly the Post Office, and forms the south-west boundary of the old burying-ground, now the compound of the New Church. At the period I mention, the lower floor was nearly as habitable as the upper one; but shortly after, a considerable part of it was rendered almost useless, in consequence of a wall being built up against the window, so close as to prevent the accession of either light or air. There is also great reason to apprehend that from the accumulation of damp between the walls and the house, and the want of a free ventilation, walls of the latter will sustain material injury.

Suffer me, therefore, to request, Gentlemen, that you will have the goodness to take the subject of this letter into consideration; and be pleased to allow that part of the wall, which stands against my house, to be taken down; or such openings to make in it, as may suffice to restore the premises to their former usefulness.—I am, Gentlemen, Your most humble servant,　　　　　　　　　ELIZA FAY.

(Quoted by Firminger from the St. John's Church records.)

[41] P. 209. WILLIAM HOSEA had been seventeen years in the Company's service; his wife's name was Mary. The *Grosvenor* met with a terrible catastrophe, to which Mrs. Fay never refers: the captain ran the ship ashore at night on the east coast of Africa, in the neighbourhood of Delagoa Bay (Aug. 4, 1782). One hundred and thirty-five people survived the wreck, including four ladies and two children. They tried to march southward to the Cape, but got into difficulties with the natives, and only three (seamen) arrived. See *Bengal Past and Present*, vol. ii. No. 3, for the official account; also Hickey, ii. 199. Rumours of young savages with light skins led to the theory that the ladies had married with their captors, and borne offspring.

Mrs. Fay nearly met with a similar disaster on the *Valentine* (p. 219).

[42] P. 212. SUFFREN AND HUGHES. They fought five engagements on the Coromandel Coast, which won the admiration of experts (Mahan, *Influence of Sea Power*, 1660–1783, ch. xii.). Suffren was a charming character and an accomplished admiral. Hughes was solid and second-rate, as his picture at Greenwich suggests, but his action was largely responsible for keeping the French out of India.

[43] P. 216. THE *VALENTINE*. The log of this vessel records the embarkation of Mrs. Fay and her luggage at Barrabola Head; also, though in guarded terms, the disgraceful muddle off the African coast. The name of the ship-surgeon who attended Mrs. Fay for colic, and with whom she was subsequently accused of flirting, was Patrick Ivory. (India Office Records: Log 452, G.)

[44] P. 221. THE *CHAPMAN*. I have ventured to repunctuate this passage. The text of 1817 reads, " On board which were Mr. Casamajor and his mother, who secured accommodations on the *Lord North*. Not

choosing to venture farther on the *Chapman*, upon which I was applied to . . ."
The grammar is too queer even for Mrs. Fay; nor does the sentence make
sense. Vaguely disapprobant, Archdeacon Firminger has, without comment,
substituted *Valentine* for *Chapman*. But try putting a comma after *Lord
North* and a full stop after *Chapman*; the situation becomes intelligible.

[45] P. 232. MR. LEWIN. Thomas Lewin (1753–1843) of the Madras
Civil Service.

[46] P. 239. MISS HICKS. Register of St. John's, Calcutta, March 19,
1785: "John Lacey, a bachelor, shopkeeper, to Avis Hicks, single woman.
T. Blanchard, Chaplain."

[47] P. 242. SLAVE GIRL AT ST. HELENA. This is the worst action re-
corded of Mrs. Fay. It roused great indignation locally (India Office Records:
St. Helena, 57). She stranded the girl on the island in 1782, probably in
payment of a bill. The girl was no fool, and, on discovering that her late
mistress was passing by on the *Henry*, she at once went to the Governor and
denounced her. In her deposition she " made oath on the Holy Evangelists
that she was called Kitty Johnson as her supposed Father was Johnson the
Governor's Groom at Calcutta, that her Mother's name was Silvia, a Free
Woman, half cast, and she believes that a woman, called Peg Chapman, her
supposed godmother, sent her to service to Mrs. Fay, then Mantua Maker
at Calcutta." Kitty goes on to say that Mrs. Fay was following her husband
to England and " was intimate with the Doctor of the Ship going home, and
as the Deponent knew of it Mrs. Fay did not like to keep her " (cf. p. 217).
She further complains that she has been left without her consent, sold into
slavery, and ill-treated; has now two children and wishes to return to her
mother who is said to be alive. The Governor then summoned Mrs. Fay.
In her statement she keeps a dignified silence about the doctor, merely remarking she left Kitty on the island " on account of her bad behaviour as a present
to Miss Betty Mason, but did not suppose she would have been sold." The
Governor took a serious view, and told Mrs. Fay she must either settle the
matter or remain to stand her trial. Accordingly she drew a Bill for £60 on
" my brother Thomas W. Preston " (presumably her brother-in-law); £10
were to purchase Kitty's freedom, £40 for her passage with her babies to
Bengal, and £10 for maintenance on arrival.

Slavery was of course still a normal part of Anglo-Oriental life. " Two
Coffree boys, who play remarkably well on the French Horn, about eighteen
years of age: belonging to a Portugese Paddrie lately deceased. For particulars enquire of the Vicar of the Portugese Church ": thus runs a Calcutta
advertisement in 1781. Cf. also William Hickey's Nabob (vol. ii.),
and the lady presented to him by Bob Pott. At St. Helena, probably
on account of this scandal, regulations were passed which compelled the
owners of slaves to teach them some useful profession and to produce

them at Divine Service at least once a fortnight. (India Office Records, as above; the volume also records the accident of the stone that fell on Ladder Hill.)

[48] P. 265. DR. HARE: eminent Calcutta doctor. He treated W. Hickey.

> What are Hartley and Hare to grim Dr. Death
> Who moves slowly, but perfects the cure?
> Their prescriptions may rob me too soon of my breath
> And heighten the pains I endure.
>
> *Bengal Gazette*, 1780.

INDEX OF MAIN REFERENCES

THE END

THE HOGARTH PRESS

This is a paperback list for today's readers – but it holds to a tradition of adventurous and original publishing set by Leonard and Virginia Woolf when they founded The Hogarth Press in 1917 and started their first paperback series in 1924.

Some of the books are light-hearted, some serious, and include Fiction, Lives and Letters, Travel, Critics, Poetry, History and Hogarth Crime and Gaslight Crime.

A list of our books already published, together with some of our forthcoming titles, follows. If you would like more information about Hogarth Press books, write to us for a catalogue:

40 William IV Street, London WC2N 4DF

Please send a large stamped addressed envelope

HOGARTH TRAVEL

Two Towns in Provence by M.F.K. Fisher

Now I Remember: A Holiday History of England
by Ronald Hamilton

A Holiday History of France by Ronald Hamilton

The Spanish Temper by V.S. Pritchett
New Introduction by the Author

The Amateur Emigrant by Robert Louis Stevenson
New Introduction by Jonathan Raban

HOGARTH HISTORY

The Ancient Economy by M.I. Finley

HOGARTH POETRY

The Complete Poems 1927-1939, Elizabeth Bishop

Collected Poems, C.P. Cavafy
Translated by Edmund Keeley and Philip Sherrard
Edited by George Savidis

Collected Poems, William Empson

Robert Louis Stevenson
The Amateur Emigrant
New Introduction by Jonathan Raban

In 1879 Fanny Osbourne telegraphed Robert Louis Stevenson in Edinburgh, begging him to join her in California. First published in 1895, this is Stevenson's traveller's notebook, a shrewd and sympathetic record not only of the people and places encountered en route but also of his spiritual journey of self-discovery. *The Amateur Emigrant* is the best account ever written of *the* great adventure of the nineteenth century, the passage to the New World.

'The best book he ever wrote – a marvellous piece of writing. . .' – *Jonathan Raban*

William Hazlitt

Liber Amoris

The Book of Love

New Introduction by Michael Neve

An extraordinary drama of sexual obsession and romantic yearning, *Liber Amoris* is Hazlitt's attempt to exorcize his infatuation with a girl half his age. Based on the letters he wrote during the 'affair', it describes their circling encounters in his rooms, his dash to Scotland for a divorce, his rising jealousy and almost insane suspicions. But in real life – as this edition shows – Hazlitt's actions were still more bizarre, and shed new light on this brilliant Romantic critic. With its breathtaking intensity, the Book of Love caused outrage on first publication, and still makes us gasp today – for here is a besotted condition all too many of us will recognise.

Samuel Butler
Notebooks

Edited by H. Festing Jones

New Introduction by P.N. Furbank

'MARRIAGE

In matrimony, to hesitate is often to be saved'

One of our most highly original thinkers and writers, Samuel Butler always carried a notebook in which he jotted such eternal epigrams, anecdotes, questions, oddities, fables – incisive comments on anything from God to Grapes, Wisdom to Window Cleaning. An instant success when first published, the *Notebooks* have long been regarded as containing some of Butler's most hilarious and pungent writing. But, despite the temptation, be warned against reading them in a dentist's waiting-room, a hushed library, or anywhere else where the sudden guffaw raises a steely glare.

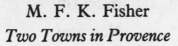

M. F. K. Fisher
Two Towns in Provence

Over the years, M. F. K. Fisher, widely regarded as one of America's finest contemporary writers and most highly esteemed of all authorities on the pleasures of the table, has spent much of her time living and travelling round France. Here she celebrates, in her uniquely perceptive, evocative fashion, Aix-en-Provence and Marseilles. Weaving together topography, history, folklore and personal memoirs with the look, the sound, the smell and (above all, perhaps) the taste of her chosen cities, M. F. K. Fisher provides the traveller, the gourmet and the lover of France and fine writing with unforgettable portraits of two remarkable and highly individual towns.